Raspberry Pi®
User Guide

2nd Edition

Eben Upton and Gareth Halfacree

WILEY

This edition first published 2014

Registered office

John Wiley & Sons Ltd., The Atrium, Southern Gate, Chichester, West Sussex, PO19 8SQ, United Kingdom

For details of our global editorial offices, for customer services and for information about how to apply for permission to reuse the copyright material in this book please see our website at www.wiley.com.

A catalogue record for this book is available from the British Library.

ISBN 978-1-118-79548-4 (Pbk); ISBN 978-1-118-79546-0 (ePDF); ISBN 978-1-118-79547-7 (ePub)

Set in 10 pt. Chaparral Pro by Indianapolis Composition Services

Printed simultaneously in Great Britain and the United States

Publisher's Acknowledgements

Some of the people who helped bring this book to market include the following:

Editorial and Production

VP Consumer and Technology Publishing Director
Michelle Leete

Associate Director–Book Content Management
Martin Tribe

Associate Publisher
Chris Webb

Executive Commissioning Editor
Craig Smith

Senior Project Editor
Sara Shlaer

Copy Editor
Kathryn Duggan, Grace Fairley

Technical Editors
Omer Kilic
Mike Cook
Russell Davis

Editorial Manager
Jodi Jensen

Editorial Assistant
Annie Sullivan

Marketing

Associate Marketing Director
Louise Breinholt

Marketing Manager
Lorna Mein

Marketing Assistant
Polly Thomas

Composition Services

Compositor
Erin Zeltner

Proofreader
Wordsmith Editorial

Indexer:
Potomac Indexing, LLC

For Liz, who made it all possible.
—Eben

For my father, the enthusiastic past,
and my daughter, the exciting future.
—Gareth

About the Authors

Eben Upton is a founder and trustee of the Raspberry Pi Foundation, and serves as its Executive Director. He is responsible for the overall software and hardware architecture of the Raspberry Pi, and for the Foundation's relationships with its key suppliers and customers. In an earlier life, he founded two successful mobile games and middleware companies, Ideaworks 3d Ltd. and Podfun Ltd., and held the post of Director of Studies for Computer Science at St John's College, Cambridge. He holds a BA, a PhD and an MBA from the University of Cambridge.

In his day job, Eben works for Broadcom as an ASIC architect and general troublemaker.

Gareth Halfacree is a freelance technology journalist and the co-author of the *Raspberry Pi User Guide* alongside project co-founder Eben Upton. Formerly a system administrator working in the education sector, Gareth's passion for open source projects has followed him from one career to another, and he can often be seen reviewing, documenting or even contributing to projects including GNU/Linux, LibreOffice, Fritzing and Arduino. He is also the creator of the Sleepduino and Burnduino open hardware projects, which extend the capabilities of the Arduino electronics prototyping system. A summary of his current work can be found at http://freelance.halfacree.co.uk.

Table of Contents

Part IV: Hardware Hacking

Introduction

"CHILDREN TODAY ARE digital natives", said a man I got talking to at a fireworks party last year. "I don't understand why you're making this thing. My kids know more about setting up our PC than I do."

I asked him if they could program, to which he replied: "Why would they want to? The computers do all the stuff they need for them already, don't they? Isn't that the point?"

As it happens, plenty of kids today aren't digital natives. We have yet to meet any of these imagined wild digital children, swinging from ropes of twisted-pair cable and chanting war songs in nicely parsed Python. In the Raspberry Pi Foundation's educational outreach work, we do meet a lot of kids whose entire interaction with technology is limited to closed platforms with graphical user interfaces (GUIs) that they use to play movies, do a spot of word-processed homework and play games. They can browse the web, upload pictures and video, and even design web pages. (They're often better at setting the satellite TV box than Mum or Dad, too.) It's a useful toolset, but it's shockingly incomplete, and in a country where 20 percent of households still don't have a computer in the home, even this toolset is not available to all children.

Despite the most fervent wishes of my new acquaintance at the fireworks party, computers don't program themselves. We need an industry full of skilled engineers to keep technology moving forward, and we need young people to be taking those jobs to fill the pipeline as older engineers retire and leave the industry. But there's much more to teaching a skill like programmatic thinking than breeding a new generation of coders and hardware hackers. Being able to structure your creative thoughts and tasks in complex, non-linear ways is a learned talent, and one that has huge benefits for everyone who acquires it, from historians to designers, lawyers and chemists.

Programming Is Fun!

It's enormous, rewarding, creative fun. You can create gorgeous intricacies, as well as (much more gorgeous, in my opinion) clever, devastatingly quick and deceptively simple-looking routes through, under and over obstacles. You can make stuff that'll have other people looking on jealously, and that'll make you feel wonderfully smug all afternoon. In my day job, where I design the sort of silicon chips that we use in the Raspberry Pi as a processor and work on the low-level software that runs on them, I basically get paid to sit around all day playing. What could be better than equipping people to be able to spend a lifetime doing that?

It's not even as if we're coming from a position where children don't want to get involved in the computer industry. A big kick up the backside came a few years ago, when we were moving quite slowly on the Raspberry Pi project. All the development work on Raspberry Pi was done in the spare evenings and weekends of the Foundation's trustees and volunteers—we're a charity, so the trustees aren't paid by the Foundation, and we all have full-time jobs to pay the bills. This meant that occasionally, motivation was hard to come by when all I wanted to do in the evening was slump in front of the *Arrested Development* boxed set with a glass of wine. One evening, when not slumping, I was talking to a neighbour's nephew about the subjects he was taking for his General Certificate of Secondary Education (GCSE, the British system of public examinations taken in various subjects from the age of about 16), and I asked him what he wanted to do for a living later on.

"I want to write computer games", he said.

"Awesome. What sort of computer do you have at home? I've got some programming books you might be interested in."

"A Wii and an Xbox."

On talking with him a bit more, it became clear that this perfectly smart kid had never done any real programming at all; that there wasn't any machine that he could program in the house; and that his information and communication technology (ICT) classes—where he shared a computer and was taught about web page design, using spreadsheets and word processing—hadn't really equipped him to use a computer even in the barest sense. But computer games were a passion for him (and there's nothing peculiar about wanting to work on something you're passionate about). So that was what he was hoping the GCSE subjects he'd chosen would enable him to do. He certainly had the artistic skills that the games industry looks for, and his maths and science marks weren't bad. But his schooling had skirted around any programming—there were no Computing options on his syllabus, just more of the same ICT classes, with its emphasis on end users rather than programming. And his home interactions with computing meant that he stood a vanishingly small chance of acquiring the skills he needed in order to do what he really wanted to do with his life.

This is the sort of situation I want to see the back of, where potential and enthusiasm is squandered to no purpose. Now, obviously, I'm not monomaniacal enough to imagine that simply making the Raspberry Pi is enough to effect all the changes that are needed. But I do believe that it can act as a catalyst. We're already seeing big changes in the UK schools' curriculum, where Computing is arriving on the syllabus and ICT is being reshaped, and we've seen a massive change in awareness of a gap in our educational and cultural provision for kids just in the short time since the Raspberry Pi was launched.

Too many of the computing devices a child will interact with daily are so locked down that they can't be used creatively as a tool—even though computing *is* a creative subject. Try using your iPhone to act as the brains of a robot, or getting your PS3 to play a game you've written. Sure, you can program the home PC, but there are significant barriers in doing that which a lot of children don't overcome: the need to download special software, and having the sort of parents who aren't worried about you breaking something that they don't know how to fix. And plenty of kids aren't even aware that doing such a thing as programming the home PC is possible. They think of the PC as a machine with nice clicky icons that give you an easy way to do the things you need to do so you don't need to think much. It comes in a sealed box, which Mum and Dad use to do the banking and which will cost lots of money to replace if something goes wrong!

The Raspberry Pi is cheap enough to buy with a few weeks' pocket money, and you probably have all the equipment you need to make it work: a TV, an SD card that can come from an old camera, a mobile phone charger, a keyboard and a mouse. It's not shared with the family; it belongs to the kid; and it's small enough to put in a pocket and take to a friend's house. If something goes wrong, it's no big deal—you just swap out a new SD card and your Raspberry Pi is factory-new again. And all the tools, environments and learning materials that you need to get started on the long, smooth curve to learning how to program your Raspberry Pi are right there, waiting for you as soon as you turn it on.

A Bit of History

I started work on a tiny, affordable, bare-bones computer about seven years ago, when I was a Director of Studies in Computer Science at Cambridge University. I'd received a degree at the University Computer Lab as well as studying for a PhD while teaching there, and over that period, I'd noticed a distinct decline in the skillset of the young people who were applying to read Computer Science at the Lab. From a position in the mid-1990s, when 17-year-olds wanting to read Computer Science had come to the University with a grounding in several computer languages, knew a bit about hardware hacking, and often even worked in assembly language, we gradually found ourselves in a position where, by 2005, those kids were arriving having done some HTML—with a bit of PHP and Cascading Style Sheets if you were lucky. They were still fearsomely clever kids with lots of potential, but their experience with computers was entirely different from what we'd been seeing before.

The Computer Science course at Cambridge includes about 60 weeks of lecture and seminar time over three years. If you're using the whole first year to bring students up to speed, it's harder to get them to a position where they can start a PhD or go into industry over the next two years. The best undergraduates—the ones who performed the best at the end of their three-year course—were the ones who weren't just programming when they'd been told to for their weekly assignment or for a class project. They were the ones who were programming in their spare time. So the initial idea behind the Raspberry Pi was a very parochial one with a very tight (and pretty unambitious) focus: I wanted to make a tool to get the small number of applicants to this small university course a kick start. My colleagues and I imagined we'd hand out these devices to schoolkids at open days, and if they came to Cambridge for an interview a few months later, we'd ask what they'd done with the free computer we'd given them. Those who had done something interesting would be the ones that we'd be interested in having in the program. We thought maybe we'd make a few hundred of these devices, or best case, a lifetime production run of a few thousand.

Of course, once work was seriously underway on the project, it became obvious that there was a lot more we could address with a cheap little computer like this. What we started with is a long way indeed from the Raspberry Pi you see today. I began by soldering up the longest piece of breadboard you can buy at Maplin with an Atmel chip at our kitchen table, and the first crude prototypes used cheap microcontroller chips to drive a standard-definition TV set directly. With only 512 K of RAM, and a few MIPS of processing power, these prototypes were very similar in performance to the original 8-bit microcomputers. It was hard to imagine these machines capturing the imaginations of kids used to modern games consoles and iPads.

There had been discussions at the University Computer Lab about the general state of computer education, and when I left the Lab for a non-academic job in the industry, I noticed that I was seeing the same issues in young job applicants as I'd been seeing at the University. So I got together with my colleagues Dr Rob Mullins and Professor Alan Mycroft (two colleagues from the Computer Lab), Jack Lang (who lectures in entrepreneurship at the University), Pete Lomas (a hardware guru) and David Braben (a Cambridge games industry leading light with an invaluable address book), and over beers (and, in Jack's case, cheese and wine), we set up the Raspberry Pi Foundation—a little charity with big ideas.

Why "Raspberry Pi"?

We get asked a lot where the name "Raspberry Pi" came from. Bits of the name came from different trustees. It's one of the very few successful bits of design by committee I've seen, and to be honest, I hated it at first. (I have since come to love the name, because it works really well—but it took a bit of getting used to since I'd been calling the project the "ABC Micro" in my head for years.) It's "Raspberry" because there's a long tradition of fruit names in computer companies (besides the obvious, there are the old Tangerine and Apricot computers—and we like to think of the Acorn as a fruit as well). "Pi" is a mangling of "Python", which we thought early on in development would be the only programming language available on a much less powerful platform than the Raspberry Pi we ended up with. As it happens, we still recommend Python as our favourite language for learning and development, but there is a world of other language options you can explore on the Raspberry Pi too.

In my new role as a chip architect at Broadcom, a big semiconductor company, I had access to inexpensive but high-performing hardware produced by the company with the intention of being used in very high-end mobile phones—the sort with the HD video and the 14-mega-pixel cameras. I was amazed by the difference between the chips you could buy for $10 as a small developer, and what you could buy as a cell-phone manufacturer for roughly the same amount of money: general purpose processing, 3D graphics, video and memory bundled into a single BGA package the size of a fingernail. These microchips consume very little power, and have big capabilities. They are especially good at multimedia, and were already being used by set-top box companies to play high-definition video. A chip like this seemed the obvious next step for the shape the Raspberry Pi was taking, so I worked on taping out a low-cost variant that had an ARM microprocessor on board and could handle the processing grunt we needed.

We felt it was important to have a way to get kids enthusiastic about using a Raspberry Pi even if they didn't feel very enthusiastic about programming. In the 1980s, if you wanted to play a computer game, you had to boot up a box that went "bing" and fed you a command prompt. It required typing a little bit of code just to get started, and most users didn't ever go beyond that—but some did, and got beguiled into learning how to program by that little bit of interaction. We realised that the Raspberry Pi could work as a very capable, very tiny, very cheap modern media centre, so we emphasised that capability to suck in the unwary—with the hope that they'd pick up some programming while they're at it.

After about five years' hard grind, we had created a very cute prototype board, about the size of a thumb drive. We included a permanent camera module on top of the board to demonstrate the sort of peripherals that can easily be added (there was no camera when we launched because it brought the price up too much, but we've now made a separate, cheap camera module available for photography projects), and brought it along to a number of meetings with the BBC's R&D department. Those of us who grew up in the UK in the 1980s had learned a lot about 8-bit computing from the BBC Microcomputer and the ecosystem that had grown up around it—with BBC-produced books, magazines and TV programmes—so I'd hoped that they might be interested in developing the Raspberry Pi further. But as it turned out, something has changed since we were kids: various competition laws in the UK and the EU meant that "the Beeb" couldn't become involved in the way we'd hoped. In a last-ditch attempt to get *something* organised with them, we ditched the R&D department idea and David (he of the giant address book) organised a meeting with Rory Cellan-Jones, a senior tech journalist, in May 2011. Rory didn't hold out much hope for partnership with the BBC, but he did ask if he could take a video of the little prototype board with his phone, to put on his blog.

The next morning, Rory's video had gone viral, and I realised that we had accidentally promised the world that we'd make everybody a $25 computer.

While Rory went off to write another blog post on exactly what it is that makes a video go viral, we went off to put our thinking caps on. That original, thumb-drive-sized prototype didn't fit the bill: with the camera included as standard, it was way too expensive to meet the cost model we'd suggested (the $25 figure came from my statement to the BBC that the Raspberry Pi should cost around the same as a text book, and is a splendid demonstration of the fact that I had no idea how much text books cost these days), and the tiny prototype model didn't have enough room around its periphery for all the ports we needed to make it as useable as we wanted it to be. So we spent a year working on engineering the board to lower cost as much as possible while retaining all the features we wanted (engineering cost down is a harder job than you might think), and to get the Raspberry Pi as useable as possible for people who might not be able to afford much in the way of peripherals.

We knew we wanted the Raspberry Pi to be used with TVs at home, just like the ZX Spectrum in the 1980s, saving the user the cost of a monitor. But not everybody has access to an HDMI television, so we added a composite port to make the Raspberry Pi work with an old cathode-ray television instead since SD cards are cheap and easy to find. We decided against microSD as the storage medium, because the little fingernail-sized cards are so flimsy in the hands of children and so easy to lose. And we went through several iterations of power supply, ending up with a micro USB cable. Recently, micro USB became the standard charger cable for mobile telephones across the EU (and it's becoming the standard everywhere), which means the cables are becoming more and more ubiquitous, and in many cases, people already have them at home.

By the end of 2011, with a projected February release date, it was becoming obvious to us that things were moving faster, and demand was higher, than we were ever going to be able to cope with. The initial launch was always aimed at developers, with the educational launch planned for later in 2012. We had a small number of very dedicated volunteers, but we needed the wider Linux community to help us prepare a software stack and iron out any early-life niggles with the board before releasing into the educational market. We had enough capital in the Foundation to buy the parts for and build 10,000 Raspberry Pis over a period of a month or so, and we thought that the people in the community who would be interested in an early board would come to around that number. Fortunately and unfortunately, we'd been really successful in building a big online community around the device, and interest wasn't limited to the UK, or to the educational market. Ten thousand was looking less and less realistic.

Our Community

The Raspberry Pi community is one of the things we're proudest of. We started with a very bare-bones blog at `www.raspberrypi.org` just after Rory's May 2011 video, and put up a forum on the same website shortly after that. That forum now has more than 60,000 members—between them they've contributed nearly 400,000 posts of wit and wisdom about the Raspberry Pi. If there's any question, no matter how abstruse, that you want to ask about the Raspberry Pi or about programming in general, someone there will have the answer (if it's not in this book, you'll find it in the forums).

Part of my job at Raspberry Pi involves giving talks to hacker groups, computing conferences, teachers, programming collectives and the like, and there's always someone in the audience who has talked to me or to my wife Liz (who runs the community) on the Raspberry Pi website—and some of these people have become good friends of ours. The Raspberry Pi website gets more than one request every single second of the day.

There are now hundreds of fan sites out there. There's also a fan magazine called *The MagPi* (a free download from `www.themagpi.com`), which is produced monthly by community members, with type-in listings, lots of articles, project guides, tutorials and more. Type-in games in magazines and books provided an easy route into programming for me—my earliest programming experience with the BBC Micro was of modifying a type-in helicopter game to add enemies and pick-ups.

We blog something interesting about the device at `www.raspberrypi.org` at least once every day. Come and join in the conversation!

There were 100,000 people on our mailing list wanting a Raspberry Pi—and they all put an order in on day one! Not surprisingly, this brought up a few issues.

First off, there are the inevitable paper cuts you're going to get boxing up 100,000 little computers and mailing them out—and the fact was that we had absolutely no money to hire people to do this for us. We didn't have a warehouse—we had Jack's garage. There was no way we could raise the money to build 100,000 units at once—we'd envisaged making them in batches of 2,000 every couple of weeks, which, with this level of interest, was going to take so long that the thing would be obsolete before we managed to fulfil all the orders. Clearly, manufacturing and distribution were something we were going to have to give up on and hand over to somebody else who already had the infrastructure and capital to do that, so we got in touch with element14 and RS Components, both UK microelectronics suppliers with worldwide businesses, and contracted with them to do the actual manufacture and distribution side of things worldwide so we could concentrate on development and the Raspberry Pi Foundation's charitable goals.

Demand on the first day was still so large that RS and element14's websites both crashed for most of the day—at one point in the day, element14 were getting seven orders a second, and for a couple of hours on February 29, Google showed more searches were made worldwide for "Raspberry Pi" than were made for "Lady Gaga". We made and sold more than a million Raspberry Pis in the first year of business, making Raspberry Pi the fastest-growing computer company in the world, ever. Things aren't slowing down: we sell more than 100,000 Pis every month. If we'd stuck with our original plans, we'd have made 100 or so of these devices for University open days, and that would have been it.

NOTE The first production Pis were made in Chinese factories, but in the last year we have managed to repatriate all of the production to the UK. Your Raspberry Pi is now made in South Wales, in an area of the country with a proud manufacturing heritage, but few remaining factories. Amazingly, it costs us the same to manufacture in Wales as it did in China, and we're able to do that manufacture without a language or cultural barrier, and with the ability to jump in the car and be on the factory floor in a few hours if necessary.

There is nothing that affects the blood pressure quite like accidentally ending up running a large computer company!

So What Can You Do with the Raspberry Pi?

This book explores a number of things you can do with your Raspberry Pi, from controlling hardware with Python, to using it as a media centre, setting up camera projects, or building games in Scratch. The beauty of the Raspberry Pi is that it's just a very tiny general-purpose computer (which may be a little slower than you're used to for some desktop applications, but much better at some other stuff than a regular PC), so you can do anything you could do on a regular computer with it. In addition, the Raspberry Pi has powerful multimedia and 3D graphics capabilities, so it has the potential to be used as a games platform, and we very much hope to see more people starting to write games for it.

We think physical computing—building systems using sensors, motors, lights and micro-controllers—is something that gets overlooked in favour of pure software projects in a lot of instances, and it's a shame, because physical computing is *massive fun*. To the extent that there was any children's computing movement when we began this project, it was a physical computing movement. The LOGO turtles that represented physical computing when we were kids are now fighting robots, quadcopters or parent-sensing bedroom doors, and we love it. However, the lack of General Purpose Input/Output (GPIO) on home PCs is a real handicap for many people getting started with robotics projects. The Raspberry Pi exposes GPIO so you can get to work straight away.

I keep being surprised by ideas the community comes up with which wouldn't have crossed my mind in a thousand years: the Australian school meteor-tracking project; the Boreatton Scouts in the UK and their robot, which is controlled via an electroencephalography headset (the world's first robot controlled by Scouting brain waves); the family who are building a robot vacuum cleaner; Manuel, the talking Christmas moose. And I'm a real space cadet, so reading about the people sending Raspberry Pis into near-earth orbit on rockets and balloons gives me goosebumps.

In the first edition of this book, I said that success for us would be another 1,000 people every year taking up Computer Science at the university level in the UK. That would not only be beneficial for the country, the software and hardware industries, and the economy; but it would be even more beneficial for every one of those 1,000 people, who, I hope, discover that there's a whole world of possibilities and a great deal of fun to be had out there. We've gotten greedy now: I'd like to see that sort of statistic replicated in many more countries across the developed world, and to see something similar starting to happen in the developing world. We've been immensely proud to see Raspberry Pi labs spring up in the most unlikely places, like a village lab in a part of Cameroon with no electricity network where the Pis run off solar power, generators and batteries, or a school high in the mountains in Bhutan.

Building a robot when you're a kid can take you to places you never imagined—I know because it happened to me!

—Eben Upton

Part I

Connecting the Board

Chapter 1
Meet the Raspberry Pi

YOUR RASPBERRY PI board is a miniature marvel, packing considerable computing power into a footprint no larger than a credit card. It's capable of some amazing feats, but there are a few things you need to know before you plunge head-first into the bramble patch.

 If you're eager to get started, skip to the next chapter to find out how to connect your Raspberry Pi to a display, keyboard and mouse, install an operating system, and jump straight in to using the Pi.

A Trip Around the Board

The Raspberry Pi is currently available as two different models, known as the Model A and the Model B. While there are differences, with the Model A sacrificing some functionality in order to reduce its cost and power requirements, both share plenty of similarities that you'll learn about in this chapter. Figure 1-1 shows a Raspberry Pi Model B.

FIGURE 1-1:
The Raspberry Pi
board

In the centre of all Raspberry Pi boards is a square *semiconductor*, more commonly known as an integrated circuit or chip. This is the Broadcom BCM2835 *system-on-chip (SoC) module*, which provides the Pi with its general-purpose processing, graphics rendering and input/output capabilities. Stacked on top of that chip is another semiconductor, which provides the Pi with *memory* for temporary storage of data while it's running programs. This type of memory is known as *random access memory (RAM)*, as the computer can read from or write to any part of the memory at any time. RAM is *volatile*, meaning that anything stored in the memory is lost when the Pi loses power or is switched off.

Above and below the SoC are the Pi's video outputs. The silver (bottom) connector is a *High Definition Multimedia Interface (HDMI)* port, the same type of connector found on media players and many satellite and cable set-top boxes. When connected to a modern TV or monitor, the HDMI port provides high-resolution video and digital audio. The yellow (top) connector is a *composite video* port, which is designed for connection to older TVs that don't have an HDMI socket. The video quality is lower than is available via HDMI, and there's no audio; instead, audio is provided as an analogue signal on the *3.5mm audio jack* to the right of the composite video socket.

The pins to the top-left of the Pi compose the *general-purpose input-output (GPIO) header*, which can be used to connect the Pi to other hardware. The most common use for this port is to connect an *add-on board*. A selection of these is described in Chapter 16, "Add-on Boards". The GPIO port is extremely powerful, but it's fragile; when handling the Pi, always take care to avoid touching these pins, and never connect anything to them while the Pi is switched on.

The plastic and metal connector below the GPIO port is the *Display Serial Interface (DSI)* port, for connecting digitally driven flat-panel display systems. These are rarely used except by professional embedded developers, as the HDMI port is more flexible. A second plastic and metal connector, found to the right of the HDMI port, is the *Camera Serial Interface (CSI)* port, which provides a high-speed connection to the Raspberry Pi Camera Module or other Pi-compatible CSI-connected camera system. For more details on the CSI port, see Chapter 15, "The Raspberry Pi Camera Module".

To the very bottom-left of the board is the Pi's *power socket*. This is a *micro-USB* socket, the same type found on most modern smartphones and tablets. Connecting a micro-USB cable to a suitable power adapter, detailed in Chapter 2, "Getting Started with the Raspberry Pi", switches the Raspberry Pi on; unlike a desktop or laptop computer, the Pi doesn't have a power switch and will start immediately when power is connected.

On the underside of the Raspberry Pi board on the left-hand side is an *SD card slot*. A Secure Digital (SD) memory card provides storage for the operating system, programs, data and other files, and is *non-volatile*; unlike the volatile RAM, it will retain its information even when power is lost. In Chapter 2, "Getting Started with the Raspberry Pi", you'll learn how to prepare an SD card for use with the Pi, including installing an operating system in a process known as *flashing*.

The right-hand edge of the Pi will have different connectors depending on which model of Raspberry Pi you have, the Model A or the Model B. Above these is a series of *Light Emitting Diodes (LEDs)*, the top two of which—marked ACT and PWR and providing an activity notification and power notification respectively—are present on all boards.

Model A

The least expensive of the Raspberry Pis, the Model A shown in Figure 1-2 is designed to be affordable yet flexible. As well as its lower cost compared to the Model B, the Model A draws less power and is a good choice for projects that use solar, wind or battery power. Although the Model A's BCM2835 SoC is just as powerful as the one found on the Model B, it comes with half the memory at 256MB. This is an important consideration when deciding which model to buy, as it can make more complex applications run slowly—in particular, those applications that turn the Pi into a *server*, as described in Chapter 10, "The Pi as a Web Server".

FIGURE 1-2:
A Raspberry Pi
Model A

The Model A has only a single port on its right-hand edge, a *Universal Serial Bus (USB)* port. This is the same type of port found on desktop and laptop computers, and allows the Pi to be connected to almost any USB-compatible peripheral. Most commonly, the USB port is used to connect a keyboard for interacting with the Pi. If you also want to use a mouse at the same time, you'll need to buy a *USB hub* to add more ports to the Model A, or alternatively, a keyboard with built-in mouse functionality.

Model B

The Raspberry Pi Model B shown in Figure 1-3 is more expensive than the Model A, but comes with considerable advantages. Internally, it includes twice the memory at 512MB, while externally there are additional ports not available on the lower-cost model. For many users, the Model B is a worthwhile investment; only those with particular requirements of weight, space or power draw should consider the Model A for general-purpose use.

FIGURE 1-3:
A Raspberry Pi
Model B

The Model B has two USB ports on the right-hand edge of the board, providing connectivity for a keyboard and mouse, and still leaving two spare ports for additional accessories such as external storage devices or hardware interfaces. Additionally, it includes an *Ethernet* port for connecting the Pi to a wired network; this allows the Pi to access the Internet, and allows other devices on the network to access the Pi—providing, that is, they know the username and password or the Pi has been set up as a server as described in Chapter 10, "The Pi as a Web Server".

A History of Model B PCB Revisions

Although the Raspberry Pi Model B currently has 512MB of memory and two USB ports, this wasn't always the case. The Model B available today is known as *Revision 2*, as it is the second board to be made with the Model B designation. If you have bought a Raspberry Pi Model B second-hand, or purchased it some time ago, you may have a Revision 1 board, which has a few differences.

Revision 1

The original Raspberry Pi Model B, the Revision 1 board has just 256MB of RAM. It also has a slightly different GPIO header, which looks identical to those of later revisions but has certain features assigned to different pins, as explained in Chapter 14, "The GPIO Port". This is the most important difference: all other Raspberry Pi revisions and models share the same GPIO layout, so if you have an original Model B Revision 1 you may need to adjust instructions and programs before they can be used successfully.

Revision 2

Introduced shortly before the launch of the Model A, the Raspberry Pi Revision 2 includes double the memory of the original at 512MB. It also introduces the new, standardised GPIO header shared with the Model A. An extra header, which is also present on Model A boards, marked P5 and located just below the GPIO header, is a sure sign that a Model B is the newer Revision 2.

A Bit of Background

Before heading into Chapter 2, "Getting Started with the Raspberry Pi", it's a good idea to familiarise yourself with some background details of the Pi and its creation. While the Pi is usable as a general-purpose computer, capable of performing the same tasks as any desktop, laptop or server—albeit more slowly—it is designed as a *single-board computer* aimed at hobbyists and educational use, and as such differs from a "normal" computer in a couple of important ways.

ARM versus x86

The processor at the heart of the Raspberry Pi system is the Broadcom BCM2835 SoC multimedia processor. This means that the vast majority of the system's components, including its central and graphics processing units along with the audio and communications hardware, are built onto that single component hidden beneath the memory chip at the centre of the board.

It's not just this SoC design that makes the BCM2835 different to the processor found in your desktop or laptop, however. It also uses a different *instruction set architecture (ISA)*, known as ARM.

Developed by Acorn Computers back in the late 1980s, the ARM architecture is a relatively uncommon sight in the desktop world. Where it excels, however, is in mobile devices: the phone in your pocket almost certainly has at least one ARM-based processing core hidden away inside. Its combination of a simple *reduced instruction set computing (RISC)* architecture and low power draw make it the perfect choice over desktop chips with high power demands and *complex instruction set computing (CISC)* architectures.

The ARM-based BCM2835 is the secret of how the Raspberry Pi is able to operate on just the 5V 1A power supply provided via the onboard micro-USB port. It's also the reason why you won't find any metal heat sinks on the device: the chip's low power draw directly translates into very little waste heat, even during complicated processing tasks.

It does mean, however, that the Raspberry Pi isn't compatible with traditional PC software. The majority of software for desktops and laptops is built with the x86 instruction set architecture in mind, as found in processors from the likes of AMD, Intel and VIA. As a result, it won't run on the ARM-based Raspberry Pi.

The BCM2835 uses a generation of ARM's processor design known as ARM11, which in turn is designed around a version of the instruction set architecture known as ARMv6. This is worth remembering: ARMv6 is a lightweight and powerful architecture, but has a rival in the more advanced ARMv7 architecture used by the ARM Cortex family of processors. Software developed for ARMv7, like software developed for x86, is sadly not compatible with the Raspberry Pi's BCM2835—although developers can usually convert the software to make it suitable, a process known as *porting*.

That's not to say you're going to be restricted in your choices. As you'll discover later in the book, there is plenty of software available for the ARMv6 instruction set and, as the Raspberry Pi's popularity continues to grow, that will only increase. In this book, you'll also learn how to create your own software for the Pi even if you have no experience with programming.

Windows versus Linux

Another important difference between the Raspberry Pi and your desktop or laptop, other than the size and price, is the operating system—the software that allows you to control the computer.

The majority of desktop and laptop computers available today run one of two operating systems: Microsoft Windows or Apple OS X. Both platforms are *closed source*, created in a secretive environment using proprietary techniques.

These operating systems are known as closed source because of the nature of their *source code*, the computer-language recipe that tells the system what to do. In closed-source software, this recipe is kept a closely guarded secret. Users are able to obtain the finished software, but never to see how it's made.

The Raspberry Pi, by contrast, is designed to run an operating system called *GNU/Linux*—hereafter referred to simply as Linux. Unlike Windows or OS X, Linux is *open source*: it's possible to download the source code for the entire operating system and make whatever changes you desire. Nothing is hidden, and all changes are made in full view of the public. This open source development ethos has allowed Linux to be altered quickly to run on the Raspberry Pi. At the time of this writing, several versions of Linux—known as *distributions*—have been ported to the Raspberry Pi's BCM2835 chip, including Raspbian, Pidora and Arch Linux.

The different distributions cater to different needs, but they all have something in common: they're all open source. They're also all, by and large, compatible with each other: software written on a Debian system will usually operate perfectly well on Arch Linux, and vice versa.

Linux isn't exclusive to the Raspberry Pi. Hundreds of different distributions are available for desktops, laptops and even mobile devices; even Google's popular Android platform is developed on top of a Linux core. If you find that you enjoy the experience of using Linux on the Raspberry Pi, you could consider adding it to other computing devices you use as well. It will happily coexist with your current operating system, allowing you to enjoy the benefits of both while giving you a familiar environment when your Pi is unavailable.

As with the difference between ARM and x86, there's a key point to make about the practical difference between Windows and OS X and Linux: software written specifically for Windows or OS X won't run on Linux. Thankfully, there are plenty of compatible alternatives for the overwhelming majority of common software products—better still, the majority are free to use and as open source as the operating system itself, and can even be installed on both Windows and OS X to provide a familiar experience across all three platforms.

Chapter 2
Getting Started with the Raspberry Pi

NOW THAT YOU have a basic understanding of how the Raspberry Pi differs from other computing devices, it's time to get started. If you've just received your Pi, take it out of its protective anti-static bag and place it on a flat, non-conductive surface before continuing with this chapter.

To use your Pi, you'll need some extra peripherals. A display will allow you to see what you're doing, while a keyboard and mouse will be your input devices. In this chapter, you'll learn how to connect these to the Pi, along with a network connection in the case of the Model B. You'll also learn how to download and install an operating system for the Pi.

Your Mileage May Vary

The information and instructions in this book give you all you need to get your Raspberry Pi up and running and to make the most of its capabilities. Be aware that some of the software for the Raspberry Pi is evolving so quickly that what you see on your screen may differ slightly from some of the images in the book, as new features and options become available.

Connecting a Display

Before you can start using your Raspberry Pi, you're going to need to connect a display. The Pi supports three different video outputs: composite video, HDMI video and DSI video. Composite video and HDMI video are readily accessible to the end user, as described in this section, while DSI video requires some specialised hardware.

Composite Video

Composite video, available via the yellow-and-silver port at the top of the Pi known as an *RCA phono connector* (see Figure 2-1), is designed for connecting the Raspberry Pi to older display devices. As the name suggests, the connector creates a composite of the colours found within an image—red, green and blue—and sends it down a single wire to the display device, typically an old cathode-ray tube (CRT) TV.

When no other display device is available, a composite video connection will get you started with the Pi. The quality isn't great, however. Composite video connections are significantly more prone to interference, lack clarity and run at a limited *resolution,* meaning that you can fit fewer icons and lines of text on the screen at once.

FIGURE 2-1:
The yellow RCA
phono
connector, for
composite video
output

RCA phono connector

HDMI Video

A better quality picture can be obtained using the *High Definition Multimedia Interface (HDMI)* connector, the only port found on the bottom of the Pi (see Figure 2-2). Unlike the analogue composite connection, the HDMI port provides a high-speed digital connection for pixel-perfect pictures on both computer monitors and high-definition TV sets. Using the HDMI port, a Pi can display images at the Full HD 1920x1080 resolution of most modern HDTV sets. At this resolution, significantly more detail is available on the screen.

If you're hoping to use the Pi with an existing computer monitor, you may find that your display doesn't have an HDMI input. That's not a disaster: the digital signals present on the HDMI cable map to a common computer monitor standard called *Digital Video Interconnect (DVI)*. By purchasing an HDMI-to-DVI cable, you'll be able to connect the Pi's HDMI port to a monitor with DVI-D connectivity.

If your monitor has a VGA input—a D-shaped connector with 15 pins, typically coloured silver and blue—the Raspberry Pi can't connect to it directly. To use this type of monitor, you will need to purchase what is known as an *adapter dongle*; look for models that convert HDMI to VGA and specifically mention Raspberry Pi compatibility when making a purchase, and simply connect the HDMI end to the Pi and your VGA monitor cable to the other end of the dongle.

FIGURE 2-2:
The silver HDMI
connector, for
high-definition
video output

HDMI connector

DSI Video

The final video output on the Pi can be found above the SD card slot on the top of the printed circuit board—it's a small ribbon connector protected by a layer of plastic. This is for a video standard known as *Display Serial Interface (DSI)*, which is used in the flat-panel displays of tablets and smartphones. Displays with a DSI connector are rarely available for retail purchase, and are typically reserved for engineers looking to create a compact, self-contained system. A DSI display can be connected by inserting a ribbon cable into the matched connector on the Pi, but for beginners, the use of a composite or HDMI display is recommended.

Connecting Audio

If you're using the Raspberry Pi's HDMI port, audio is simple: when properly configured, the HDMI port carries both the video signal and a digital audio signal. This means that you can connect a single cable to your display device to enjoy both sound and pictures.

Assuming you're connecting the Pi to a standard HDMI display, there's very little to do at this point. For now, it's enough simply to connect the cable.

If you're using the Pi with a DVI-D monitor via an adapter or cable, audio will not be included. This highlights the main difference between HDMI and DVI: while HDMI can carry audio signals, DVI cannot and is instead used exclusively for video signals.

For those with DVI-D monitors, or those using the composite video output, a black *3.5 mm audio jack* located on the top edge of the Pi next to the yellow phono connector provides analogue audio (see Figure 2-1). This is the same connector used for headphones and microphones on consumer audio equipment, and it's wired in exactly the same way. If you want, you can simply connect a pair of headphones to this port for quick access to audio.

While headphones can be connected directly to the Raspberry Pi, you may find the volume a little lacking. If possible, connect a pair of powered speakers instead. The amplifier inside will help boost the signal to a more audible level, while many will also provide a physical volume control.   **TIP**

If you're looking for something more permanent, you can either use standard PC speakers that have a 3.5 mm connector or buy some adapter cables. For composite video users, a *3.5 mm to RCA phono cable* is useful. This provides the two white-and-red RCA phono connections that sit alongside the video connection, each carrying a channel of the stereo audio signal to the TV.

For those connecting the Pi to an amplifier or stereo system, you'll either need a 3.5 mm to RCA phono cable or a 3.5 mm to 3.5 mm cable, depending on what spare connections you have on your system. Both cable types are readily and cheaply available at consumer electronics shops, or can be purchased even cheaper from online retailers such as Amazon.

Connecting a Keyboard and Mouse

Now that you've got your Raspberry Pi's output devices sorted, it's time to think about input. At a bare minimum, you're going to need a keyboard, and for the majority of users, a mouse or trackball is a necessity too.

First, some bad news: if you've got a keyboard and mouse with a PS/2 connector—a round plug with a horseshoe-shaped array of pins—then you're going to have to go out and buy a replacement. The old PS/2 connection has been superseded, and the Pi expects your peripherals to be connected over the *Universal Serial Bus (USB) port*. An alternative is to buy a *USB to PS/2 adapter,* although be aware that some particularly old keyboards may not operate correctly through such an adapter.

Depending on whether you purchased the Model A or Model B, you'll have either one or two USB ports available on the right side of the Pi (see Figure 2-3). If you're using a Model B, you can connect the keyboard and mouse directly to these ports. If you're using a Model A, you'll need to purchase an *external USB hub* in order to connect two USB devices simultaneously.

FIGURE 2-3:
The Raspberry Pi
Model B's two
USB ports

USB ports

A USB hub is a good investment for any Pi user: even if you've got a Model B, you'll use up both your available ports just connecting your keyboard and mouse, leaving nothing free for additional devices such as an external optical drive, storage device or joystick. Make sure you buy a powered USB hub: passive models are cheaper and smaller, but lack the ability to run current-hungry devices like CD drives and external hard drives.

> **TIP** If you want to reduce the number of power sockets in use, connect the Raspberry Pi's USB power lead to your powered USB hub. This way, the Pi can draw its power directly from the hub, rather than needing its own dedicated power socket and mains adapter. This will only work on hubs with a power supply capable of providing 700mA to the Pi's USB port—more than will be available on cheaper hub models—along with whatever power is required by other peripherals.

Connecting the keyboard and mouse is as simple as plugging them into the USB ports, either directly in the case of a Model B or via a USB hub in the case of a Model A.

A Note on Storage

As you've probably noticed, the Raspberry Pi doesn't have a traditional hard drive. Instead, it uses a *Secure Digital (SD) memory card*, a solid-state storage system typically used in digital cameras. Almost any SD card will work with the Raspberry Pi, but because it holds the entire operating system, you need a card with at least 4 GB in capacity to store all the required files.

SD cards with the operating system preloaded are available from the official Raspberry Pi Store as well as with numerous other sites on the Internet. If you've purchased one of these, or received it in a bundle with your Pi, you can simply plug it into the SD card slot on the bottom side of the left-hand edge.

Some SD cards work better than others, with some models refusing to work at all with the Raspberry Pi. For an up-to-date list of SD card models known to work with the Pi, visit the eLinux Wiki page at `http://www.elinux.org/RPi_SD_cards`.

Installing NOOBS on an SD Card

The Raspberry Pi Foundation supplies a software tool for the Pi known as *New Out-Of-Box Software*, or *NOOBS*. This tool, is intended to make it as easy as possible to get started with using the Pi, and is available pre-installed on SD cards bundled with Raspberry Pi boards as well as separately and as a free download. It provides a selection of different operating systems for installation on the Pi, along with tools for changing its configuration.

If you have purchased an SD card with NOOBS already installed on it, you need do nothing at this stage. If not, download the latest version of the NOOBS software from the Raspberry Pi Foundation at `www.raspberrypi.org/downloads`. Note that this is a large file, and can take some considerable time to download; if you are on a capped Internet connection of around 1 GB a month, you will be unable to download the file. In this case, invest in an SD card with NOOBS preloaded from any Raspberry Pi-carrying retailer.

To use NOOBS, you'll need an SD card of at least 4 GB capacity, and preferably at least 8 GB to give you room to install additional software as you use the Pi. You'll also need an existing computer with an SD card reader, either built-in as with some models of laptop or an add-on device. To begin, insert the SD card into the card reader. If you have previously used your SD card with another device, such as a digital camera or games console, follow the link on the Raspberry Pi Downloads page to the SD Card Association's formatting tool and use this to *format* the SD card, preparing it for the installation. If the card is new, you can safely skip this step.

The NOOBS software is provided as a *Zip archive*. This is a file format where the data is *compressed*, so that it takes up less space and is quicker to download. Double-clicking on the file should be enough to open it on most operating systems; if not, download an archive utility like 7Zip (www.7-zip.org) and try again.

When you have opened the file, use your archive software's *extract* or *copy* function to transfer the files from within the archive to your SD card (see Figure 2-4). This can take some time to complete, thanks to the number and size of the files involved. Be patient, and when the extraction has finished and the activity light—if applicable—has gone off, use your operating system's Eject option to remove the SD card, and then insert the card into the Pi's SD card slot.

FIGURE 2-4:
Extracting
NOOBS to the
SD card

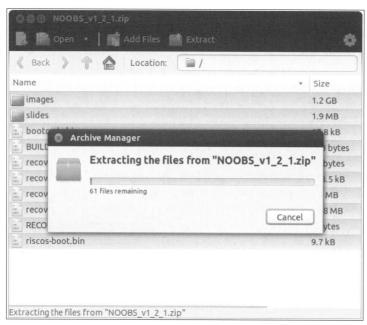

Connecting External Storage

While the Raspberry Pi uses an SD card for its main storage device—known as a boot device—you may find that you run into space limitations quite quickly. Although large SD cards holding 32 GB, 64 GB or more are available, they are often prohibitively expensive.

Thankfully, there are devices that provide an additional hard drive capacity to any computer when connected via a USB cable. Known as *USB Mass Storage (UMS) devices*, these can be physical hard drives, solid-state drives (SSDs) or even portable pocket-sized flash drives (see Figure 2-5).

The majority of USB Mass Storage devices can be read by the Pi, whether or not they have existing content. In order for the Pi to be able to access these devices, their drives must be mounted—a process you will learn in Chapter 3, "Linux System Administration". For now, it's enough to connect the drives to the Pi in readiness.

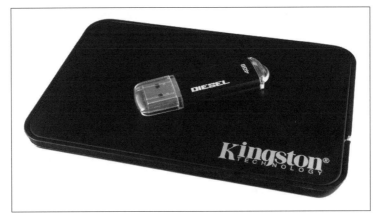

FIGURE 2-5: Two USB Mass Storage devices: a pen drive and an external hard drive

Connecting the Network

While the majority of these setup instructions are equally applicable to both the Raspberry Pi Model A and the Model B, networking is a special exception. To keep the component count—and therefore the cost—as low as possible, the Model A doesn't feature any onboard networking. Thankfully, that doesn't mean you can't network the Model A, only that you'll need some additional equipment to do so.

Networking the Model A

To give the Model A the same networking capabilities as its more expensive Model B counterpart, you'll need a USB-connected Ethernet adapter. This connects to a free USB port on the Raspberry Pi or a connected hub, and provides a wired Ethernet connection with an RJ45 connector, the same as is available on the Model B.

A 10/100 USB Ethernet adapter—with the numbers referring to its two-speed mode, 10 Mb/s and 100 Mb/s—can be purchased from online retailers for very little money. When buying an Ethernet adapter, be sure to check that Linux is listed as a supported operating system. There are a few models that only work with Microsoft Windows and are incompatible with the Raspberry Pi.

Don't be tempted to go for a gigabit-class adapter, which may be referred to as a 10/100/1000 USB Ethernet adapter. Standard USB ports, as used on the Raspberry Pi, can't cope with the speed of a gigabit Ethernet connection, and you'll see no benefit from the more expensive adapter.

Wired Networking

To get your Raspberry Pi on the network, you'll need to connect an *RJ45 Ethernet patch cable* between the Pi and a switch, router or hub. If you don't have a router or hub, you can get your desktop or laptop talking to the Pi by connecting the two directly together with a patch cable.

Usually, connecting two network clients together in this way requires a special cable, known as a *crossover cable*. In a crossover cable, the receive and transmit pairs are swapped so that the two devices are prevented from talking over each other—a task usually handled by a network switch or hub.

The Raspberry Pi is cleverer than that, however. The RJ45 port on the side of the Pi (see Figure 2-6) includes a feature known as *auto-MDI*, which allows it to reconfigure itself automatically. As a result, you can use any RJ45 cable—crossover or not—to connect the Pi to the network, and it will adjust its configuration accordingly.

FIGURE 2-6:
The Raspberry Pi
Model B's
Ethernet port

Ethernet port

If you do connect the Pi directly to a PC or laptop, you won't be able to connect out onto the Internet by default. To do so, you'll need to configure your PC to **bridge** the wired Ethernet port and another (typically wireless) connection. Doing so is outside the scope of this book, but if you are completely unable to connect the Pi to the Internet in any other way, you can try searching your operating system's help file for "bridge network" to find more guidance.

With a cable connected, the Pi will automatically receive the details it needs to access the Internet when it loads its operating system through the *Dynamic Host Configuration Protocol (DHCP)*. This assigns the Pi an *Internet Protocol (IP)* address on your network, and tells it the gateway it needs to use to access the Internet (typically the IP address of your router or modem).

For some networks, there is no DHCP server to provide the Pi with an IP address. When connected to such a network, the Pi will need manual configuration. You'll learn more about this in Chapter 5, "Network Configuration".

Wireless Networking

Current Raspberry Pi models don't feature any form of wireless network capability onboard, but—as with adding wired Ethernet to the Model A—it's possible to add Wi-Fi support to any Pi using a USB wireless adapter (see Figure 2-7).

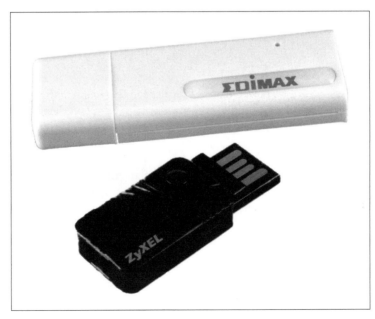

FIGURE 2-7: Two USB wireless adapters, suitable for use with the Raspberry Pi

Using such a device, the Pi can connect to a wide range of wireless networks, including those running on the latest 802.11n high-speed standard. Before purchasing a USB wireless adapter, check the following:

○ Ensure that Linux is listed as a supported operating system. Some wireless adapters are provided with drivers for Windows and OS X only, making them incompatible with the Raspberry Pi. A list of Wi-Fi adapters known to work with the Raspberry Pi can be found on the following website: `http://elinux.org/RPi_USB_Wi-Fi_Adapters`.

○ Ensure that your Wi-Fi network type is supported by the USB wireless adapter. The network type will be listed in the specifications as a number followed by a letter. If your network type is 802.11a, for example, an 802.11g wireless adapter won't work.

○ Check the frequencies supported by the card. Some wireless network standards, like 802.11a, support more than one frequency. If a USB wireless adapter is designed to work on a 2.4GHz network, it won't connect to a 5GHz network.

○ Check the encryption type used by your wireless network. Most modern USB wireless adapters support all forms of encryption, but if you're buying a second-hand or older model, you may find it won't connect to your network. Common encryption types include the outdated WEP and more modern WPA and WPA2.

Configuration of the wireless connection is done within Linux, so for now it's enough simply to connect the adapter to the Pi (ideally through a powered USB hub). You'll learn how to configure the connection in Chapter 5, "Network Configuration".

Connecting Power

The Raspberry Pi is powered by the small *micro-USB connector* found on the lower left side of the circuit board. This connector is the same as is found on the majority of smartphones and many tablet devices.

Many chargers designed for smartphones will work with the Raspberry Pi, but not all. The Pi is more power-hungry than most micro-USB devices, and requires up to 700 mA of current in order to operate. Some chargers can only supply up to 500 mA, causing intermittent problems in the Pi's operation (see Chapter 4, "Troubleshooting").

Connecting the Pi to the USB port on a desktop or laptop computer is possible, but not recommended. As with smaller chargers, the USB ports on a computer can't provide the power required for the Pi to work properly. Connect the micro-USB power supply only when you are ready to start using the Pi. With no power button on the device, it will start working the instant power is connected.

To safely turn the Raspberry Pi off, issue a *shutdown* command at the console or terminal by typing:

```
sudo shutdown -h now
```

For more information on using the terminal, see Chapter 3, "Linux System Administration".

If you have prepared or purchased your SD card with the NOOBS tool, as described earlier in this chapter, the Pi will load this tool and wait for your instructions; if not, powering the Pi on with a blank SD card will result in a blank screen or a coloured test pattern. In this case, switch off the power and remove the SD card before following the manual installation instructions from the following section, "Installing the Operating System".

Installing the Operating System

If you purchased your Raspberry Pi with a bundled SD card featuring a preloaded operating system, or followed the instructions for installing NOOBS earlier in this chapter, you can simply insert the card into the SD card slot on the underside of the Pi. If you bought the Pi by itself, you will need to install an operating system on the SD card before the Pi is ready to use.

Installing Using NOOBS

If you have installed NOOBS on your SD card, or purchased an SD card with NOOBS pre-installed, powering on the Raspberry Pi will display a menu (see Figure 2-8). This menu provides a list of operating systems suitable for the Pi, any one (or more) of which can be installed. You can also choose to change the interface language by clicking the arrow next to Language at the bottom of the screen, or choose a different keyboard layout using the arrow next to Keyboard.

If this is your first time running NOOBS on that SD card, there will be a delay while the SD card's *partition* is resized to make room for your chosen operating system; do not unplug the Pi's power while this is in progress, as you will risk damaging your SD card.

FIGURE 2-8:
The NOOBS
operating
system menu

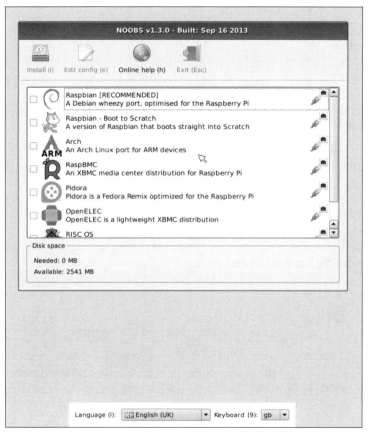

TIP

If you see only a blank screen, but the Pi's ACT and PWR lights are on, you may need to choose a different *display mode*. Press 1 on the keyboard for standard HDMI mode, 2 for a 'safe' mode with a lower resolution, 3 if you are using the composite port in a PAL region or 4 if you are using the composite port in an NTSC region. If you're not sure which is suitable, try all the options until you find one that works for you. The chosen display mode will also be passed to the installed operating system automatically.

Using the keyboard or mouse, browse through the list of operating systems and click on the box by its name to mark it for installation. Note that you can install multiple operating systems if your SD card is large enough: simply tick two or more operating systems from the list. For beginners, we recommend the Raspbian operating system. The remainder of this book will be written with Raspbian in mind, but much of what you'll learn is applicable to almost any Linux-based operating system both on the Pi and on other devices.

To begin the installation process, click the Install icon at the top-left of the menu and, when asked, confirm that the SD card can be overwritten when asked. As with installing NOOBS itself, this process can take a long time to complete; be patient, watch the progress bar and slideshow (see Figure 2-9) and don't remove the power cable or SD card from the Pi until it is finished. When the operating system is installed, click the OK button to reboot and load your chosen operating system.

FIGURE 2-9:
Installing an operating system via NOOBS

If you have installed more than one operating system, NOOBS will bring up a menu asking which one to boot: if you don't make a choice, the last operating system chosen—or the first in the list, if you haven't booted into an OS before—will automatically boot after 10 seconds.

For more information on using NOOBS after the operating system is installed, to either install a different operating system or to change the Pi's various settings, see Chapter 7, "Advanced Raspberry Pi Configuration".

Installing Manually

Installing an operating system manually is a more complicated procedure than using the NOOBS tool, but is sometimes preferable. By installing the software manually—a process known as *flashing*—you can choose to install operating systems that aren't available through NOOBS or newer versions that the tool doesn't yet have available.

To prepare a blank SD card for use with the Raspberry Pi, you'll need to flash an operating system onto the card, using your desktop or laptop computer. While this is slightly more complicated than simply dragging and dropping files onto the card, it shouldn't take more than a few minutes to complete.

First, you'll need to decide which Linux distribution you would like to use with your Raspberry Pi. Each has its advantages and disadvantages. Don't worry if you change your mind later and want to try a different version of Linux: an SD card can be flashed again with a new operating system at any point, and if you choose you can have multiple cards each with a different operating system installed.

The most up-to-date list of Linux releases compatible with the Pi is available from the Raspberry Pi website at `http://www.raspberrypi.org/downloads`.

The Foundation provides *BitTorrent* links for each distribution. These are small files that can be used with BitTorrent software to download the files from other users. Using these links is an efficient and fast way to distribute large files, and keeps the Foundation's download servers from becoming overloaded.

To use a BitTorrent link, you'll need to have a compatible *client* installed. If you don't already have a BitTorrent client installed, download one and install it before trying to download the Raspberry Pi Linux distribution. One client for Windows, OS X and Linux is μTorrent, available from `http://www.utorrent.com/downloads`.

Which distribution you choose to download is up to you. Instructions in the rest of the book will be based on the Raspbian Raspberry Pi distribution, a good choice for beginners. Where possible, we'll give you instructions for other distributions as well.

Linux distributions for the Raspberry Pi are provided as a single *image file*, compressed to make it faster to download. Once you've downloaded the Zip archive (a compressed file, which takes less time to download than the uncompressed files would) for your chosen distribution, you'll need to decompress it somewhere on your system. In most operating systems, you can simply double-click the file to open it, and then choose Extract or Unzip to retrieve the contents.

After you've decompressed the archive, you'll end up with two separate files. The file ending in `sha1` is a *hash*, which can be used to verify that the download hasn't been corrupted in transit. The file ending in `img` contains an exact copy of an SD card set up by the distribution's creators in a way that the Raspberry Pi understands. This is the file that needs to be flashed to the SD card.

| **WARNING** | In the following instructions, you'll be using a software utility called *dd*. Used incorrectly, *dd* will happily write the image to your main hard drive, erasing your operating system and all your stored data. Make sure you read the instructions in each section thoroughly and note the device address of your SD card carefully. Read twice, write once! |

Flashing from Linux

If your current PC is running a variant of Linux already, you can use the dd command to write the contents of the image file out to the SD card. This is a text-interface program operated from the command prompt, known as a *terminal* in Linux parlance. Follow these steps to flash the SD card:

1. Open a terminal from your distribution's applications menu.

2. Plug your blank SD card into a card reader connected to the PC.

3. Type sudo fdisk -l to see a list of disks. Find the SD card by its size, and note the device address: /dev/sdX, where X is a letter identifying the storage device. Some systems with integrated SD card readers may use the alternative format /dev/mmcblkX—if this is the case, remember to change the target in the following instructions accordingly.

4. Use cd to change to the directory with the .img file you extracted from the Zip archive.

5. Type sudo dd if=*imagefilename*.img of=/dev/sdX bs=2M to write the file *imagefilename*.img to the SD card connected to the device address from step 3. Replace *imagefilename.img* with the actual name of the file extracted from the Zip archive. This step takes a while, so be patient! During flashing, nothing will be shown on the screen until the process is fully complete (see Figure 2-10).

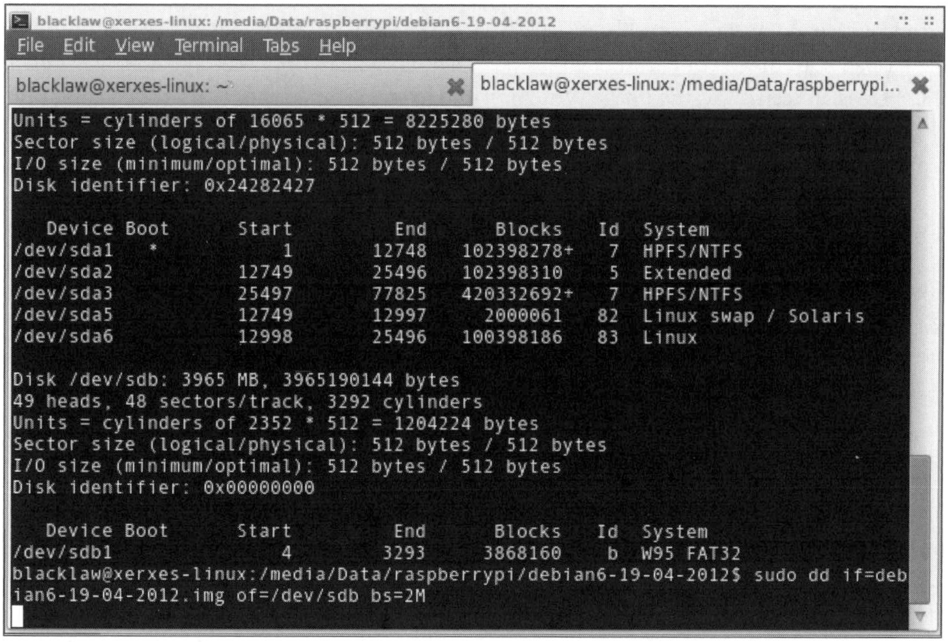

FIGURE 2-10:
Flashing the SD card using the dd command in Linux

Flashing from OS X

If your current computer is a Mac running Apple OS X, you'll be pleased to hear that things are just as simple as with Linux. Thanks to a similar ancestry, OS X and Linux both contain the dd utility, which you can use to flash the system image to your blank SD card as follows:

1. Select Utilities from the Application menu, and then click on the Terminal application.

2. Plug your blank SD card into a card reader connected to the Mac.

3. Type `diskutil list` to see a list of disks. Find the SD card by its size, and note the device address (`/dev/diskX`, where *X* is a letter identifying the storage device).

4. If the SD card has been automatically mounted and is displayed on the desktop, type `diskutil unmountdisk /dev/diskX` to unmount it before proceeding.

5. Use `cd` to change to the directory with the `.img` file you extracted from the Zip archive.

6. Type `dd if=imagefilename.img of=/dev/diskX bs=2m` to write the file `imagefilename.img` to the SD card connected to the device address from step 3. Replace `imagefilename.img` with the actual name of the file extracted from the Zip archive. This step takes a while, so be patient!

Flashing from Windows

If your current PC is running Windows, things are slightly trickier than with Linux or OS X. Windows does not have a utility like dd, so some third-party software is required to get the image file flashed onto the SD card. Although it's possible to install a Windows-compatible version of dd, there is an easier way: the Image Writer for Windows. Designed specifically for creating USB or SD card images of Linux distributions, this features a simple graphical user interface that makes the creation of a Raspberry Pi SD card straightforward.

The latest version of Image Writer for Windows can be found at the official website: `https://sourceforge.net/projects/win32diskimager/`. Follow these steps to download, install and use the Image Writer for Windows software to prepare the SD card for the Pi:

1. Click the green Download button to download the Image Writer for Windows Zip file, and extract it to a folder on your computer.

2. Plug your blank SD card into a card reader connected to the PC.

3. Double-click the `Win32DiskImager.exe` file to open the program, and click the blue folder icon to open a file browse dialogue box.

4. Browse to the *imagefilename*.img file you extracted from the distribution archive, replacing *imagefilename.img* with the actual name of the file extracted from the Zip archive, and then click the Open button.

5. Select the drive letter corresponding to the SD card from the Device drop-down dialogue box. If you're unsure which drive letter to choose, open My Computer or Windows Explorer to check.

6. Click the Write button to flash the image file to the SD card. This process takes a while, so be patient!

No matter which operating system you're writing from, it's important to ensure you leave the   **WARNING**
SD card connected until the image has been completely written. If you don't, you may find
that Pi doesn't *boot* when the SD card is connected. If this happens, start the process again.

When the image has been flashed onto the SD card, remove it from the computer and insert it
into the Raspberry Pi's SD card slot, located underneath the circuit board. The SD card should
be inserted with the label facing away from the board and pushed fully home to ensure a good
connection.

Chapter **3**
Linux System Administration

THE MAJORITY OF modern Linux distributions are user-friendly, with a *graphical user interface (GUI)* that provides an easy way to perform common tasks. It is, however, quite different to both Windows and OS X, so if you're going to get the most out of your Raspberry Pi, you'll need a quick primer in using the operating system.

Linux: An Overview

As briefly explained in Chapter 1, "Meet the Raspberry Pi", Linux is an open source project that was originally founded to produce a *kernel* that would be free for anyone to use. The kernel is the heart of an operating system, and handles the communication between the user and the hardware.

Although only the kernel itself is rightly called Linux, the term is often used to refer to a collection of different open source projects from a variety of companies. These collections come together to form different *flavours* of Linux, known as *distributions*.

The original version of Linux was combined with a collection of tools created by a group called GNU. The resulting system, known as *GNU/Linux*, was basic but powerful. Unlike many mainstream operating systems of the era, it offered facilities like multiple user accounts where several users can share a single computer. That's something rival closed-source operating systems have taken on board, with both Windows and OS X now supporting multiple user accounts on the same system. It's also still present in Linux, and provides security and protection for the operating system.

In Linux, you'll spend most of your time running a *restricted* user account. This doesn't mean you're being limited in what you can do; instead, it prevents you from accidentally doing something that will break the software on your Raspberry Pi. It also prevents *viruses* and other *malware* from infecting the system by locking down access to critical system files and directories.

Before you can get started, it's worth becoming familiar with some of the terms and concepts used in the world of Linux, as defined in Table 3-1. Even if you're experienced with other operating systems, it's a good idea to review this table before booting up your Pi for the first time.

Table 3-1 **The Quick Linux Glossary**

Term/Concept	Definition
Bash	The most popular *shell* choice, used in the majority of Linux distributions.
Bootloader	Software responsible for loading the Linux kernel. The most common is GRUB.
Console	A version of the terminal that is always available, and the first thing you see on the Pi.
Desktop environment	Software to make the GUI look pretty. GNOME and KDE are popular desktop environments.
Directory	The Linux term for what Windows calls *folders*, where files are stored.
Distribution	A particular version of Linux. Pidora, Arch and Raspbian are distributions.
Executable	A file that can be run as a program. Linux files must be marked executable in order to run.
EXT2/3/4	The EXTended file system, the most common file system used in Linux.
File system	The way a hard drive or other storage device is formatted so it's ready for file storage.
GNOME	One of the most common Linux desktop environments.
GNU	A free software project, which provides many of the tools used in Linux distributions.
GRUB	The GRand Unified Bootloader, created by GNU and used to load the Linux kernel.
GUI	A graphical user interface, in which the user operates the computer via a mouse or touch.
KDE	Another extremely popular Linux desktop environment.
Linux	Properly, the kernel used by GNU/Linux. Popularly, an open source operating system.
Live CD	A Linux distribution provided as a CD or DVD, which doesn't require installation.
Package	A collection of files required to run an application, typically handled by the package manager.
Package manager	A tool for keeping track of, and installing new, software.
Partition	A section of a hard drive that is ready to have a file system applied to it for storage.
Root	The main user account in Linux, equivalent to the Windows administrator account. Also called the *superuser*.
Shell	A text-based command prompt, loaded in a terminal.
sudo	A program that allows restricted users to run a command as the root user.
Superuser	See *Root*.
Terminal	A text-based command prompt in which the user interacts with a *shell* program.
X11	The X Window system, a package that provides a graphical user interface (GUI).

The Terminal and the GUI

As in OS X and Windows, there are typically two main ways to achieve a given goal in Linux: through the graphical user interface (GUI) and through the command line (known in Linux parlance as the *console* or the *terminal*).

The appearance of various Linux distributions can be quite different, depending on the desktop environment in use. In this book, the recommended Raspbian distribution is used, but most of the commands you will be learning are entered at the *terminal* and are typically the same across all distributions.

Where other distributions differ, you will be given alternative methods of achieving the same goals.

Linux Basics

Although there are hundreds of different Linux distributions available, they all share a common set of tools known as *commands*. These tools, which are operated via the terminal, are analogous to similar tools on Windows and OS X. To get started, you'll need to learn the following commands:

- **ls**—Short for *listing*, `ls` provides a list of the contents of the current directory. Alternatively, it can be called with the directory to be listed as an argument. As an example, typing `ls /home` will provide a list of the contents of `/home`, regardless of your current directory. The Windows equivalent is `dir`.

- **cd**—An initialism of *change directory*, `cd` allows you to navigate your way through the file system. Typing `cd` on its own puts you back in your home directory. Typing the command along with the name of the directory you wish to move to, by contrast, switches to that directory. Note that directories can be absolute or relative: `cd boot` will move you to the directory called `boot` under your current directory, but `cd /boot` will move you straight to the `/boot` directory wherever you are.

- **mv**—The *move* command has two purposes in Linux: it allows a file to be moved from one directory to another, and it also allows files to be renamed. That latter feature may seem out of place, but in Linux terms, the file is being moved from one name to another. The command is called as `mv oldfile newfile`.

- **rm**—Short for *remove*, `rm` deletes files. Any file—or list of files—provided after the command name will be deleted. The Windows equivalent is `del`, and the two share a common requirement that care should be taken to ensure the right file is deleted.

○ **rmdir**—By itself, rm cannot usually remove directories. As a result, rmdir is provided to delete directories once they have been emptied of files by rm.

○ **mkdir**—The opposite of rmdir, the mkdir command creates new directories. For example, typing mkdir myfolder at the terminal will create a new directory called myfolder under the current working directory. As with cd, directories provided to the command can be relative or absolute.

Introducing Raspbian

Raspbian is the name given to a customised variant of the popular Debian Linux distribution. Debian is one of the longest-running Linux distributions, and concentrates on high compatibility and excellent performance even on modest hardware—making it a great partner for the Raspberry Pi. Raspbian takes Debian as its base, or *parent distribution*, and adds custom tools and software to make using the Raspberry Pi as easy as possible.

To keep the download size to a minimum, the Raspberry Pi image for Raspbian includes only a subset of the software you'd find on a regular desktop version. This includes tools for browsing the web, programming in Python and using the Pi with a GUI. Additional software can be quickly installed through the use of the distribution's package manager, *apt*, or purchased through the Raspberry Pi Store link on the desktop. Raspbian includes a desktop environment known as the *Lightweight X11 Desktop Environment (LXDE)*. Designed to offer an attractive user interface using the *X Window System* software, LXDE provides a familiar point-and-click interface that will be immediately accessible to anyone who has used Windows, OS X or other GUI-based operating systems in the past.

The GUI doesn't load by default in most Raspberry Pi distributions, and Raspbian is no exception. To quickly load it and leave the text-based console behind, log in, type startx and then press the Enter key. To return to the console, while leaving the GUI running in the background, hold down Ctrl + Alt and press F1 before releasing all three keys.

TIP

If you're using the recommended Raspbian distribution, you'll find that you have plenty of preinstalled software to get started. While hardly an exhaustive example of the software available for the Pi, which numbers in the thousands of *packages*, it's a good introduction to precisely what the system can do.

The software provided with the Raspbian distribution is split into themed categories. To view these categories, left-click the menu icon, the arrow located on the bottom-left of the screen in LXDE (see Figure 3-1).

FIGURE 3-1:
The LXDE
desktop, as
loaded on the
Raspbian
distribution on a
Raspberry Pi

The following lists describe the software packages, grouped by category. There is also a category not covered here, dubbed "Other", into which numerous system tools are grouped. If you have installed a program and can't find it anywhere else, try the Other menu.

Accessories

○ **Debian Reference**—A built-in reference guide, this provides a detailed explanation of the Debian Linux distribution and how programmers can contribute to its development.

○ **File Manager**—The PCManFM file manager provides a graphical browser for files stored on the Pi or any connected storage device.

○ **Galculator**—An open source scientific calculator, offering a variety of functions for both quick and complex sums.

○ **Image Viewer**—The GPicView lets you view images, such as those from a digital camera or on a connected storage device.

○ **Leafpad**—This is a simple text editor, which is useful for making quick notes or writing simple programs.

○ **LXTerminal**—This LXDE terminal package allows you to use the Linux command line in a window without leaving the graphical user interface.

○ **Root Terminal**—Similar to LXTerminal, the Root Terminal automatically logs you in as the *root* superuser account in order to carry out system maintenance tasks unavailable to a regular user account.

○ **Xarchiver**—If you need to create or extract compressed files, such as Zip archives, this is the tool for the job.

Education

○ **Scratch**—A graphical programming language aimed at young children. You'll learn more about Scratch and its capabilities in Chapter 11, "An Introduction to Scratch".

○ **Squeak**—The platform on which Scratch runs. You will rarely need to use this menu entry, and should instead use the Scratch entry above.

Internet

○ **Dillo**—One of the fastest web browsers available for the Pi, but somewhat basic compared to Midori.

○ **Midori**—A fast yet lightweight web browser, Midori is equivalent to Internet Explorer in Windows or Safari on OS X.

○ **Midori Private Browsing**—Clicking on this menu entry loads the Midori web browser in private mode, meaning that sites you visit aren't saved into the browser's history.

○ **NetSurf Web Browser**—An alternative to Midori, NetSurf can perform better on certain types of web page. Trying both will allow you to experiment and find the one that works best for you.

○ **wps_gui**—A graphical user interface for configuring a Raspberry Pi with optional USB Wireless Adapter to connect to a Wireless Protected System (WPS) encrypted network.

Programming

○ **IDLE**—An *integrated development environment (IDE)* written specifically for Python. You'll learn more about using IDLE to write your own Python programs in Chapter 12, "An Introduction to Python".

○ **IDLE 3**—Clicking this entry loads IDLE configured to use the newer Python 3 programming language, rather than the default Python 2.7 language. Both are largely compatible with each other, but some programs may require features of Python 3.

○ **Scratch**—This shortcut opens the Scratch educational language, and is the same as the Scratch entry found in the Education category. Either can be used to start the program.

○ **Squeak**—As with Scratch, this is a duplicate of the shortcut found in the Education category. You will rarely want to click this directly, and should instead use the Scratch shortcut.

System Tools

○ **Task Manager**—A tool for checking the amount of free memory available on the Pi and the current workload of the processor, and for closing programs that have crashed or are otherwise unresponsive.

Preferences

○ **Customise Look and Feel**—A toolkit for adjusting the appearance of the GUI, including the style and colour of windows.

○ **Desktop Session Settings**—A tool for changing how the system works when the user is logged in, including what programs are automatically loaded and which window manager—the software that draws the borders and title bars of windows—is used.

○ **Keyboard and Mouse**—A tool for adjusting input devices. If your keyboard is typing the wrong characters for certain keys, or your mouse is too sensitive, the settings can be altered here.

○ **Monitor Settings**—The resolution that the monitor or TV connected to the Pi runs at can be altered here, although advanced changes require modification of configuration files. You'll learn about this in Chapter 7, "Advanced Raspberry Pi Configuration".

○ **Openbox Configuration Manager**—The LXDE GUI uses a desktop environment called *Openbox*, which can be adjusted here. Using this tool, you can apply new themes to change the GUI's appearance, or alter how certain aspects of the interface operate.

○ **Preferred Applications**—A tool for changing which applications are opened for particular file types. If you choose to use an alternative web browser, the system default can be changed here.

Finding Help

Linux is designed to be as user-friendly as possible to new users, even at the terminal command prompt. Although you'll learn the most common ways to use each command in this chapter, not every option will be covered—to do so would require a much larger book.

If you find yourself stuck, or if you want to learn more about any of the tools that are discussed in the following pages, there's a command you should learn: man.

Each Linux application comes with a help file known as a *man page*—short for "manual page". It provides background on the software as well as details on what its options do and how to use them.

To access the man page for a given tool, just type man followed by the command name. To see the man page for ls, a tool for listing the contents of directories, just type man ls.

About Raspbian's Parent, Debian

Raspbian is based on one of the original Linux distributions, Debian. Named after its creator and his girlfriend—Ian and Deb—Debian is a popular distribution in its own right. It is common in the world of open source software, however, for projects to start up based on refining, customising or tweaking existing projects in a process known as *forking*. Raspbian is a *fork* of Debian, but it isn't alone: Ubuntu Linux from Canonical is also based on Debian, while Linux Mint, one of the most popular distributions for desktops and laptops, is based in turn on Ubuntu.

This process of forking and forking again is something unique to open source software. With a closed-source package, like Microsoft Windows, it's not possible to customise it to your individual requirements. This is one of the biggest strengths of open source software, and is brilliantly demonstrated by the ease with which Raspbian was tailored to the requirements of the Raspberry Pi.

Alternatives to Raspbian

While Raspbian is the recommended Linux distribution for the Raspberry Pi, there are alternatives. The most popular are available from the Raspberry Pi Foundation's Downloads page at http://www.raspberrypi.org/downloads, and most can be installed easily using NOOBS, as described in Chapter 2, "Getting Started with the Raspberry Pi".

Next to Raspbian, the most common distributions installed are RaspBMC and OpenELEC, which both turn the Pi into a dedicated home theatre system, as demonstrated in Chapter 8, "The Pi as a Home Theatre PC". The next most popular is Pidora, a distribution based on the Fedora Linux project, which, in turn, has Red Hat as its parent distribution. Finally, Arch Linux is designed for those already familiar with Linux; unlike the others in the list, it doesn't include a graphical user interface by default.

One entry in the NOOBS list is not a variant of Linux at all: RiscOS. Originally produced by Acorn Computers in the late 1980s for its Archimedes range of personal computers—which, like the Raspberry Pi, were based on an ARM processor—RiscOS is a fast, easy-to-use operating system with a clean appearance to its graphical user interface. While the breakup of Acorn in 1998 saw the popularity of RiscOS decline, the platform still has its fans, who were quick to add support for the Raspberry Pi.

Running RiscOS on the Raspberry Pi results in an environment that is significantly more responsive than any of the other operating systems on offer, thanks to its origins as a platform designed specifically for the ARM instruction set architecture. Sadly, that speed comes at a cost: RiscOS can only run applications written specifically for RiscOS, of which there are far fewer than those written for Linux.

Using External Storage Devices

The Pi's SD card, which stores all the various Pi files and directories, isn't very big. The largest available SD card at the time of writing is 256 GB, which is tiny compared to the 4,000 GB (4 TB) available from the largest full-size desktop hard drives.

If you're using your Pi to play back video files (see Chapter 8, "The Pi as a Home Theatre PC") you'll likely need more storage than you can get from an SD card. As you learned in Chapter 1, "Meet the Raspberry Pi", it's possible to connect USB Mass Storage (UMS) devices to the Pi in order to gain access to more storage space.

Before these external devices are accessible, however, the operating system needs to know about them. In Linux, this process is known as *mounting*. If you're running a version of Linux with a desktop environment loaded—like the recommended Raspbian distribution's LXDE, loaded from the console with the `startx` command—this process is automatic. Simply connect the device to a free USB port on the Pi or a USB hub, and the device and its contents will immediately be accessible (see Figure 3-2).

FIGURE 3-2:
LXDE
automatically
mounting a USB
mass storage
device

From the console, things are only slightly more difficult. To make a device accessible to Linux when the desktop environment isn't loaded, follow these steps:

| TIP | Where you see a ↲ symbol, this means the command has been split over multiple lines due to the size of the book's pages. Enter the command as a single line, continuing to type for each line that ends in a ↲ and only pressing Enter at the very end of the command. |

1. Connect the USB storage device to the Pi, either directly or through a connected USB hub.

2. Type sudo fdisk -1 to get a list of drives connected to the Pi, and find the USB storage device by size. Note the device name: /dev/sd*XN*, where *X* is the drive letter and *N* is the partition number. If it is the only device connected to the Pi, this will be /dev/sda1.

3. Before the USB storage device is accessible, Linux needs a mount point for it. Create this by typing sudo mkdir /media/externaldrive.

4. Currently, the device is only accessible to the root user. To make it accessible to all users, type the following as a single line:

```
sudo chgrp -R users /media/externaldrive && ⏎
 sudo chmod -R g+w /media/externaldrive
```

5. Type the following command to mount the USB storage device to gain access to the device and its contents:

```
sudo mount /dev/sdXN /media/externaldrive -o=rw
```

Creating a New User Account

Unlike many desktop operating systems, which were originally designed for use by a single individual, Linux is at heart a social operating system designed to accommodate numerous users. By default, Raspbian is configured with two user accounts: *pi*, which is the normal user account, and *root*, which is a superuser account with additional permissions.

Don't be tempted to log in as *root* all the time. Using a nonprivileged user account, you're **TIP** protected against accidentally wrecking your operating system and from the ravages of viruses and other malware downloaded from the Internet.

While it's certainly possible for you to use the *pi* account, it's better if you create your own dedicated user account. Further accounts can also be created, for any friends or family members who might want to use the Pi.

Creating a new account on the Pi is straightforward, and is roughly the same on all distributions, except for the username and password used to log in to the Pi initially. Just follow these steps:

1. Log in to the Pi using the existing user account (user name pi and password raspberry if you're using the recommended Raspbian distribution).

2. Type the following as a single line with no spaces after any of the commas:

```
sudo useradd -m -G adm,dialout,cdrom,audio,plugdev,users, ↵
  lpadmin,sambashare,vchiq,powerdev username
```

This creates a new, blank user account.

3. To set a password on the new account, type sudo passwd *username* followed by the new password when prompted.

To explain what just happened: the command sudo tells the operating system that the command you're typing should be run as if you were logged in as the *root* account. The useradd command says you want to create a new user account. The –m section—known as a *flag* or an *option*—tells the useradd program to create a home directory where the new user can store his or her files. The big list following the –G flag is the list of groups of which the user should be a member.

Users and Groups

In Linux, each user has three main attributes: their *User ID (UID)*, their *Group ID (GID)* and a list of supplementary group memberships. A user can be a member of as many groups as he or she pleases, although only one of these can be the user's primary group. This is usually a self-named group matching the user name.

Group membership is important. While users can be granted direct access to files and devices on the system, it's more common for a user to receive access to these via group membership. The group audio, for example, grants all members the ability to access the Pi's sound playback hardware. Without that membership, the user won't be listening to any music.

To see a user's group memberships, type groups *username* at the terminal. If you use this on the default user *pi*, you'll see the list of groups any new member should join to make use of the Pi. This is where the information used in step 2 of the preceding procedure was found.

File System Layout

The content of the SD card is known as its *file system* and is split into multiple sections, each with a particular purpose. Although it's not necessary for you to understand what each section does in order to use the Raspberry Pi, it can be helpful background knowledge should anything go wrong.

Logical Layout

The way Linux deals with drives, files, folders and devices is somewhat different to other operating systems. Instead of having multiple drives labelled with a letter, everything appears as a branch beneath what is known as the *root file system*.

If you log in to the Pi and type `ls /` you'll see various directories displayed (see Figure 3-3). Some of these are areas of the SD card for storing files, while others are *virtual directories* for accessing different portions of the operating system or hardware.

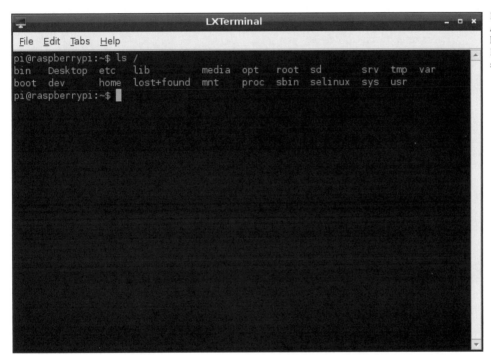

FIGURE 3-3:
A directory listing for the Pi's root file system

The directories visible on the default Raspbian distribution are as follows:

- **boot**—This contains the Linux kernel and other packages needed to start the Pi.

- **bin**—Operating system-related binary files, like those required to run the GUI, are stored here.

- **dev**—This is a virtual directory, which doesn't actually exist on the SD card. All the devices connected to the system—including storage devices, the sound card and the HDMI port—can be accessed from here.

- **etc**—This stores miscellaneous configuration files, including the list of users and their encrypted passwords.

- **home**—Each user gets a subdirectory beneath this directory to store all their personal files.

- **lib**—This is a storage space for *libraries*, which are shared bits of code required by numerous different applications.

- **lost+found**—This is a special directory where *file fragments* are stored if the system crashes.

- **media**—This is a special directory for removable storage devices, like USB memory sticks or external CD drives.

- **mnt**—This folder is used to manually *mount* storage devices, such as external hard drives.

- **opt**—This stores optional software that is not part of the operating system itself. If you install new software to your Pi, it will usually go here.

- **proc**—This is another virtual directory, containing information about running programs, which are known in Linux as *processes*.

- **selinux**—Files related to *Security Enhanced Linux*, a suite of security utilities originally developed by the US National Security Agency.

- **sbin**—This stores special binary files, primarily used by the root (superuser) account for system maintenance.

- **sys**—This directory is where special operating system files are stored.

- **tmp**—Temporary files are stored here automatically.

- **usr**—This directory provides storage for user-accessible programs.

- **var**—This is a virtual directory that programs use to store changing values or *variables*.

Physical Layout

Although the preceding list is how the file system appears to the Linux operating system, it's not how it's laid out on the SD card itself. For the default Raspbian distribution, the SD card is organised into two main sections, known as *partitions* because they split the device into different areas in much the same way as the chapters of this book help to organise its contents.

The first partition on the disk is a small (approximately 75 MB) partition formatted as VFAT, the same partition format used by Microsoft Windows for removable drives. This is *mounted*, or made accessible, by Linux in the /boot directory and contains all the files required to configure the Raspberry Pi and to load Linux itself.

The second partition is far larger and formatted as EXT4, a native Linux file system designed for high-speed access and data safety. This partition contains the main chunk of the distribution. All the programs, the desktop, the users' files and any software that you install yourself are stored here. This takes up the bulk of the SD card.

Installing and Uninstalling Software

The default software installed with the Raspbian distribution is enough to get you started, but chances are you're going to want to customise your Pi according to your own requirements.

Obtaining Software from the Pi Store

Installing new software onto the Pi is simple, thanks to the inclusion of the Raspberry Pi Store. This is a custom shopfront where Pi programmers can offer their software for quick download and installation. To get started, double-click the Pi Store icon on the desktop. The window that appears provides access to all software currently available through the Pi Store (see Figure 3-4).

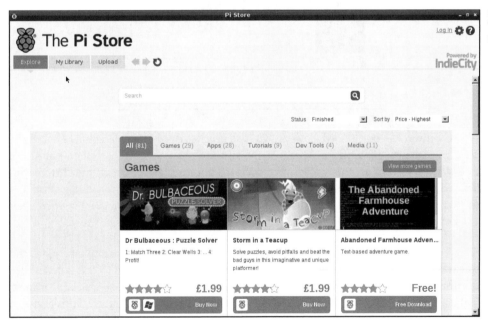

FIGURE 3-4:
The Pi Store
main window

Software on the Pi Store is split into categories, ranging from games to tutorials and even media like videos, books and magazines. Clicking on a category across the top will show the software from that category in a grid, which can be scrolled using the keyboard or mouse. Clicking on a piece of software will provide access to more information and a download link to automatically install the software (see Figure 3-5).

FIGURE 3-5:
Viewing
software in the
Pi Store

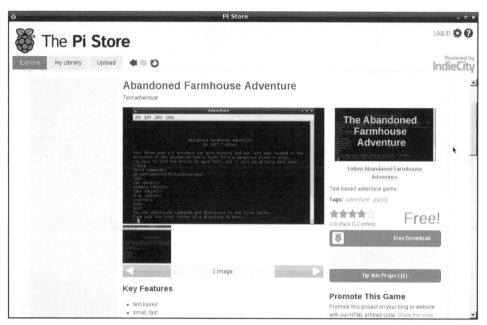

Before software can be installed, however, you will need to register for an account. The Pi Store is run by digital distribution specialist IndieCity; if you already have an account on IndieCity's own website, you can use this by clicking the Log In option at the top right of the Pi Store window and entering your email address and password. If not, when you try to download any software you will be asked to register: simply click the Register button and fill in your email address, followed by typing a password for your account in the two boxes provided.

Some software on the Pi Store requires payment. If this is the case, attempting to install the software will prompt you for your name, address and payment details. These details are transmitted across an *encrypted connection*, meaning that they cannot be seen during transit, and used by the Pi Store's operator IndieCity to take payment for the item. Once payment has been made, the software can be downloaded as normal.

All software you install through the Pi Store is placed in the My Library section (see Figure 3-6). This provides an easy way to uninstall software, or to install software that you have previously used but since removed. Downloads are tied to your account; if you log in to the Pi Store on a different Raspberry Pi, you can use the My Library to quickly find and install your favourite software.

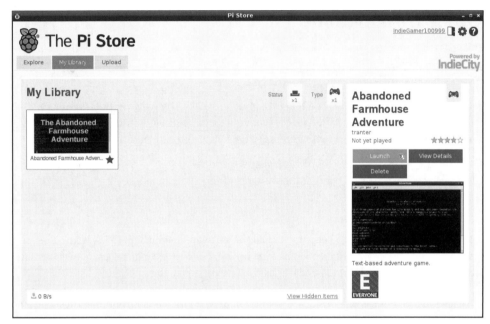

FIGURE 3-6:
The Pi Store My
Library screen

As you learn to use the Raspberry Pi, and especially if you're learning to program, you may find yourself writing software of your own. Whether it's a game, a productivity application or even a tutorial, you can quickly and easily list it for download on the Pi Store by clicking the Upload option and filling in the form that appears.

If you have any trouble with the Pi Store, either for downloading software or publishing your own, click the question mark icon at the top right of the window to access help.

Obtaining Software from Elsewhere

For a larger selection of packages, the Raspbian distribution includes a tool called apt, which is a powerful *package manager*. Packages are what Linux calls a piece of software, or a collection of different pieces of software designed to work together.

Although apt is designed to be operated from the command line, it's very user-friendly and easy to learn. There are GUIs for apt, such as the popular Synaptic Package Manager, but they often struggle to run on the Pi due to the lack of memory. As a result, we recommend that software be installed at the terminal.

Other Distributions

Raspbian, in common with most Debian-based distributions, uses a tool called apt as the package manager. It's not the only tool out there, and other distributions make different choices. Pidora, for example, uses the pacman tool.

Pacman is no more difficult to use than apt, but its syntax (the way it expects you to phrase instructions to install new software or remove existing software) is different. For instructions on how to use pacman instead of apt, type man pacman at the Pidora terminal.

Other distributions may use the yum package manager. If you're trying a distribution that uses yum, simply type man yum at the terminal for instructions.

A package manager's job is to keep track of all the software installed on the system. It doesn't just install new software—it also keeps tabs on what is currently installed, allows old software to be removed and installs updates as they become available.

Package management is one of the areas where Linux differs greatly from operating systems like Windows or OS X. Although it's possible to manually download new software to install, it's far more common to use the built-in package management tools instead.

TIP   Before trying to install new software or upgrade existing software, you need to make sure the apt *cache* is up to date. To do this, simply type the command sudo apt-get update.

Finding the Software You Want

The first step to installing a new piece of software is to find out what it's called. The easiest way to do this is to search the *cache* of available software packages. This cache is a list of all the software available to install via apt, stored on Internet servers known as *repositories*.

The apt software includes a utility for managing this cache, called apt-cache. Using this software, it's possible to run a search on all the available software packages for a particular word or phrase.

For example, to find a game to play, you can type the following command:

```
apt-cache search game
```

That tells `apt-cache` to search its list of available software for anything that has the word "game" in its title or description. For common search terms, you can end up with quite a list (see Figure 3-7), so try to be as specific as you can.

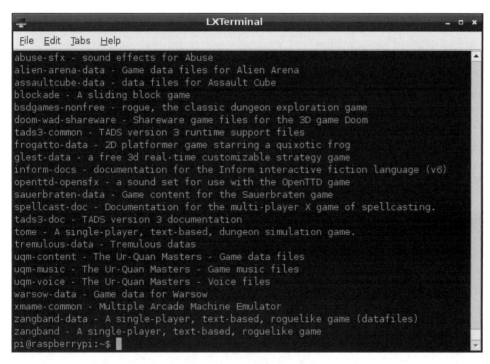

```
abuse-sfx - sound effects for Abuse
alien-arena-data - Game data files for Alien Arena
assaultcube-data - data files for Assault Cube
blockade - A sliding block game
bsdgames-nonfree - rogue, the classic dungeon exploration game
doom-wad-shareware - Shareware game files for the 3D game Doom
tads3-common - TADS version 3 runtime support files
frogatto-data - 2D platformer game starring a quixotic frog
glest-data - a free 3d real-time customizable strategy game
inform-docs - documentation for the Inform interactive fiction language (v6)
openttd-opensfx - a sound set for use with the OpenTTD game
sauerbraten-data - Game content for the Sauerbraten game
spellcast-doc - Documentation for the multi-player X game of spellcasting.
tads3-doc - TADS version 3 documentation
tome - A single-player, text-based, dungeon simulation game.
tremulous-data - Tremulous datas
uqm-content - The Ur-Quan Masters - Game data files
uqm-music - The Ur-Quan Masters - Game music files
uqm-voice - The Ur-Quan Masters - Voice files
warsow-data - Game data for Warsow
xmame-common - Multiple Arcade Machine Emulator
zangband-data - A single-player, text-based, roguelike game (datafiles)
zangband - A single-player, text-based, roguelike game
pi@raspberrypi:~$
```

FIGURE 3-7:
The last few results for an `apt-cache` "game" search

> **TIP** If your search term brings up too many different packages to see on a single screen display, you can tell Linux that you want it to pause on each screenful by *piping* the output of `apt-cache` through a tool called `less`. Simply change the command to `apt-cache search game | less` and use the cursor keys to scroll through the list. Press the letter Q on the keyboard to exit.

Installing Software

Once you know the name of the package you want to install, switch to the `apt-get` command in order to install it. Installing software is a privilege afforded only to the *root* user, as it affects all users of the Raspberry Pi. As a result, the commands will need to be prefaced with sudo to tell the operating system that it should be run as the *root* user.

For example, to install the package nethack-console (a console-based randomly generated role-playing game), you would simply use the install command with apt-get as follows:

```
sudo apt-get install nethack-console
```

Some packages rely on other packages in order to operate. A programming language may depend on a compiler, a game engine on graphics files, or an audio player on codecs for playing back different formats. These are known in Linux terms as *dependencies*.

Dependencies are one of the biggest reasons for using a package manager like apt rather than installing software manually. If a package depends on other packages, apt will automatically find them (see Figure 3-8) and prepare them for installation. If this happens, you'll be shown a prompt asking whether you want to continue. If you do, type the letter Y and press the Enter key.

FIGURE 3-8:
Apt listing the dependencies for the OpenOffice.org package

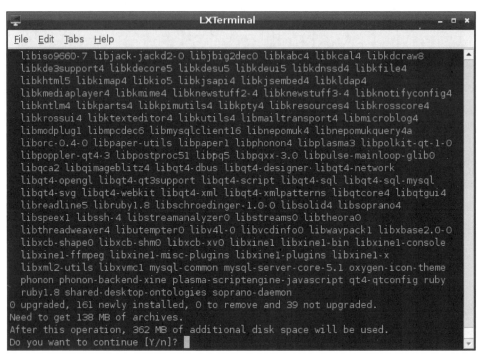

Uninstalling Software

If you decide you no longer want a piece of software, `apt-get` also includes a `remove` command that cleanly uninstalls the package along with any dependencies that are no longer required. When you're using a smaller SD card with the Pi, the ability to try out software and quickly remove it is extremely useful.

To remove `nethack-console`, simply open the terminal and type the following command:

```
sudo apt-get remove nethack-console
```

The `remove` command has a more powerful brother in the form of the `purge` command. Like `remove`, the `purge` command gets rid of software you no longer require. Where `remove` leaves the software's configuration files intact, however, `purge` removes everything. If you've got yourself into a mess customising a particular package and it no longer works, `purge` is the command to use. For example, to purge `nethack-console`, you would just type this:

```
sudo apt-get purge nethack-console
```

Upgrading Software

In addition to installing and uninstalling packages, `apt` can be used to keep them up to date. Upgrading a package through `apt` ensures that you've received the latest updates, bug fixes and security patches.

Before trying to upgrade a package, make sure the `apt` cache is as fresh as possible by running an update:

```
sudo apt-get update
```

When upgrading software, you have two choices: you can upgrade everything on the system at once or upgrade individual programs. If you just want to keep your distribution updated, the former is achieved by typing the following:

```
sudo apt-get upgrade
```

To upgrade an individual package, simply tell `apt` to install it again. For example, to install a `nethack-console` upgrade, you would type this:

```
sudo apt-get install nethack-console
```

If the package is already installed, apt will treat it as an in-place upgrade. If you're already running the latest version available, apt will simply tell you it cannot upgrade the software, and will then exit.

Shutting the Pi Down Safely

Although the Pi doesn't have a power switch like a traditional computer, that doesn't mean that you can simply pull the power cable out when you're finished. Even when it doesn't appear to be doing anything, the Pi is often reading from or writing to the SD card, and if it loses power while this is happening the contents of the card can become *corrupt* and unreadable.

To shut down using the terminal, type the following command:

```
sudo shutdown -h now
```

The Pi will close all open applications, prompting you to save any open files if you haven't done so already, and shut itself down, at which point the screen will go black and the ACT light will switch off. Once the light has gone off, it's safe to remove the micro-USB cable or switch the Pi off at the wall.

When you want to switch the Pi back on, or if you accidentally shut the Pi down without meaning to, simply reconnect the power and it will start to boot automatically.

Chapter 4
Troubleshooting

SOMETIMES, THINGS DON'T go entirely smoothly. The more complex the device, the more complex the problems that can occur—and the Pi is an extremely complex device indeed.

Thankfully, many of the most common problems are straightforward to diagnose and fix. In this chapter, we'll look at some of the most common reasons for the Pi to misbehave and how to fix them.

Keyboard and Mouse Diagnostics

Perhaps the most common problem that users experience with the Raspberry Pi is when the keyboard repeats certain characters. For example, if the command startx appears onscreen as sttttttttttartxxxxxxxxxxxx, it will, understandably, fail to work when the Enter key is pressed.

There are typically two reasons why a USB keyboard fails to operate correctly when connected to the Raspberry Pi: it's drawing too much power, or its internal chipset is conflicting with the USB circuitry on the Pi.

Check the documentation for your keyboard, or the label on its underside, to see if it has a power rating given in *milliamps (mA)*. This is how much power the keyboard attempts to draw from the USB port when it's in use.

The Pi's USB ports have a component called a *polyfuse* connected to them, which protects the Pi in the event that a device attempts to draw too much power. When this polyfuse is tripped, it causes the USB port to shut off, at around 150 mA. If your keyboard draws anywhere around that much power, it may operate strangely—or not at all. This can be a problem for keyboards that have built-in LED lighting, which require far more power to operate than a standard keyboard.

If you find that your USB keyboard may be drawing too much power, try connecting it to a powered USB hub instead of directly to the Pi. This will allow the keyboard to draw its power from the hub's power supply unit, instead of from the Pi itself. Alternatively, swap the keyboard out for a model with lower power demands. The repeating-letter problem may also be traced to an inadequate power supply for the Pi itself, which is addressed in the next section, "Power Diagnostics".

The issue of compatibility, sadly, is harder to diagnose. While the overwhelming majority of keyboards work just fine with the Pi, a small number exhibit strange symptoms. These range from intermittent response, the repeating-letter syndrome or even crashes that prevent the Pi from operating. Sometimes, these issues don't appear until other USB devices are connected to the Pi. If your keyboard was working fine until another USB device, in particular a USB wireless adapter, was connected, you may have an issue of incompatibility.

If possible, try swapping the keyboard out for another model. If the new keyboard works, your old one may be incompatible with the Pi. For a list of known-compatible keyboards, visit the eLinux wiki at `http://elinux.org/RPi_USB_Keyboards`.

The same advice on checking compatibility in advance applies to problems with the mouse: the majority of USB mice and trackballs work fine, but some exhibit incompatibility with the Pi's own USB circuitry. This usually results in symptoms like a jerky or unresponsive mouse pointer, but it can sometimes lead to the Pi failing to load or crashing at random intervals. If you're looking to buy a new mouse, an up-to-date list of models known to work with the Pi is available at the eLinux wiki site at `http://elinux.org/RPi_USB_Mouse_devices`.

Power Diagnostics

Many problems with the Raspberry Pi can be traced to an inadequate power supply. The Model A requires a 5 V supply capable of providing a 500 mA current, while the Model B's extra components bump up the current requirement to 700 mA. Not all USB power adapters are designed to offer this much power, even if their labelling claims otherwise.

The formal USB standard states that devices should draw no more than 500 mA, with even that level of power only available to the device following a process called *negotiation*. Because the Pi doesn't negotiate for power, it's unlikely that it will work if you connect it to the USB ports on a desktop or laptop computer.

TIP

If you're having intermittent problems with your Pi—particularly if it works until you connect something to a USB port or start a processor-intensive operation like playing video—the chances are that the power supply in use is inadequate. The Pi provides a relatively easy way to check if this is the case in the form of two *voltage test points*.

To use the voltage test points, you'll need a *voltmeter* or *multimeter* with direct current (DC) voltage measuring capabilities. If your meter has multiple inputs for different voltages, use an appropriate setting.

WARNING Avoid touching the test probes to anything not labelled as a test point. It's possible to bridge the 5 V supply that comes in to the Pi to the internal 3.3 V supply, creating a short circuit which can damage the device. Be especially careful around exposed header pins.

The two test points are small, copper-clad holes known as *vias*, which are connected to the Pi's 5 V and ground circuits. Put the positive (red) meter probe on TP1, located to the left of the board just above a small black component called a *regulator* labelled RG2. Connect the black (negative) meter probe to TP2, located between the copper GPIO pins and the yellow-and-silver RCA phono connector at the top-left of the board (see Figure 4-1).

FIGURE 4-1:
The two voltage
test points,
labelled TP1 and
TP2, on a
Raspberry Pi
Model B
Revision 1

The reading on the voltmeter should be somewhere between 4.8 V and 5 V. If it's lower than 4.8 V, this indicates that the Pi is not being provided with enough power. Try swapping the USB adapter for a different model, and check that the label says it can supply 700 mA or more. A model rated at 1A is recommended, but beware of cheap models—they sometimes have inaccurate labelling, and fail to supply the promised current. Genuine branded mobile phone chargers rarely have this problem, but cheap unbranded devices—often sold as *compatible adapters*—should be avoided

If your voltmeter reads a negative number, don't worry: this just means you've got the positive and negative probes in the wrong place. Either swap them around or just ignore the negative sign when noting your reading.

Display Diagnostics

Although the Pi is designed to work with almost any HDMI, DVI or composite video display device, it simply may not work as expected when you plug it in. For example, you may find that your picture is shifted to the side or not fully displayed, or is only visible as a postage-stamp-sized cut-out in the middle of the screen or in black-and-white—or even missing entirely.

First, check the type of device to which the Pi is connected. This is especially important when you're using the composite RCA connection to plug the Pi into a TV. Different countries use different standards for TV video, meaning that a Pi configured for one country may not work in another. This is the usual explanation for a Pi showing black-and-white video. You'll learn how to adjust this setting in Chapter 7, "Advanced Raspberry Pi Configuration".

When you use the HDMI output, the display type is usually automatically detected. If you're using an HDMI to DVI adapter to plug the Pi into a computer monitor, this occasionally goes awry. Common symptoms include snow-like static, missing picture portions or no display at all. To fix this, note the resolution and refresh rate of your connected display, and then jump to Chapter 7, "Advanced Raspberry Pi Configuration", to find out how to set these manually.

Another issue is a too-large or too-small image, either missing portions at the edge of the screen or sitting in the middle of a large black border. This is caused by a setting known as *overscan*, which is used when the Pi is connected to TVs to avoid printing to portions of the display which may be hidden under a bezel. As with other display-related settings, you will learn how to adjust—or even completely disable—overscan in Chapter 7.

Boot Diagnostics

The most common cause for a Pi to fail to boot is a problem with the SD card. Unlike a desktop or laptop computer, the Pi relies on files stored on the SD card for everything. If Pi can't talk to the card, it won't display anything on the screen or show any signs of life at all.

If your Pi's power light glows when you connect the micro-USB power supply, but nothing else happens and the OK light remains dark, you have an SD card problem. First, ensure that the card works when you connect it to a PC, and that it shows the partitions and files expected of a well-flashed card. (For more details, see Chapter 3, "Linux System Administration", particularly the section titled "File System Layout" in that chapter.)

If the card works on a PC but not in the Pi, it may be a compatibility problem. Some SD cards—especially high-speed cards marked as *Class 10* on their labelling—don't operate correctly when connected to the Pi's onboard SD card reader. A list of cards known to be compatible with the Pi can be found on the eLinux wiki at `http://elinux.org/RPi_SD_cards`.

Sadly, if you have an incompatible card, you will probably need to replace it with a different card in order for the Pi to work. As the Pi's software base is developed, however, work is being carried out to ensure that a wider range of cards operate correctly with the Pi. Before giving up on a high-speed card completely, check to see if an updated version of your chosen Linux distribution is available. (See Chapter 1, "Meet the Raspberry Pi", for more information about distributions.)

If you've been changing the speed of your Raspberry Pi by overclocking (see Chapter 6, "The Raspberry Pi Software Configuration Tool"), this can also stop it from booting correctly. To temporarily disable the overclock and run the Pi at its default speed, hold down the Shift key as you turn the Pi on.

Network Diagnostics

The most useful tool for diagnosing network problems is `ifconfig`. If you're using a wireless network connection, jump to Chapter 5, "Network Configuration", for information on a similar tool for those devices. Otherwise, read on.

Designed to provide information on connected network ports, `ifconfig` is a powerful tool for controlling and configuring the Pi's network ports. For its most basic usage, simply type the tool's name in the terminal:

```
ifconfig
```

Called in this manner, `ifconfig` provides information on all the network ports it can find (see Figure 4-2). For the standard Raspberry Pi Model B, there are two ports: the physical Ethernet port on the right side of the board, and a virtual *loopback* interface that allows programs on the Pi to talk to each other.

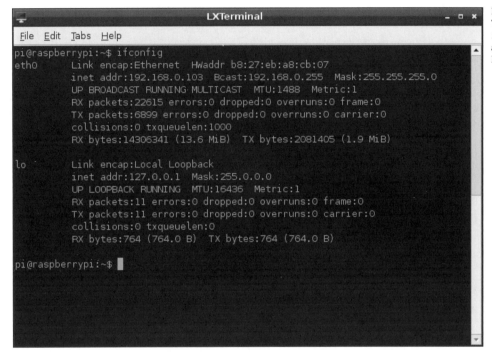

FIGURE 4-2:
The output of
`ifconfig` on
a Raspberry Pi
Model B

The output of `ifconfig` is split into the following sections:

○ **Link encap**—The type of *encapsulation* used by the network, which on the Model B will either read `Ethernet` for the physical network port or `Local Loopback` for the virtual loopback adaptor.

○ **Hwaddr**—The *Media Access Control (MAC) address* of the network interface, written in hexadecimal. This is unique for every device on the network, and each Pi has its own MAC address, which is set at the factory.

○ **inet addr**—The *internet protocol (IP) address* of the network interface. This is how you find the Pi on the network if you're using it to run a network-accessible service, such as a web server or file server.

○ **Bcast**—The *broadcast address* for the network to which the Pi is connected. Any traffic sent to this address will be received by every device on the network.

○ **Mask**—The *network mask*, which controls the maximum size of the network to which the Pi is connected. For most home users, this will read 255.255.255.0.

○ **MTU**—The *maximum transmission unit* size, which is how big a single packet of data can be before the system needs to split it into multiple packets.

○ **RX**—This section provides feedback on the received network traffic, including the number of errors and dropped packets recorded. If you start to see errors appearing in this section, there's something wrong with the network.

○ **TX**—This provides the same information as the RX section, but for transmitted packets. Again, any errors recorded here indicate a problem with the network.

○ **collisions**—If two systems on the network try to talk at the same time, you get a *collision* which requires them to retransmit their packets. Small numbers of collisions aren't a problem, but a large number here indicates a network issue.

○ **txqueuelen**—The length of the *transmission queue*, which will usually be set to 1000 and rarely needs changing.

○ **RX bytes, TX bytes**—A summary of the amount of traffic the network interface has passed.

If you're having problems with the network on the Pi, you should first try to disable and then re-enable the network interface. The easiest way to do this is with two tools called `ifup` and `ifdown`.

If the network is up, but not working correctly—for example, if `ifconfig` doesn't list anything in the `inet addr` section—start by disabling the network port. From the terminal, type the following command:

```
sudo ifdown eth0
```

Once the network is disabled, make sure that the cable is inserted tightly at both ends, and that whatever network device the Pi is connected to (hub, switch or router) is powered on and working. Then bring the interface back up again with the following command:

```
sudo ifup eth0
```

You can test the networking by using the ping command, which sends data to a remote computer and waits for a response. If everything's working, you should see the same response as shown in Figure 4-3. If not, you may need to manually configure your network settings, which you'll learn how to do in Chapter 5, "Network Configuration".

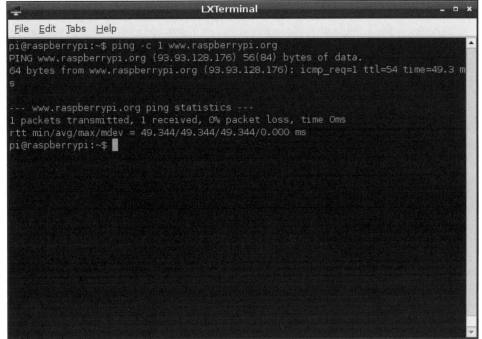

FIGURE 4-3: The result of a successful test of the network, using the ping command

The Emergency Kernel

The Linux kernel is the heart of the operating system that drives the Pi. It's responsible for everything from making sure that you can access your files to allowing programs to talk to other programs.

When switched on, your Pi will load the normal, default kernel. There's also a second kernel included in most distributions, which sits unused. This is the *emergency kernel*, and as the name suggests, it is typically used only when the normal kernel isn't working.

It's highly unlikely that you'll ever need to boot a Pi using the emergency kernel, but it's worth learning how to do so just in case. This is especially important if you're upgrading your kernel or are using a new and potentially poorly tested distribution. Sometimes, newly released software can have *bugs* which aren't spotted before its release. When encountering strange errors after upgrading, the emergency kernel can be used to narrow down the problem to the new kernel version.

The Linux kernel is a single file located in the `/boot` directory called `kernel.img`. When the Pi is first switched on and begins to load the operating system, it looks for this file, and if the file is missing, the Pi won't work. The emergency kernel is a second file, again in the `/boot` directory, called `kernel_emergency.img`.

The emergency kernel is, in most cases, almost identical to the standard kernel. When changes are made to the standard kernel, to boost performance or add new features for example, the emergency kernel is left unaltered. This way, if the changes to the standard kernel cause stability problems, a user can simply tell the Pi to load the emergency kernel instead.

There are two ways to boot into the emergency kernel, and both require the use of a PC and an SD card reader if the Pi can't boot. Otherwise, the following steps can be carried out on the Pi itself.

The easiest way to boot the emergency kernel is to rename the existing `kernel.img` file to `kernel.img.bak`, and then rename the `kernel_emergency.img` file to `kernel.img`. When the Pi loads, it will now load the emergency kernel by default. To go back to the standard kernel, simply reverse the process: rename `kernel.img` to `kernel_emergency.img` and `kernel.img.bak` to `kernel.img`.

An alternative method to load the emergency kernel is to edit the `cmdline.xt` file (located in the `/boot` directory) by adding the following entry at the end of the existing command line:

```
kernel=kernel_emergency.img
```

This tells the Pi that it should load the kernel named `kernel_emergency.img` instead of the usual `kernel.img`. Reversing the process is as simple as opening `cmdline.txt` again and removing the entry.

You'll learn more about `cmdline.txt` and how it affects the operation of the Raspberry Pi in Chapter 7, "Advanced Raspberry Pi Configuration".

Chapter 5
Network Configuration

FOR MOST USERS, configuring the Raspberry Pi's network is as easy as plugging a cable into the Model B's Ethernet port—or a USB Ethernet adapter, in the case of the Model A. For others, however, the network requires manual configuration.

If you know that your network doesn't have a *Dynamic Host Configuration Protocol (DHCP)* server—a system that tells the Pi and other devices on the network how they should connect—or if you want to use a USB wireless adapter with the Pi, read on.

Wired Networking

In some instances, in order for the Pi's network to operate correctly you may need to configure it manually. Normally, the network in a home, school or office has a DHCP server that tells the Pi and other devices on the network how they should connect. Some networks don't have a DHCP server, however, and need to be set up manually.

The list of network interfaces, along with information about how they should be configured, is stored in a file called `interfaces` located in the folder `/etc/network`. This is a file only the *root* user can edit, because removing a network interface from this list will cause it to stop working.

From the terminal, you can edit this file using a variety of different text editors. For simplicity, the nano text editor should be used for this process. Open the file for editing with the following command:

```
sudo nano /etc/network/interfaces
```

Nano is a powerful yet lightweight text editor, with a simple user interface (see Figure 5-1). You can move your cursor around the document with the arrow keys, save the file by holding down the CTRL key and pressing O, and quit by holding down the CTRL key and pressing X.

The line you need to edit for manual configuration starts with `iface eth0 inet`. Delete dhcp from the end of this line and replace it with `static`, press Enter to start a new line, and then fill in the remaining details in the following format with a tab at the start of each line:

```
[Tab] address xxx.xxx.xxx.xxx
[Tab] netmask xxx.xxx.xxx.xxx
[Tab] gateway xxx.xxx.xxx.xxx
```

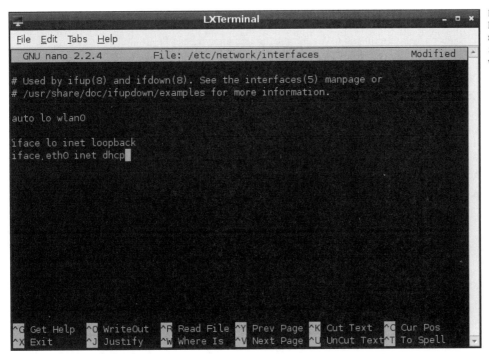

FIGURE 5-1:
Editing /etc/
network/
interfaces
with nano

Make sure that you press the Tab key at the start of each line, and don't actually type *[Tab]*. The *x* characters in the configuration lines represent network addresses you'll need to enter. For address, you should enter the static IP address that you want to assign to the Pi. For netmask, you should enter the network mask—which controls the size of the connected network—in what is known as *dotted-quad format*. If you're using a home network, this is typically 255.255.255.0. For gateway, you should enter the IP address of your router or cable modem.

As an example, the settings for a common home network would look like this:

```
iface eth0 inet static
[Tab] address 192.168.0.10
[Tab] netmask 255.255.255.0
[Tab] gateway 192.168.0.254
```

When you've finished editing the file, press CTRL + O to save it, and then press CTRL + X to leave nano and return to the terminal. To use your new network settings, restart the *networking service* by typing the following:

```
sudo /etc/init.d/networking restart
```

If you need to return to automatic settings via DHCP, you need to edit the `interfaces` file again and delete the `address`, `netmask` and `gateway` settings. Replace `static` with `dhcp` at the end of the `iface` line, and then restart the networking service again.

Setting a manual IP address isn't quite enough to get your Pi connected to the outside world. Computers on modern networks have both a numerical address identifier—known as an IP address—and a hostname or domain name. It's this latter, friendly name that allows you simply to type `www.raspberrypi.org` into your browser, instead of trying to remember `93.93.128.176`.

A system called a *Domain Name Service (DNS) server* is responsible for looking up the friendly names you supply and converting them into the numbers required to access the system. It operates much like an automated telephone directory. Before you'll be able to access Internet-connected systems via their domain names, you'll need to tell the Pi which DNS servers to use.

The list of DNS servers, known as *nameservers* in Linux parlance, is stored in `/etc/resolv.conf`. When the system gets its details through DHCP, this file is automatically filled in; but when you set an address manually, you need to provide the addresses of the nameservers on your network. Normally, this would be the address of your router as found in the `gateway` line from the `interfaces` file (described earlier in this chapter).

To set the nameservers, open the file with `nano` by typing the following command at the terminal:

```
sudo nano /etc/resolv.conf
```

Add each nameserver on a separate line, prefaced with `nameserver` and a space. As an example, the `resolv.conf` configuration for a network that uses Google's publicly accessible nameservers to resolve domain names would appear like this:

```
nameserver 8.8.8.8
nameserver 8.8.4.4
```

You'll notice that the nameserver addresses need to be supplied as IP addresses, rather than domain names. If you provided domain names instead, the Pi would enter an infinite loop of trying to find a nameserver to ask how it can find the nameservers.

Save the file by pressing CTRL + O, and then quit nano by pressing CTRL + X. Restart the networking interface by typing the following:

```
sudo /etc/init.d/networking restart
```

Then test the settings by either opening a web browser or using the following `ping` command (see Figure 5-2):

```
ping -c 1 www.raspberrypi.org
```

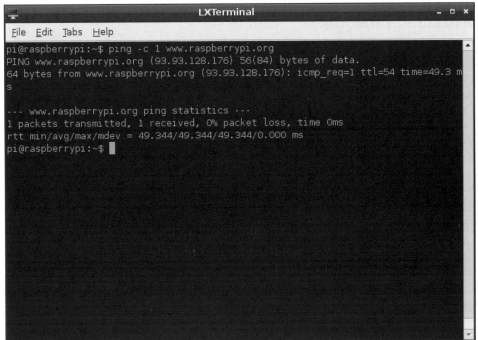

FIGURE 5-2:
A successful test
of networking
on the
Raspberry Pi
Model B

Wireless Networking

Although no current models of the Raspberry Pi include Wi-Fi networking hardware onboard, it's possible to add wireless connectivity with a simple USB Wi-Fi adapter. However, you will need to configure the adapter before you can use it to get your Pi online.

USB Wi-Fi adapters are very power-hungry. If you connect one directly to the Pi's USB port, it may not work. Instead, connect a powered USB hub to the Pi, and then insert the Wi-Fi adapter into that.

TIP

Before you start to set up the wireless interface, you'll need to know the *Service Set Identifier* *(SSID)*—also known as the *network name*—of the wireless router to which you want to connect, along with the type of encryption in use and the password required. You'll also need to know what type of wireless network it is. A USB adapter designed for 802.11a Wi-Fi may not connect to an 802.11g network, and vice versa.

Installing Firmware

In order for the USB wireless adapter to be addressed by the system, a software bundle known as a *firmware* is required. While some distributions include a selection of the most common Wi-Fi firmware installed by default, others do not. Raspbian includes most common wireless firmware packages, and if this is the operating system you are using you can skip ahead to the section on "Connecting to a Wireless Network via wpa_gui"; otherwise, read on for instructions on installing firmware packages.

In order to download the firmware files, the Pi must be connected to the Internet. If you can spare a wired port on your router or gateway for a few minutes, that's not a problem. However, if wireless is your only way of getting online, you'll need to manually download the firmware installation package on a different computer, and then transfer it across to the Pi by either copying it to the Pi's SD card or connecting an external storage device such as a USB flash drive.

To find the correct firmware file to download, you'll need to know what type of wireless adapter you have. Although various companies sell branded USB wireless adapters, the number of companies that actually manufacture the components is a lot smaller. Several different manufacturers may use the same type of chip inside their USB wireless adapters, making them all compatible with the same firmware. As a result, the labelling on a device or its packaging is not enough to know which firmware you should install. Instead, you'll need to connect the device to the Pi and check the *kernel ring buffer* for error messages. If you've already connected the wireless adapter as instructed in Chapter 2, "Getting Started with the Raspberry Pi", you can continue. If not, connect the adapter now.

The kernel ring buffer is a special portion of memory used by the Linux kernel to store its human-readable output. It's an important part of the Linux operating system: the text flashes by too quickly to read while the Pi boots, so it's critical that users are able to view the messages at a later date to read errors and diagnose problems.

With the adapter connected but no wireless firmware packages installed, the kernel will print a series of error messages to the ring buffer. To read these messages, you can use the dmesg command to print the contents of the buffer to the screen. At the terminal, or at the console if you haven't loaded the desktop environment, simply type the following command to view the buffer:

```
dmesg
```

This will print out the entire kernel ring buffer, which will contain all messages output by the kernel since the Pi was switched on. If the Pi has been running a while, that can be a lot of text. To locate error messages particular to the wireless adapter, it can help to send the output of dmesg through a tool called grep. Using grep, you can search through the buffer for text relating to missing firmware. By *piping* the output of dmesg through grep with a search term, things become significantly clearer. Type the following at the terminal:

```
dmesg -t | grep ^usb
```

The | symbol is known as a *pipe*, and it tells Linux to send the output of one program—which would normally go to a file or the screen—to the input of another. Multiple programs can be chained this way. In this example, grep is being told to search through the output of dmesg—the screens full of text from the earlier command—for any use of the term usb at the start of the line (denoted by the ^ character).

The exact output of that search will depend on the manufacturer of your USB wireless adapter. In Figure 5-3, the output is shown with a Zyxel NWD2015 Wireless USB Adapter connected to the Pi.

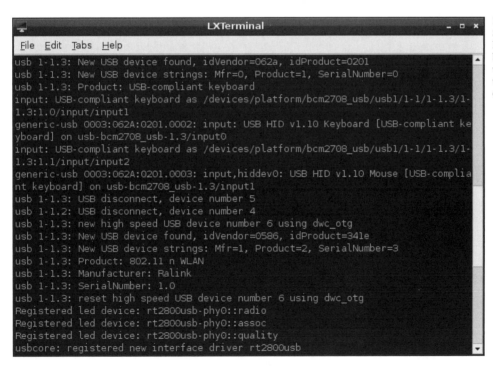

FIGURE 5-3: Searching the kernel ring buffer for usb with a Zyxel wireless adapter connected

The important part of this output is the line that reads `Manufacturer`. In the case of the example Zyxel NWD2105, this reads `Ralink`, which is the company that makes the actual chip found inside Zyxel USB wireless adapter. It's this company's firmware that must be installed for the wireless adapter to work.

TIP   If you couldn't find anything using `usb` as a search term, you can try the same command using the search term `firmware`, `wlan` or `wireless`. If you still can't see anything useful, type `lsusb` for a list of all USB devices connected to the system.

Using the manufacturer name from `dmesg`, search for the firmware files using the `apt-cache` search tool introduced earlier in this chapter. For the example Zyxel NWD2015 adapter, the `apt-cache` command would be:

```
apt-cache search ralink
```

If `apt-cache` fails to find the firmware, you may need to make a guess based on the firmware packages in the following list. Don't worry if you install the wrong one—any firmware can be quickly uninstalled using `apt-get remove`, and having multiple firmware packages does no harm. The following wireless firmware packages are available in the recommended Raspbian distribution on the Raspberry Pi:

- **atmel-firmware**—for devices based on the Atmel AT76C50X chipset
- **firmware-atheros**—for devices based on Atheros chipsets
- **firmware-brcm80211**—for devices based on Broadcom chipsets
- **firmware-intelwimax**—for devices based on Intel's WiMAX chipsets
- **firmware-ipw2x00**—for Intel Pro Wireless adapters (including 2100, 2200 and 2915)
- **firmware-iwlwifi**—for other Intel wireless adapters (including 3945, 4965 and the 5000 series)
- **firmware-ralink**—for devices based on Ralink chipsets
- **firmware-realtek**—for devices based on Realtek chipsets
- **zd1211-firmware**—for devices based on the ZyDAS 1211 chipset

The firmware for the example Zyxel wireless adapter is provided by the `firmware-ralink` package in this list. This package can be installed using `apt-get`, but only while the Pi is connected to the Internet through its wired Ethernet port or a USB Ethernet adapter. When connected, install the firmware by typing the following:

```
sudo apt-get install firmwarepackage
```

Replace *firmwarepackage* in this command with the name of the package that you found by using `apt-cache`. For the example Zyxel NWD2105, the full command would be `sudo apt-get install firmware-ralink`.

Installing Wireless Firmware Offline

If you can't connect the Pi to the Internet using any method other than a wireless connection, you'll need to download the firmware on a different computer. In a web browser, load a search engine and type the name of the firmware package followed by the name of the distribution you're using and its version.

If you're using the recommend Raspbian distribution, the firmware for the Ralink RT2x00 chipset from the example can be found by searching for `firmware-ralink debian wheezy`. The search will lead you to a *package file* to download. In the case of Debian and Raspbian, this is a `.deb` file. For Pidora, the same firmware is provided as a `.rpm` file.

Download this file, and then copy it to the Pi's SD card in the `/home/pi` directory, or onto a USB flash drive or other external storage device. Load the Pi, and then when it is time to install the firmware, replace the package name with the name of the file you downloaded. For the example Zyxel NWD2105 card, the command would be the following:

```
sudo apt-get install firmware-ralink_0.35_all.deb
```

With the firmware installed, disconnect the USB wireless adapter and reconnect it to the Pi. This will restart the kernel's search for the firmware files, which it will now be able to find. These files will remain in place, and load automatically when the USB wireless adapter is connected. You will only have to perform the installation process once.

Connecting to a Wireless Network via wpa_gui

The simplest way to connect to a wireless network from the Raspberry Pi is to use the *wpa_gui* tool. This provides a graphical user interface for software that would otherwise require the use of the terminal, and is accessed from the desktop by double-clicking on the icon labelled WiFi Config.

The main wpa_gui window has two drop-down lists, labelled Adapter and Network (see Figure 5-4). The first should be already filled with your wireless network dongle's identifier, wlan0. If you have more than one dongle connected, you can click on the arrow to choose which you are configuring; if nothing is listed, turn back a few pages and make sure the firmware for your dongle is correctly installed.

FIGURE 5-4:
The wpa_gui
application

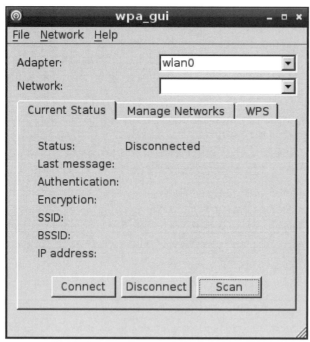

Finding a wireless network is a process known as *scanning*, which in wpa_gui is activated by clicking the Scan button at the bottom-right of the window. This will pop up a second window, showing the results of the scan (see Figure 5-5). Look through the list to find the name of your wireless network—which, hopefully, will also be the strongest in the list, as shown by the signal column—and double-click on its entry.

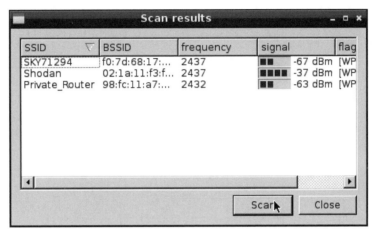

FIGURE 5-5: Choosing a wireless network in wpa_gui

The window that appears when you double-click on a network asks for several different settings, which will depend on the type of network to which you are trying to connect (see Figure 5-6). For an unencrypted network—which is a bad thing to be running as it allows anybody within range to use your network—wpa_gui will require no additional settings; just click the Add button at the bottom.

If your network uses encryption, you will need to choose the type of encryption, using the Authentication and Encryption drop-down lists. In most cases, wpa_gui will have selected these values automatically. If so, simply type in the password—known as a *pre-shared key*—in the box labelled PSK and click Add . If the network encryption is *Wired Equivalent Privacy (WEP)* rather than the more secure *Wireless Protected Access* (WPA) type, you will need to fill in at least one key in the WEP keys section. If you use an authenticated enterprise network, you can also add the details of your identity, password and encryption certificate, but most home users will not need these fields.

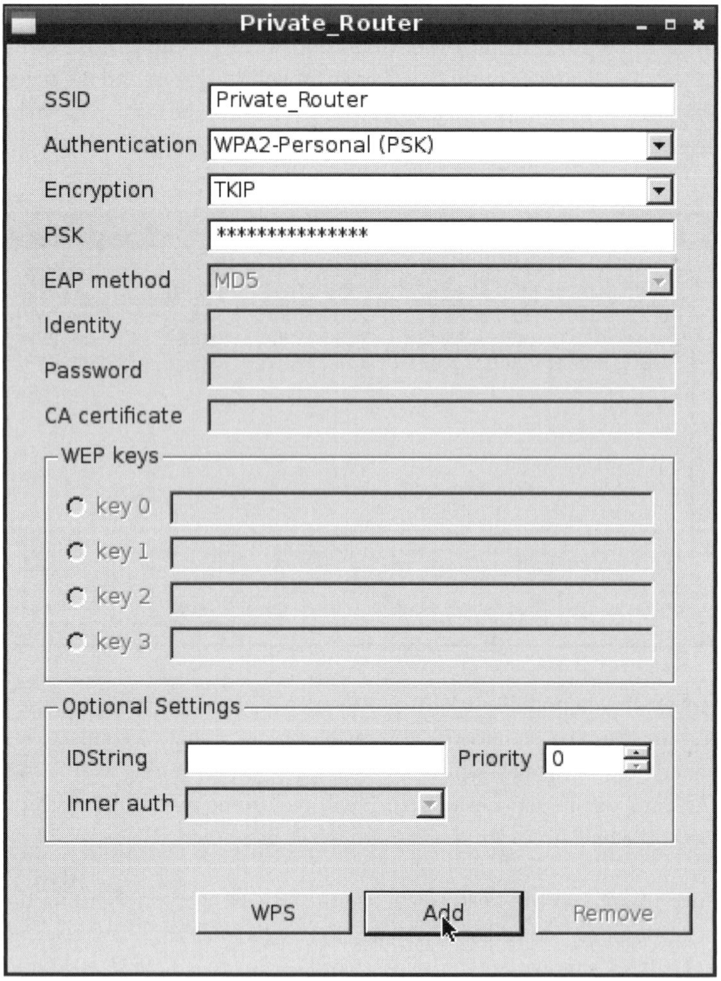

FIGURE 5-6:
Adding a
network to
wpa_gui

If your network includes a *Wi-Fi Protected Setup (WPS)* option, you can click the WPS button at the bottom-left of the window to perform a one-click setup. Simply press the WPS button on your router or access point, and then click the WPS button in wpa_gui to connect automatically.

When you have filled in the details of your network, click Add. This will close the window and return you to the main wpa_gui window—but now the Network drop-down should have an entry, named after your wireless access point. At this point, wpa_gui will automatically connect you to the wireless network and an IP address should appear at the bottom of the screen (see Figure 5-7).

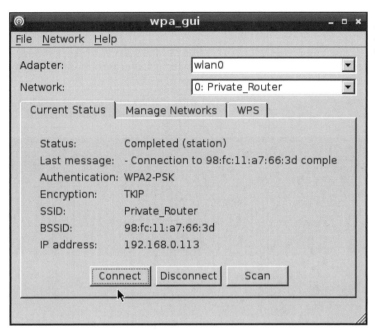

FIGURE 5-7:
Connected to a
wireless network
via wpa_gui

If you need to connect to a different network in the future, simply start the process again from the beginning. Connecting to a new network won't cause wpa_gui to forget the old network; both will appear in the drop-down list, and you can connect to any network in range simply by choosing it from the list, once configured.

You can also use wpa_gui to disconnect from a wireless network without having to remove the wireless dongle physically. Simply click the Disconnect button at the bottom of the main window and after a few seconds your Pi should be removed from the network. To reconnect, click the Connect button.

Connecting to a Wireless Network via the Terminal

If you are running your Pi without a graphical user interface, you can also connect to wireless networks at the terminal or console. First, check that the USB wireless adapter is working as it should by using the iwlist command to scan for nearby wireless access points. This list will probably be larger than a single screen, so pipe the command's output through less to pause after each screenful, like this:

```
sudo iwlist scan | less
```

This command will return a list of all the wireless networks reachable from the Pi, together with their details (see Figure 5-8). If you receive an error message at this point—in particular, one that claims the network or interface is down—check that you have installed the correct firmware, and that the USB wireless adapter is connected to a powered USB hub.

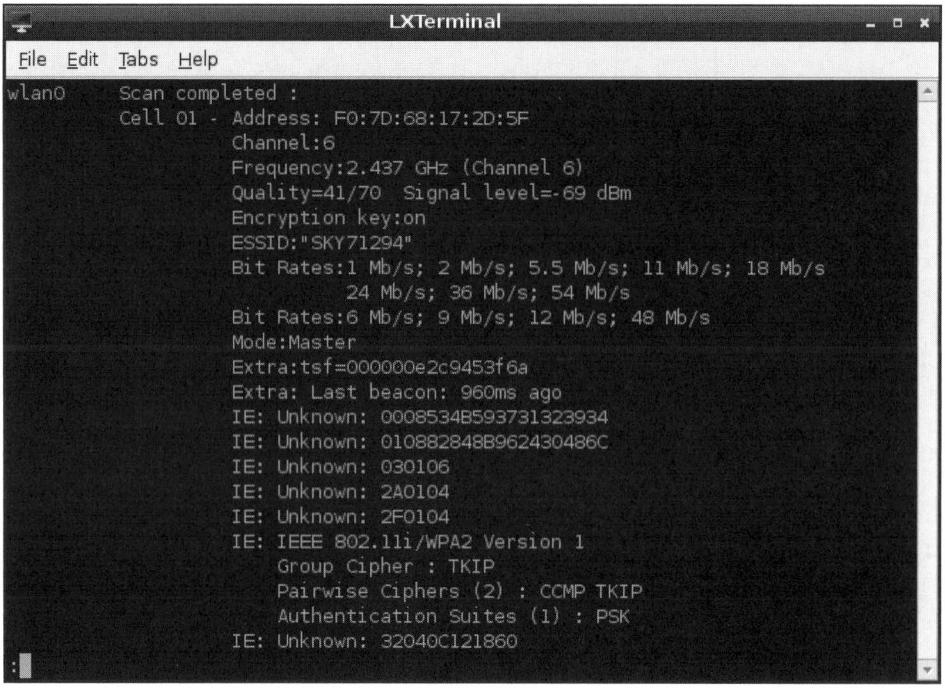

FIGURE 5-8:
Scanning for
wireless
networks with
iwlist

```
wlan0     Scan completed :
          Cell 01 - Address: F0:7D:68:17:2D:5F
                    Channel:6
                    Frequency:2.437 GHz (Channel 6)
                    Quality=41/70  Signal level=-69 dBm
                    Encryption key:on
                    ESSID:"SKY71294"
                    Bit Rates:1 Mb/s; 2 Mb/s; 5.5 Mb/s; 11 Mb/s; 18 Mb/s
                           24 Mb/s; 36 Mb/s; 54 Mb/s
                    Bit Rates:6 Mb/s; 9 Mb/s; 12 Mb/s; 48 Mb/s
                    Mode:Master
                    Extra:tsf=000000e2c9453f6a
                    Extra: Last beacon: 960ms ago
                    IE: Unknown: 0008534B593731323934
                    IE: Unknown: 010882848B962430486C
                    IE: Unknown: 030106
                    IE: Unknown: 2A0104
                    IE: Unknown: 2F0104
                    IE: IEEE 802.11i/WPA2 Version 1
                        Group Cipher : TKIP
                        Pairwise Ciphers (2) : CCMP TKIP
                        Authentication Suites (1) : PSK
                    IE: Unknown: 32040C121860
```

You can check the current status of the network using the `iwconfig` command. Like `ifconfig`, the `iwconfig` command allows you to check the status of a network interface and issue configuration commands. Unlike `ifconfig`, however, `iwconfig` is specifically designed for wireless networks and includes specific features for this. Type the command name at the terminal as follows:

```
iwconfig
```

The output of `iwconfig`, as shown in Figure 5-9, is split into the following sections:

○ **Interface Name**—Each device has its own interface name, as with wired networks. If the interface is a wireless connection, additional details will be shown. The default name for a Pi's wireless connection is `wlan0`.

○ **Standard**—The IEEE 802.11 wireless standards have a variety of different types, distinguished by a letter suffix. This section lists the standards supported by the USB wireless adapter. For the example adapter, this reads `IEEE 802.11bgn` for the network types it can address.

○ **ESSID**—The SSID of the network to which the adapter is connected. If the adapter is not currently connected to a network, this will read `off/any`.

○ **Mode**—The mode that the adapter is currently operating in, which will be one of the following:

   • **Managed**—A standard wireless network, with clients connecting to access points. This is the mode used for almost all home and business networks.

   • **Ad-Hoc**—A device-to-device wireless network, with no access points.

   • **Monitor**—A special mode in which the card listens out for all traffic whether or not it is the addressee. This mode is typically used in network troubleshooting for capturing wireless network traffic.

   • **Repeater**—A special mode that forces a wireless card to forward traffic on to other network clients, to boost signal strength.

   • **Secondary**—A subset of the Repeater mode, which forces the wireless card to act as a backup repeater.

○ **Access Point**—The address of the access point to which the wireless adapter is currently connected. If the adapter isn't connected to a wireless access point, this will read `Not-Associated`.

○ **Tx-Power**—The transmission power of the wireless adapter. The number displayed here indicates the strength of the signal that the adapter is sending: the higher the number, the stronger the signal.

○ **Retry**—The current setting for the wireless adapter's transmission retry, used on congested networks. This does not normally need changing, and some cards won't allow it to be changed.

○ **RTS**—The adapter's current setting for *Ready To Send* and *Clear To Send (RTS/CTS)* handshaking, used on busy networks to prevent collisions. This is normally set by the access point on connection.

○ **Fragment**—The maximum fragment size, used on busy networks to split packets up into multiple fragments. This is normally set by the access point on connection.

○ **Power Management**—The current status of the adapter's power management functionality, which reduces the device's power demands when the wireless network is idle. This has little effect on the Pi, but is typically enabled for battery-powered devices like a laptop.

FIGURE 5-9:
The output of
iwconfig
when not
connected to a
wireless network

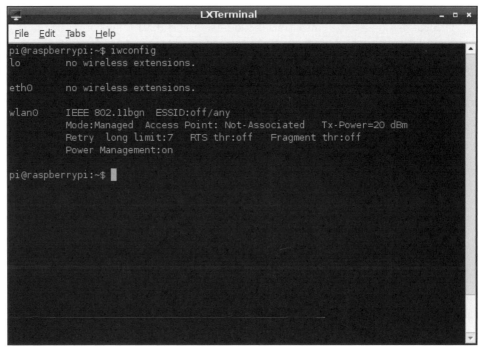

To connect the Pi to a wireless network, you will need to add some lines into the /etc/net-work/interfaces file. (For full details on how this file is laid out, see the "Wired Networking" section earlier in this chapter.)

First, open the file in the nano text editor:

```
sudo nano /etc/network/interfaces
```

At the bottom of the file, create a new entry for the USB wireless adapter that reads as follows (see Figure 5-10):

```
auto wlan0
iface wlan0 inet dhcp
wpa-conf /etc/wpa.conf
```

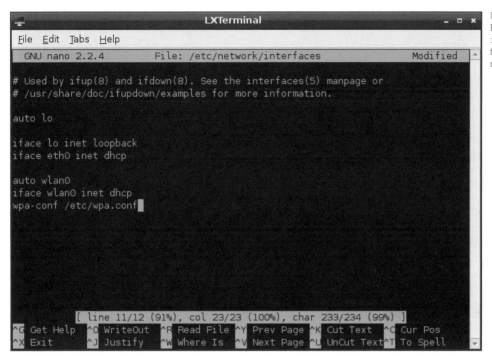

FIGURE 5-10:
Editing the
interfaces
file for wireless
network access

Once the entry is in place, save the file by pressing CTRL + O and then quit nano with CTRL + X.

> The device ID of wlan0 is correct if this is the first wireless device you've set up on your Pi. If it isn't, the number at the end will be different. Type iwconfig to see a current list of wireless devices, and change the lines in the preceding code example accordingly.

TIP

The last line of the interfaces file makes reference to a configuration file, wpa.conf, which does not yet exist. This file is used by a tool known as wpasupplicant, designed to provide Linux with an easy way to connect to networks secured *with Wireless Protected Access (WPA)* encryption.

Using wpasupplicant, you can connect the Pi to almost any wireless network—regardless of whether it's protected by WPA or its newer replacement WPA2—in both *Advanced Encryption Standard (AES)* and *Temporal Key Integrity Protocol (TKIP)* modes. Despite its name, wpasupplicant also allows connection to wireless networks using the older *Wired Equivalent Privacy (WEP)* encryption standard.

The wpasupplicant program stores its configuration in a file called wpa.conf, located in the /etc directory. To begin configuring the Pi for wireless access, first open a new blank file for editing by typing the following:

```
sudo nano /etc/wpa.conf
```

Enter the following two lines, which, again, are the same for any wireless network type. Replace Your_SSID with the SSID for the wireless network to which you want to connect, and then finish the file with the lines that match your network's encryption type:

```
network={
[Tab] ssid="Your_SSID"
```

At this point in the configuration file, the details required differ depending on the type of wireless network you are configuring. The following subsections provide instructions for completing the configuration for unencrypted, WEP and WPA networks.

No Encryption

If your wireless network has no encryption in place, finish the wpa.conf file as follows:

```
[Tab] key_mgmt=NONE
}
```

Save the file with CTRL + O, and then exit nano with CTRL + X.

WEP Encryption

If your wireless network uses WEP encryption, finish the wpa.conf file as follows:

```
[Tab] key_mgmt=NONE
[Tab] wep_key0="Your_WEP_Key"
}
```

Replace Your_WEP_Key with the ASCII key for your wireless network's WEP encryption. Save the file with CTRL + O, and then exit nano with CTRL + X.

TIP   WEP encryption is extremely insecure. Readily available software can break the encryption on a WEP-protected network in just a few minutes, allowing a third party to use your network. If you're still running WEP, consider switching to WPA or WPA2 for better security.

WPA/WPA2 Encryption

If your wireless network uses WPA or WPA2 encryption, finish the wpa.conf file as follows:

```
[Tab] key_mgmt=WPA-PSK
[Tab] psk="Your_WPA_Key"
}
```

Replace *Your_WPA_Key* with the pass phrase for your wireless network's encryption. Figure 5-11 shows an example configuration for a wireless network with the SSID "Private_Router" and the WPA pass phrase "Private Wireless Network". Save the file with CTRL + O, and then exit nano with CTRL + X.

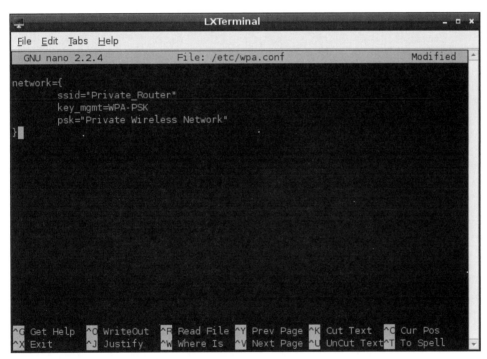

FIGURE 5-11: Editing the wpa.conf file for a WPA-protected network

Connecting to the Wireless Network

The Pi's wireless networking is now configured, and will begin the next time the Pi is restarted. To start the wireless network without rebooting, type the following:

```
sudo ifup wlan0
```

To make sure that the network is operational, unplug the Pi's Ethernet cable (if attached) and type the following:

```
ping -c 1 www.raspberrypi.org
```

> **TIP** If you start having problems with your Pi following the installation of a USB wireless adapter, it could be due to a conflict with other USB devices. Some adapter models are known to cause problems with certain USB keyboards. For an up-to-date list of adapters that are known to be good, as well as those that are known to cause conflicts, visit `www.element14.com/community/docs/DOC-44703/1/raspberry-pi-wifi-adapter-testing` or the eLinux wiki at `http://elinux.org/RPi_USB_Wi-Fi_Adapters`.

Chapter 6
The Raspberry Pi Software Configuration Tool

THE RASPBERRY PI is designed to be as controllable as possible, through the editing of configuration files found in the /boot directory of the SD card. For beginners, these files can seem dauntingly complex—although, with a little time, they soon give up their secrets—but without them some of the more advanced features of the Pi are unavailable.

The Raspberry Pi Software Configuration Tool, raspi-config, is designed to solve this problem. Offering access to the majority of common configuration tasks through a simple, menu-based interface, raspi-config makes it easy for newcomers to adjust system performance, change the memory split, alter overscan settings or simply change the keyboard layout at the console.

At the time of writing, raspi-config is exclusive to the Raspbian Linux distribution. Work is in progress to bring the tool's functionality to other operating systems but for now it is recommended that beginners stick with the well-supported Raspbian platform in order to take advantage of this most useful of configuration tools.

WARNING   Although raspi-config is designed to be safe, some settings—in particular the overclock option—can leave your Raspberry Pi unable to boot. Make sure you read each section in this chapter carefully before you use raspi-config to make any changes to your Raspberry Pi.

Running the Tool

The Raspberry Pi Software Configuration Tool edits a number of files that are important to the running of the Raspberry Pi. As a result, the tool can only be run as the *root user*, using the sudo command. To load the tool, type the following command:

```
sudo raspi-config
```

If you receive an error message stating that the command is not recognised, it means that you don't have raspi-config installed. This is usually the result of using an outdated version of Raspbian. To update your Pi, either download the latest release from the Raspberry Pi website or run the following command:

```
sudo apt-get update && sudo apt-get upgrade
```

The text-based menu of raspi-config is navigated using the cursor keys: the Up and Down arrow keys move the red selection band through the available options, while the Left and Right arrow keys move between the option list and the Select and Finish buttons below it.

The Enter key is used to activate an option when it is highlighted by the red band. The default action is always Select, so if you've highlighted an option in the menu, there's no need to press the Right arrow key to choose Select before pressing the Enter key.

Some of the options in `raspi-config` take a short while to run, particularly the Update and Expand Filesystem options. During this time, it's important to ensure that you don't unplug the Pi; doing so can leave you with a damaged file system, which will mean reinstalling your operating system from scratch.

The Setup Options Screen

The initial menu presented by `raspi-config` is the Setup Options screen (see Figure 6-1), which provides access to most of the basic functionality of the tool. If you've launched the tool by accident, simply press the Right arrow key twice followed by Enter to exit back to the console or terminal. Otherwise, choose the option corresponding to the feature you're trying to enable or change, as per the following descriptions.

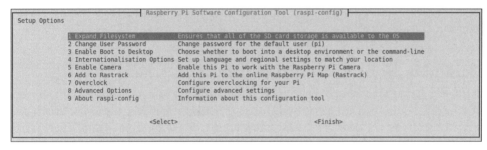

FIGURE 6-1: The raspi-config Setup Options screen

1 Expand Filesystem

The first option, Expand Filesystem, offers the capability to grow the Raspbian file system to take up the full space available on the SD card. When you first install Raspbian, it asks you whether or not you wish to do this when it first boots; as a result, you should only ever need to choose this option if you've cloned your installation to a larger SD card.

To run the filesystem expansion, make sure the red highlight bar is on the Expand Filesystem option and hit Enter. The `raspi-config` menu will disappear and a series of console messages will appear on the screen. Once the initial resize has finished, press Enter to dismiss the message that appears about rebooting the Pi, and then press the Right arrow key twice followed by Enter to exit the tool. When prompted, press Enter to reboot the Pi.

When the Pi reboots, it will perform the remainder of the filesystem expansion. On larger or slower cards, this can take a little time. It's important that the Pi is not disturbed during this process because if the power is lost, the Pi's filesystem can be corrupted. If this happens, you will lose any files you have stored on the Pi's SD card and will need to reinstall your operating system from scratch. The card itself, however, will not be damaged.

2 Change User Password

By default, Raspbian includes a single non-root user account named *pi*. This account is used for the day-to-day operation of the Pi, and comes with the default password *raspberry*. Although this is fine for private use, if you have your Pi on a publicly-accessible network—including a Wi-Fi hotspot or other Internet connection—it's a good idea to change at least the password, if not the username, to improve security.

While it's possible to change the password manually using the `passwd` command (see Chapter 3, "Linux System Administration" for details), beginners may find it easier to change the password using `raspi-config`. Highlight this option by moving the red bar with the cursor keys and then press Enter. When prompted, enter a new password and then confirm the change by entering the password again. To exit `raspi-config`, press the Right arrow key twice followed by Enter.

3 Enable Boot to Desktop

Normally, Raspbian loads into the text-based command line interface known as the console. It does this to ensure that the Pi is ready to use as quickly as possible, and also to save memory. Many common uses of the Pi—including using it as a web server or recording video or still images with the Raspberry Pi Camera Module—work fine at the console without the need to load the desktop graphical user interface.

If you use your Pi as a general-purpose computer, however, you may find it annoying that you need to type `startx` to load the desktop environment. Choosing the Enable Boot to Desktop option with the cursor keys and pressing Enter will prompt you as to whether the Pi should boot straight into the desktop or not. If you choose Yes with the cursor keys and press Enter, the graphical interface will load as soon as the Pi has finished booting—the equivalent of typing `startx` every time it loads. If you choose No, the usual text-based console will load instead.

When you have made your choice, press the Right arrow key twice followed by Enter to exit `raspi-config`.

4 Internationalisation Options

This menu option provides a way for users in countries other than the UK to configure the Pi for their needs (see Figure 6-2). By default, Raspbian sets itself to use UK English language settings, time zone settings and keyboard layout. Users in other countries will find that certain keys on their keyboards don't type the right characters, particularly those using non-QWERTY keyboard layouts such as AZERTY or QWERTZ.

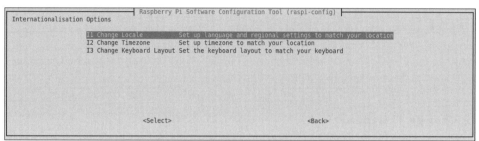

Use the cursor keys to select the Internationalisation Options choice and press Enter. This loads a submenu that provides access to three different location-based settings: Change Locale, Change Timezone and Change Keyboard Layout.

I1 Change Locale

This option, selected with the cursor keys and Enter, provides a list of all the languages available to the Pi. The list is extensive and includes most common languages. Use the cursor keys to scroll through the list that appears, and press the spacebar to put a * symbol next to the language or languages you would like to use.

Each language is named in a particular way: the first two characters represent the language name based on the International Organisation for Standardisation's two-letter identifier. Next comes an underscore, followed by another two characters that represent the country-specific identifier for that language. The prefix en_GB, for example, specifies the variant of English used in Great Britain; en_US, by contrast, is English as used in the United States of America.

Following the language and country identifier is a string that shows the *character encoding* used by the language. Most languages will have more than one option here, but the majority of users will only need to select one: the UTF-8. This specifies the Unicode Transformation Format 8-bit encoding—the most common and compatible encoding standard.

When you have chosen your locales, press Enter to confirm the changes and select your default. This allows you to have multiple locales installed at the same time without difficulty, although be aware that each locale will take up space on the Pi's SD card. Choose a default locale with the cursor keys, and confirm your selection with the Enter key.

If you have selected multiple locales, the change may take some time to complete. When the `raspi-config` menu reappears, choose Finish with the cursor keys and press Enter to exit.

| TIP | Changing the locale of the system won't translate all applications into your native language. Where a translation is available, it will be used; otherwise, English text will be displayed as the default. Changing the locale will also have no effect on command names: echo will still be called echo, for example, regardless of your locale. |

I2 Change Timezone

The system clock of the Raspberry Pi is set to Greenwich Mean Time by default. If you live in a different time zone, this means your Pi will be displaying the wrong time. Choosing the Change Timezone menu option with the cursor keys and pressing Enter will present you with a third menu, listing geographic areas like the Indian Ocean, the US and Europe. Use the cursor keys to select your local area and then press Enter.

The next screen displays a list of cities or regions in that area. Scroll through the list with the cursor keys and press Enter to select your city. If your city does not appear in the list, choose the closest city geographically, or your country's capital city if no other city is listed. When you have confirmed your change, press the Right arrow key twice to choose Finish and press Enter to quit `raspi-config`.

I3 Change Keyboard Layout

This is one of the most important options in the internationalisation menu, allowing you to alter the expected layout of your keyboard. By default, the Pi is configured to expect a British English keyboard in the standard QWERTY layout. If you use a different keyboard, choose this option with the cursor keys and press Enter to load the keyboard layout selection menu.

Using the cursor keys, choose the layout that corresponds to your particular keyboard and activate it with the Enter key. When you have been returned to the main Setup Options menu, press the Right arrow key twice followed by Enter to quit `raspi-config`.

5 Enable Camera

This option should be used only if you have a Raspberry Pi Camera Module (see Chapter 15, "The Raspberry Pi Camera Module") installed in your system. Choose the Enable Camera option with the cursor keys, press Enter, and then press Enter again to confirm the change. This will ensure that your Pi is configured to use the Camera Module, including downloading and installing the companion software if required.

If you remove the Camera Module from your Raspberry Pi, choose the Enable Camera menu option with the cursor keys, press Enter, and then use the Right arrow key to select No before pressing Enter again. Although this isn't strictly speaking required—having the Raspberry Pi configured for a camera that isn't connected will do no harm—it can help to keep things tidy.

Note that you will need to ensure that your Pi has at least 128MB available to the graphics processing unit (GPU) in order to use the Camera Module for video recording; see the section "A3 Memory Split" later in this chapter for how to configure this option.

6 Add to Rastrack

Rastrack is an interactive map of Raspberry Pi created by Ryan Walmsley. It is designed to help enthusiasts in close proximity to find each other, and to demonstrate areas of the world that have a large concentration of Raspberry Pi users. The service is voluntary and is not connected with the Raspberry Pi Foundation.

To appear on the Rastrack map, a Raspberry Pi must be registered. This is an optional process, and if you have any concerns about privacy you can skip it without losing any features or functionality. If you would like your Pi to appear on the map, however, choose the Add to Rastrack option with the cursor keys and press Enter. Note that you will need an Internet connection to continue.

Press Enter to confirm you have read the message that appears, then enter your name—or a nickname—followed by Enter. Enter an email address next, followed by Enter again to add your Raspberry Pi to the map. You don't need to give your location because the software uses your Internet connection to place your Pi on the map. It will not give your exact location at street level, but it will show others roughly where in the world you and your Pi are located.

Finally, press Enter to return to the main `raspi-config` screen, press the Right arrow key twice and then Enter to quit the tool and return to the console or terminal. To see the map, visit the website at `rastrack.co.uk`.

7 Overclock

Overclocking refers to the process of running a device at a speed higher than its manufacturers intended. The Raspberry Pi's BCM2835 processor can be run above its default speed of 700MHz to boost the performance of the system. Such performance comes at a price, however, in that the chip will run hotter than before, will draw more power and may suffer from a shorter lifespan than a Pi running at its default speed.

Although it's possible to alter the performance of the BCM2835 processor manually (see Chapter 7, "Advanced Raspberry Pi Configuration") the safest way is to use `raspi-config`. This limits you to a selection of preconfigured overclock settings (see Figure 6-3) that are known to be safe for use with most Raspberry Pis.

FIGURE 6-3: The pre-set overclock options included in raspi-config

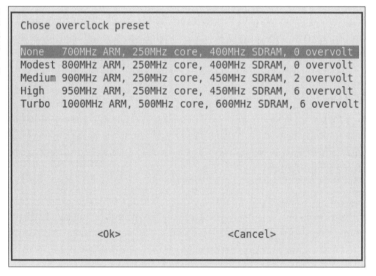

WARNING   While the overclock settings available to `raspi-config` are reasonably safe and will not harm your warranty, not all Raspberry Pis can reach the top speeds. If you find your Pi is unstable—particularly if you are experiencing files on the SD card becoming corrupt—drop down to the setting below the one you're currently using, or return the Pi to its default 700MHz speed.

To overclock your Raspberry Pi, highlight the Overclock option with the cursor keys and press Enter. Carefully read the message that appears and then press Enter to confirm that you wish to continue. If you have changed your mind, you can just press Enter as soon as the next screen appears to keep the stock speed of the Raspberry Pi intact.

If you want to try overclocking your Pi, use the cursor keys to select an option from one of the pre-set overclocks that appear on the next screen: None, Modest, Medium, High and Turbo. Almost all Raspberry Pi models should be able to use the Modest setting, which simply increases the processor's clock speed to 800MHz. Many will be able to use Medium, which increases the voltage applied to the processor to reach 900MHz and additionally increases the memory speed from 400MHz to 450MHz.

The remaining two settings may not work on all Raspberry Pi models. The BCM2835 processor is a complex circuit that will differ in its ability to be overclocked from unit to unit —even two Pis from the same batch. The High setting increases the speed to 950MHz but requires significantly more voltage than Medium or Modest to do so, which means more heat output and a lower lifespan for the processor. The Turbo setting increases the processor to 1000MHz while also doubling the graphics clock to 500MHz and increasing the memory clock to 600MHz. This offers the best performance, but has been linked to SD card corruption— where files become unreadable—on certain Raspberry Pi models.

If you wish to make use of the Turbo mode, make sure you have backed up any important files stored on the Pi beforehand. If you do start to have problems, drop down to the High setting or lower and your Pi should return to normal.

When you have made your selection, press the Enter key and then press the Enter key again to reboot the Pi at its new speed.

If you select a speed higher than the Pi can accept, it may not boot correctly. If you find your Pi loads to a black screen or constantly restarts itself without prompting you to log in, you have chosen too high a speed. Hold down the Shift key on the keyboard; this will temporarily bypass the overclocking setting, loading the Pi at its stock speed. Once the Pi has booted, release the Shift key and log in, then load `raspi-config` and enter the Overclock menu to choose a more conservative setting.

8 Advanced Options

Choosing the Advanced Options entry with the cursor keys and pressing Enter will load the Advanced Options menu (see Figure 6-4), which provides access to additional settings not found on the Setup Options menu. If you enter this menu by mistake, you can go back by pressing the Right arrow key twice followed by Enter to return to the main Setup Options menu.

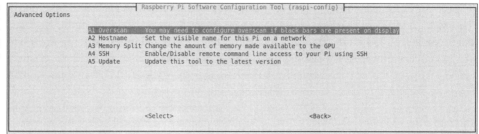

FIGURE 6-4:
The raspi-
config
Advanced
Options screen

A1 Overscan

Many TV sets feature *overscan*, which means the visible picture area is slightly smaller than the transmitted picture. In broadcast TV, this is often used to hide additional data such as time code information but in computing, it can result in the edges of the display becoming hidden. By contrast, using a TV signal with a modern monitor can reveal the previously hidden edges with their additional data.

You may need to adjust the overscan for one of two reasons: the image from your Pi is surrounded by black bars, in which case the overscan needs to be reduced or disabled altogether; or the image from your Pi extends beyond the visible edges of your screen, in which case the overscan needs to be increased. The latter is most common when using the Pi's composite video output (see Chapter 2, "Getting Started with the Raspberry Pi") with an older TV set.

To adjust the overscan setting, highlight the Overscan option with the cursor keys and press Enter. A menu will appear asking whether the overscan should be enabled or disabled. If you are using a monitor or TV using the Pi's HDMI port, choose Disable by pressing Enter; otherwise, press the Right arrow key to select Enable and confirm with the Enter key. To exit raspi-config, press the Right arrow key twice to highlight Finish and press Enter. You will be prompted to reboot to apply the new setting; confirm with Enter.

The Overscan menu in raspi-config only allows you to enable or disable the setting; to control the size of the overscan to maximise the visible screen area on an old TV, see Chapter 7, "Advanced Raspberry Pi Configuration".

A2 Hostname

A system's *hostname* is the name it uses to identify itself on the network. When you use the console or terminal on the Pi, you'll see the hostname as part of the prompt that accepts your command. Hostnames should be unique, which can cause a problem if you have more than one Raspberry Pi on your network. You can change a Pi's hostname at any time using the Hostname option of `raspi-config`'s Advanced Options menu, selected by highlighting it with the cursor keys and pressing the Enter key.

When you access the Hostname setting, `raspi-config` will inform you of the rules of a hostname. Because hostnames adhere to an international standard, known as a *request for comments* or *RFC*, certain characters aren't allowed: a hostname should only contain letters and numbers, and can include hyphens as long as they aren't at the beginning or end. Confirm you've read this message by pressing Enter.

Using the Backspace key, delete the current hostname in the box that appears and type in your new choice. You can opt for a descriptive hostname such as "living-room-pi" or name your devices based on a theme such as "bladerunner" for science fiction films. When you have chosen your name, press Enter to confirm. To exit `raspi-config`, press the Right arrow key twice to highlight Finish and press Enter. You'll be prompted to reboot the Pi; press Enter to confirm.

A3 Memory Split

Depending on your Raspberry Pi model, you will have either 512MB or 256MB of memory available to the system. This memory is split between the BCM2835 chip's general-purpose processor, known as the *central processing unit (CPU)*, and the graphics processor, known as the *graphics processing unit (GPU)*. By default, 128MB of memory is reserved for the GPU while the remainder is given over to the CPU.

If you're not using the graphics processor, such as when the Pi is used as a web server with no display connected, you can reduce the amount of memory reserved for the GPU using the Memory Split option in `raspi-config`. Highlight this option with the cursor keys and press Enter to load the menu.

Using the Backspace key, delete the current value listed in the box that appears and enter a new choice. The minimum you should give to the GPU to ensure proper operation is 16MB, which should be entered simply as the number 16. If you have a Raspberry Pi model with 512MB of memory, you can increase the split to 256MB, which may improve performance when using the GPU to render complex 3D scenes in games.

You can choose other values but you should restrict this to doubling the value at each step: for example, 16MB can be increased to 32MB, 32MB to 64MB, 64MB to 128MB and so on.

Choosing an uneven value, such as 17MB, will not harm the Pi but may result in a different value being used than the one selected.

When you have chosen a memory split, press the Enter key to confirm. To apply the setting, exit `raspi-config` by pressing the Right arrow key twice followed by Enter, and then press Enter again to confirm that you want the Pi to reboot.

A4 SSH

The *Secure Shell*, also known as *SSH*, is a way of accessing the Raspberry Pi's terminal over the network. It's most commonly used when running the Pi as a standalone server, as it doesn't require you to have a keyboard or monitor attached. SSH allows the user to access the text-based terminal, and also to transfer files to or from the Pi.

Some users may wish to improve the security of their Pi by turning this feature off. Highlight the SSH option using the cursor keys and press the Enter key. In the window that appears, choose either Enable or Disable to turn SSH on or off. Even if you don't need it, it's a good idea to keep SSH enabled for future troubleshooting; a better way of improving security is to ensure that you have changed the password for the *pi* user.

A5 Update

The Update menu option ensures that you are running the very latest version of `raspi-config`. The tool is updated frequently as new features are enabled on the Pi or different settings added to the menu, so it's always a good idea to ensure that your version is up to date.

Choosing this menu option with the cursor keys and pressing Enter will begin the update process. This requires an Internet connection to complete, so if you are using a Raspberry Pi Model A you will need to connect a USB network adapter to continue.

Note that this option will only update `raspi-config`, not any other aspect of the system. To update everything, including `raspi-config`, see the instructions in Chapter 3, "Linux System Administration".

When the update has completed, exit `raspi-config` by pressing the Right arrow key twice followed by the Enter key.

9 About raspi-config

The final menu option available in `raspi-config` simply introduces the tool. Choosing this option with the cursor keys and pressing Enter will launch a window explaining the purpose of the tool (see Figure 6-5) and will make no changes to the system. The message can be dismissed by pressing Enter, and `raspi-config` can be closed by pressing the Right arrow key twice followed by the Enter key.

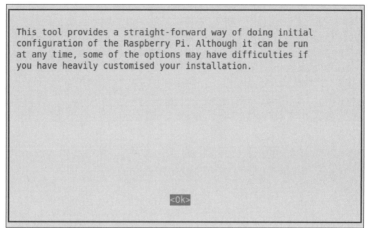

FIGURE 6-5:
About the
`raspi-config`
software tool

Chapter 7

Advanced Raspberry Pi Configuration

OWING TO ITS origins in embedded computing, the BCM2835 chip at the heart of the Raspberry Pi doesn't have anything like a PC's *Basic Input-Output System (BIOS)* menu where various low-level system settings can be configured. Instead, it relies on text files containing configuration strings that are loaded by the chip when the power is switched on.

Before taking a look at the various options available in these files—`config.txt` and `cmdline.txt`—a word of warning: changing some of these settings away from their defaults can result in a Pi that doesn't boot until the files are reverted, in the best case, and can physically damage the system, in the worst case. These potentially dangerous settings will be highlighted with warnings in this chapter.

TIP   If you're using the Raspbian distribution, the easiest way of changing the majority of settings is to use the `raspi-config` utility (see Chapter 6, "The Raspberry Pi Software Configuration Tool"). These instructions are provided for those on other distributions or who would prefer to do things manually.

Editing Configuration Files via NOOBS

If you have edited your configuration files in such a way that your operating system no longer boots, the easiest way to restore them is to use the NOOBS software (see Chapter 2, "Getting Started with the Raspberry Pi"). If your operating system was installed via NOOBS, you can use the tool to edit the configuration files; if you installed your operating system manually, you will need to remove the SD card and use a second computer to edit the files.

To load NOOBS after you have used it to install your operating system, hold down the Shift key as you apply power to the Pi. This will bypass the loading of the operating system and instead boot into NOOBS, but with a new option: the Edit Config button at the top of the menu (see Figure 7-1).

Clicking the Edit Config button (or pressing the E key) will load a text editor window with the two configuration files—`config.txt` and `cmdline.txt`—pre-loaded (see Figure 7-2). You can make changes as described in this chapter in the text editor with your keyboard and mouse, and click the OK button at the bottom-right to save your changes to the SD card. When you've finished making changes, click Exit on the main window to reboot the Pi with its new settings.

TIP   If you have a Raspberry Pi Model B that is connected to the Internet, you can also click the Online Help button or press the H key on the keyboard to load a web browser that will take you to the Raspberry Pi Forums. This is an invaluable resource if your Pi isn't working properly, allowing you to find help or post a question to get your Pi computing back on track.

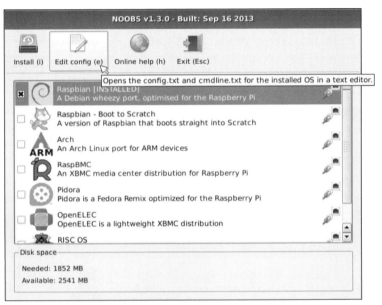

FIGURE 7-1:
The Edit Config
button in
NOOBS

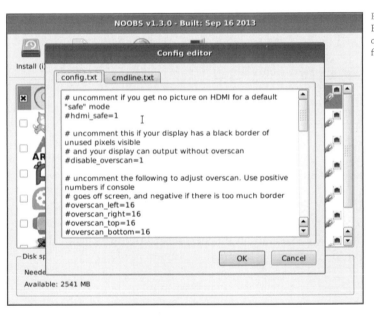

FIGURE 7-2:
Editing
configuration
files in NOOBS

Hardware Settings—config.txt

The Pi's hardware is controlled by settings contained in a file called `config.txt`, which is located in the `/boot` directory (see Figure 7-3). This file tells the Pi how to set up its various inputs and outputs, and at what speed the BCM2835 chip and its connected memory module should run.

FIGURE 7-3:
The contents of
the /boot
directory, with
config.txt
highlighted

If you're having problems with graphics output, such as the image not filling the screen or spilling over the edge, `config.txt` is where you'll be able to fix it. Normally, the file is empty or, on some distributions, simply not present; this just means that the Pi will operate using its pre-set defaults. If you want to make changes and the file isn't there, just create a new text file called `config.txt` and fill in the settings you want to change.

The `config.txt` file can control almost all aspects of the Pi's hardware, with the exception of the way the central processing unit (CPU) and graphics processing unit (GPU) sections of the BCM2835 apportion the memory. You'll learn how to alter that split in the "Memory Partitioning" section, later in this chapter.

The `config.txt` file is only read when the system first starts up. Any changes made while the Pi is running won't take effect until the system is restarted, or switched off and back on again. In the event that the changes are unwanted, simply deleting the file from the `/boot` directory should be enough to restore the defaults once more. If the Pi won't boot with your new settings, just remove the SD card and delete `config.txt` from the `boot` partition on another PC, and then reinsert the card into the Pi and try again.

Modifying the Display

Usually, the Raspberry Pi will detect the type of display that's connected and alter its settings accordingly. Sometimes, however, this automatic detection doesn't work. This is often the case when a Raspberry Pi from one country is connected to an older TV from another country. If you connect your Pi to your TV and there's nothing to see, you may need to override these defaults.

Various settings in the `config.txt` file can be used to improve or alter the video output. These settings, and their possible values, are described in the following list.

Manually adjusting the High Definition Multimedia Interface (HDMI) or composite video output   **WARNING**
settings can leave your Pi unable to communicate with your monitor. It's usually best to use
the automatically detected settings, unless you're unable to see a picture in the first place.

- **overscan_left**—This setting moves the picture inwards a set number of pixels to compensate for a TV's *overscan*. If the text on the Pi is disappearing off the edge of the screen, adjusting the overscan will fix it. Values should be given as the number of pixels to skip.

- **overscan_right**—This setting does the same job as `overscan_left`, but on the right side of the screen.

- **overscan_top**—Again, this setting ignores a certain number of pixels, but this time on the top of the screen.

- **overscan_bottom**—This setting can be used to skip a number of pixels from the bottom of the display. Typically, the values for all the `overscan_` settings would be the same, creating a regular border around the display.

- **disable_overscan**—If you use a monitor or TV via HDMI, you may find that your image has a black border around it. To get rid of this border, any default overscan settings can be disabled by setting this value to 1.

- **framebuffer_width**—This value is measured in pixels, and adjusting it will change the width of the console. If text appears too small on your screen, try changing this to a lower value than the default width of the connected display.

- **framebuffer_height**—This setting affects the size of the console in the same way as `framebuffer_width`, but vertically rather than horizontally.

- **framebuffer_depth**—Controls the colour depth of the console in bits per pixel. The default is 16 bits per pixel, which gives 65,536 colours. Other values, including 8 bits per pixel (256 colours), 24 bits per pixel (around 16.7 million colours) and 32 bits per pixel (around 1 billion colours) are valid, but may cause graphical corruption.

○ **framebuffer_ignore_alpha**—Set to 1, this value disables the *alpha channel*, which controls transparency in the console. Disabling the alpha channel is not normally required, but it may correct graphical corruption caused when setting `framebuffer_depth` to 32 bits per pixel.

○ **sdtv_mode**—This value affects the analogue composite video output of the Pi, adjusting it to operate in various countries. By default, the Pi uses the North American version of the NTSC video standard; users in other countries may need to change this value to get a picture on an analogue TV. Possible values are:

- **0**—NTSC, the North American video standard

- **1**—NTSC-J, the Japanese video standard

- **2**—PAL, the video standard for the UK and other countries

- **3**—PAL-M, the Brazilian video standard

○ **sdtv_aspect**—Controls the aspect ratio of the analogue composite output. If the picture looks stretched or squished, alter this to correspond to your TV's aspect ratio. Possible values are:

- **1**—4:3 aspect ratio, common on older sets

- **2**—14:9 aspect ratio, common for smaller widescreen TVs

- **3**—16:9 aspect ratio, common for modern widescreen TVs

○ **hdmi_mode**—In addition to setting the video mode for the analogue composite output, it's also possible to override automatic resolution detection on the HDMI port. This is handy if you want to run your Pi at a lower resolution than the display's native resolution in order to make things more readable from a distance. Appendix C, "HDMI Display Modes", lists the possible values for this setting.

○ **hdmi_drive**—It's also possible to alter the voltage output by the HDMI port. This is important when you're using an HDMI to DVI adapter, because HDMI and DVI voltages differ slightly. If you find that your picture is snowy or blown out with too bright an image, try altering this setting. Possible values are:

- **1**—DVI output voltages. In this mode, no audio is included on the HDMI cable.

- **2**—HDMI output voltages. In this mode, audio is included on the HDMI cable.

○ **hdmi_force_hotplug**—Forces the Raspberry Pi to use the HDMI port, even if it doesn't detect a connected display. A value of 0 allows the Pi to attempt to detect the display, while a value of 1 forces the Pi to use HDMI regardless.

○ **hdmi_group**—Sets the HDMI group mode to CEA or DMT. You should change this setting according to the display type you're trying to connect, before using `hdmi_mode` to control the output resolution and frequency. The two possible values are:

  - **1**—Sets the HDMI group to that defined by the Consumer Electronics Association of America (CEA). Use this setting when the Pi is connected to a high-definition television (HDTV) over HDMI and use the first settings list from Appendix C, "HDMI Display Modes".

  - **2**—Sets the HDMI group to that defined by the Video Electronics Standards Association (VESA) in the Display Monitor Timings (DMT) specification. Use this setting when the Pi is connected to a computer monitor over DVI and use the second settings list from Appendix C, "HDMI Display Modes".

○ **hdmi_safe**—Forces the Pi to use a pre-set collection of HDMI settings designed to provide maximum compatibility with displays connected to the HDMI port. Setting this to a value of 1 is the equivalent of setting `hdmi_force_hotpug=1`, `config_hdmi_boost=4`, `hdmi_group=1`, `hdmi_mode=1` and `disable_overscan=0`.

○ **config_hdmi_boost**—Some monitors require more power on the HDMI output to operate. If your picture looks snowy, try increasing this value in stages from 1 (for short cables) to 7 (for long cables).

Each option in `config.txt` should be on its own line, with the option name followed by an equals sign (=) and then the required value. For example, to tell the Pi to use a PAL-format analogue TV with a 4:3 aspect ratio and a 20-pixel overscan on all sides, put the following lines into `config.txt`:

```
sdtv_mode=2
sdtv_aspect=1
overscan_left=20
overscan_right=20
overscan_top=20
overscan_bottom=20
```

To tell the Pi to use a DVI display through the HDMI port in the 720p60 format with no overscan at all, use the following values instead:

```
hdmi_group=1
hdmi_mode=4
hdmi_drive=1
disable_overscan=1
```

For the changes to take effect, the Pi must be restarted. If you find that your changes have disabled the Pi's video output on your monitor, simply insert the SD card into another computer and either modify the `config.txt` file with new settings or delete it altogether to restore the defaults.

Boot Options

The `config.txt` file can also be used to control how Linux is loaded on the Raspberry Pi. Although the most common method for controlling the loading of the Linux kernel is to use a separate file called `cmdline.txt` (which you'll learn about later in this chapter), it is possible to use just `config.txt`. The following options control the boot process:

○ **disable_commandline_tags**—This tells the `start.elf` module that loads first during the Pi's boot process to skip filling in memory locations past 0x100 before loading the Linux kernel. This option should not be disabled, as doing so can cause Linux to load incorrectly and crash.

○ **cmdline**—The command line parameters to be passed to the Linux kernel. This can be used in place of the `cmdline.txt` file, usually found in the `/boot` directory.

○ **kernel**—The name of the kernel file to be loaded. This can be used as a way to load the emergency kernel (see Chapter 4, "Troubleshooting").

○ **ramfsfile**—The name of the initial RAM file system (RAMFS) to be loaded. This should rarely be modified, unless you've built a new initial file system with which to experiment.

○ **init_uart_baud**—The speed of the serial console, in bits per second. The default is 115200, but lower values may improve the connection if the Pi is used with an older hardware serial terminal.

Overclocking the Raspberry Pi

The `config.txt` file not only controls the graphics outputs of the Pi's BCM2835 processor but also enables you to control the chip in other ways. In particular, it allows you to alter the speed at which the chip runs, increasing its performance at the expense of the part's lifespan—a process known as *overclocking*.

WARNING   Adjusting any of the settings listed in this section can result in damage to your Pi. In particular, changing settings corresponding to memory, GPU or CPU voltages will set a fuse in the chip, which invalidates the Raspberry Pi's warranty even if the setting is returned to normal before any damage is done. Damage caused when using these settings will not be put right by the Raspberry Pi Foundation or by the retailer from whom you purchased your Pi. If in doubt, *don't alter these settings*: the performance gains through overclocking are rarely worth the risk to the Pi.

The BCM2835 multimedia processor at the heart of the Pi is a system-on-chip (SoC) design split into two main parts: the graphics processor (GPU) and the central processor (CPU). Simply put, the CPU handles all the day-to-day processing tasks while the GPU handles drawing things on the screen, in both 2D and 3D.

Using `config.txt`, you can overclock one or both parts of the BCM2835. You can also increase the speed at which the memory module—located on top of the chip in a package-on-package (PoP) mounting format—operates.

Boosting the operating frequency of these components results in a small increase in the Pi's performance: an increase to the GPU's clock frequency means that 3D graphics (such as game graphics) will render at a faster pace, and video will be decoded quicker for smoother playback; and increasing the CPU's clock frequency will boost overall performance of the device, as will increasing the memory's frequency.

The reason the Pi isn't provided with higher operating speeds in the first place is related to the chip's lifespan. The BCM2835 is rated by its manufacturer, Broadcom, to operate at a speed of 700 MHz. Increasing the speed above this officially rated level may work, but it will also have a deleterious effect on the lifespan of the chip. Unlike a desktop processor, SoC designs rarely have much headroom for overclocking.

Overclocking Settings

If you're willing to take the risk of breaking the Pi—a process known as *bricking* in embedded device circles—for the sake of a small performance gain, there are settings in `config.txt` that can help. The following settings control performance of the Pi's SoC:

- **arm_freq**—Sets the core clock frequency of the CPU portion of the BCM2835, for a boost in general-purpose performance. The default speed is 700 MHz.

- **gpu_freq**—Sets the clock frequency of the GPU portion of the BCM2835, for a boost in graphics performance across all operations. The default speed is 250 MHz. Additionally, you can adjust individual portions of the GPU's hardware using the following options:

  - **core_freq**—Sets the core clock frequency of the GPU, leaving the other frequencies alone, to improve overall GPU performance. The default speed is 250 MHz.

  - **h264_freq**—Sets the clock frequency of the GPU's hardware video decoder to improve playback of H.264 video data. The default speed is 250 MHz.

- **isp_freq**—Sets the clock frequency of the image sensor pipeline, for improving the capture rate of connected video hardware (such as a camera). The default speed is 250 MHz.

- **v3d_freq**—Sets the clock frequency of the GPU's 3D rendering hardware, for a boost in visualisation and gaming performance. The default speed is 250 MHz.

○ **sdram_freq**—Sets the clock speed of the random access memory (RAM) chip on the Pi, to give the entire system a small increase in performance. The default speed is 400 MHz.

○ **init_uart_clock**—Sets the default clock speed of the *Universal Asynchronous Receiver/ Transmitter (UART)*, used to control the serial console. The default is 3000000, which sets a speed of 3 MHz. Altering this is likely to have little effect beyond corrupting the output of the serial console.

○ **init_emmc_clock**—Sets the default clock speed of the SD card controller. The default is 80000000, which sets a speed of 80 MHz. Increasing this value can result in faster reading and writing from the SD card, but can also lead to data corruption.

As an example, to overclock the CPU to 800 MHz, the GPU to 280 MHz and the RAM to 420 MHz, enter the following options into `config.txt`, one per line:

```
arm_freq=800
gpu_freq=280
sdram_freq=420
```

As with adjusting the display configuration, any changes made regarding overclocking won't take effect until the Pi is restarted. To return the settings to normal, you can either delete the entire `config.txt` file or—if you're using it to control the display settings as well—simply delete the lines that deal with overclocking, and then restart the Pi.

If you have overclocked your Pi and it no longer boots, either place the SD card into another computer to edit the configuration and then try again, or hold down the Shift key while the Pi boots to temporarily disable your new settings and run the Pi at its normal clock speed.

Overvoltage Settings

If you're overclocking your Pi, you will eventually hit a brick wall past which the device won't go. The precise point at which the Pi won't reliably overclock depends on the individual device, due to natural variations in the chip introduced during the manufacturing stage. For some users, this limit may be as low as 800 MHz; others may find that they can push their Pi as high as 1 GHz (1,000 MHz) without issue.

If you want to eke a little more performance out of your Pi, there is a way to potentially boost this upper limit: a process known as *overvoltage* or *overvolting*. The Pi's BCM2835 system-on-chip processor and the associated memory module usually run at 1.2 V. It's possible, although potentially inadvisable, to override this default and force the components to run at higher or lower voltages. Boosting the voltage means boosting the signal within the chip, making it more likely to hit higher speeds—it also means that the chip runs hotter, reducing its lifespan dramatically compared to overclocking alone.

Setting any of the voltage options in `config.txt` causes a fuse within the BCM2835 to trip in a way that cannot be reset. It's a foolproof way to tell if someone has been attempting to overclock the chip outside its rated specifications, and *renders your warranty null and void—* even if the cause of failure is unrelated to overclocking. If you return a Pi for replacement under warranty and the fuse is tripped, *it will not be replaced.* Do not attempt to overvolt a Pi that you cannot afford to replace yourself.

WARNING

Unlike the previously described settings, which are provided in `config.txt` as absolute values, the voltage adjustment is carried out using values relative to the Pi's stock 1.2 V setting. For each whole number above zero, the voltage is increased by 0.025 V from stock. For each whole number below zero, the voltage is decreased by 0.025 V from stock.

The voltage adjustment settings have upper and lower limits of 8 and -16, equivalent to 0.2 V above stock voltage or 1.4 V absolute and 0.4 V below stock voltage or 0.8 V absolute. The voltage must be adjusted in whole numbers, and it cannot be adjusted below 0.8 V (-16) or above 1.4 V (8.)

The following settings are accessible from `config.txt`:

○ **over_voltage**—Adjusts the BCM2835's core voltage. Values are given as a whole number (an integer) corresponding to 0.025 V above or below the default value (0,) with a lower limit of -16 and an upper limit of 8.

○ **over_voltage_sdram**—Adjusts the voltage given to the memory chip on the Pi. As with `over_voltage`, values are given as a whole number corresponding to 0.025 V above or below the stock (0,) with a lower limit of -16 and an upper limit of 8. Additionally, you can adjust voltages for individual memory components using the following options:

    • **over_voltage_sdram_c**—Adjusts the voltage given to the memory controller. Acceptable values are the same as with `over_voltage_sdram`.

    • **over_voltage_sdram_i**—Adjusts the voltage given to the memory's input/output (I/O) system. Acceptable values are the same as with `over_voltage_sdram`.

    • **over_voltage_sdram_p**—Adjusts the voltage given to the memory's physical layer (PHY) components. Acceptable values are the same as with `over_voltage_sdram`.

As an example, the following lines entered into `config.txt` will give the BCM2835 a small boost of 0.05 V to 1.25 V and the memory chip a bigger boost of 0.1 V to 1.3 V:

```
over_voltage=2
over_voltage_sdram=4
```

As with other settings, deleting the lines from `config.txt` or deleting the file itself will return things to normal. Unlike the other settings in this section, however, the evidence will remain in the form of a blown fuse in the BCM2835, rendering the Pi's warranty null and void even after the default settings are restored.

Disabling L2 Cache

The Pi's BCM2835 SoC processor has 128 KB of *Layer 2 cache memory* onboard. Although this memory is small, it's extremely fast. It's used to temporarily store—or *cache*—data and instructions between the slower main memory and the processor itself to improve performance.

Because of the BCM2835's origins as a multimedia processor targeted at set-top boxes, this L2 cache is designed to be used by the GPU portion of the chip alone. Unlike a traditional processor, the CPU doesn't have any L2 cache of its own.

Using `config.txt`, you can tell the BCM2835 to allow or disallow its CPU portion access to the L2 cache memory. In some cases, this can improve performance. In other cases it can harm performance, due to the physical location of the cache being a relatively long distance away from the CPU section of the chip and closer to the GPU.

Use of the L2 cache memory also requires a Linux distribution that has been compiled with the cache memory in mind. Raspbian is one such distribution, and comes with the L2 cache enabled for improved performance. It should be left this way, and only disabled if it causes problems with alternative operating systems.

To switch the L2 cache off for CPU access, simply add the following line to the `config.txt` file:

```
disable_l2cache=1
```

As with all `config.txt` settings, the system must be rebooted before the change will take place. To enable the CPU's access to the cache memory, replace the 1 with a 0.

Enabling Test Mode

This final option in `config.txt` is one the overwhelming majority of Pi users won't need to touch, but it is included here for completeness: test mode. Used during production of the Raspberry Pi at the factory, the test mode—combined with special hardware used to electrically check the board—allows the factory staff to make sure the Pi is operating as it should.

Enabling test mode won't do any permanent damage, but the Pi won't boot into its operating system until the mode is disabled again and the power to the Pi is switched off and back on.　**WARNING**

If you're curious to see what the Pi looks like to factory staff, you can enable test mode by entering the following option into the `config.txt` file:

```
test_mode=1
```

As with other `config.txt` settings, test mode won't be enabled until the Pi is restarted. Test mode can be disabled again by removing the line in `config.txt`, deleting the file altogether, or replacing the 1 with a 0.

Memory Partitioning

Although the Raspberry Pi has either a 256 MB or 512 MB memory chip, that memory can be apportioned to the hardware in a variety of ways. The BCM2835 is split into two main sections: the general-purpose CPU and the graphics-oriented GPU. Both of these sections require memory to operate, meaning that the 256 MB or 512 MB of memory on the Raspberry Pi needs to be shared between the two.

The typical split is chosen by the maintainers of the Linux distribution installed on the Pi. Some choose to provide 128MB to the GPU, ensuring that the graphics hardware can perform to its fullest potential. Others allow the CPU to have a larger share in order to improve general-purpose performance.

Previously, the memory split was controlled by using different versions of a firmware file called *start.elf*, where different files were used to supply different amounts of memory to the CPU. These files have now been replaced by a single line in `config.txt`, which can be edited to control the memory split.

WARNING Applications that do heavy graphics work, such as 3D games and high-definition video playback software, typically need 128 MB of memory for the GPU. Reducing this can result in a dramatic drop in performance. The Raspberry Pi Camera Module is unable to record video with less than 128 MB of graphics memory.

The memory split is changed by editing config.txt as with other hardware settings, and editing or inserting the line marked gpu_mem. This line tells the Pi how much of the total memory—256 MB on the Model A, 512 MB on the Model B—should be given to the GPU, with the remainder going to the CPU.

The value can be set to 16 MB as a minimum, or 128 MB as a maximum. The setting should be adjusted in 16 MB increments and written without the MB suffix—giving possible values of 16, 32, 48, 64, 80, 96, 112 and 128. To give the GPU the minimum 16 MB of memory, for example, edit the line as follows:

```
gpu_mem=16
```

Software Settings—cmdline.txt

In addition to config.txt, which controls various features of the Pi's hardware, there's another important text file in the /boot directory: cmdline.txt (see Figure 7-4). This file contains what is known as the *kernel mode line*—options passed to the Linux kernel as the Pi boots up.

FIGURE 7-4:
The cmdline.
txt file in
/boot

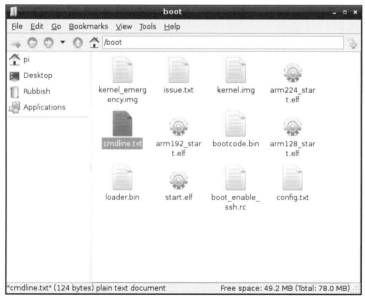

In a Linux-based desktop or laptop, these options are normally passed to the kernel by a tool known as a *bootloader*, which has its own configuration file. On the Pi, the options are simply entered directly into `cmdline.txt` to be read by the Pi at startup.

Almost any kernel option supported by Linux can be entered into the `cmdline.txt` file, to alter things like the appearance of the console or which kernel is loaded. As an example, here is the `cmdline.txt` file from the Raspbian distribution, which should be written in the file as one continuous line:

```
dwc_otg.lpm_enable=0 console=ttyAMA0,115200 ↵
  kgdboc=ttyAMA0,115200 console=tty1 root=/dev/mmcblk0p2 ↵
  rootfstype=ext4 rootwait
```

The first option, `dwg_otc.lpm_enable`, tells the Pi to disable the *On-The-Go (OTG)* mode of its USB controller, to prevent problems that can occur when the functionality is enabled without proper support in the operating system. The majority of Linux distributions for the Pi disable this mode.

The `console` option tells Linux that it should create a serial console—device `ttyAMA0`—and at what speed it should operate. In most cases, the speed should be left at the default of 115,200 bps (bits per second). If the Pi is being used to communicate with older devices, this can be reduced accordingly.

The `kgdboc` kernel option enables debugging of the Linux kernel over the serial console created using the `console` parameter. For most users, this is unnecessary. For developers, having access to kernel debugging over a serial connection is most useful. Many distributions leave this enabled just in case.

The second `console` entry creates the device `tty1`, which is the text-filled screen you see when you first boot the Pi. Without this entry, you wouldn't be able to use the Pi without connecting something to the serial console created by the first `console` option.

The `root` option tells the Linux kernel where it can find its *root file system*, containing all the files and directories required for the system to operate. In the case of the default Raspbian distribution, this is on the second partition of the SD card—device `mmcblk0p2`. This option can be altered to address an external storage device connected over USB, which can speed up the operation of the Pi considerably compared to having the root file system stored on the SD card.

In addition to telling the kernel where to find its root file system, it also needs to know what format the partition was created in. Because Linux supports a variety of different file systems, the `rootfstype` option specifically tells the Raspbian distribution to use an EXT4 file system.

Finally, the `rootwait` parameter tells the kernel that it should not try to boot the system any further until the device containing the root file system is available. Without this option, the Pi can get stuck as it begins to boot before the relatively slow SD card is fully ready for access.

With the exception of the `dwc_otg` setting, none of these kernel parameters are unique to the Pi. The bootloader configuration of any Linux distribution will include a list of options very similar to those of `cmdline.txt`.

Typically, you should leave the `cmdline.txt` file alone. It's created by the distribution maintainers specifically for that version of Linux, and may differ from one distribution to the next. Entries that work on Pidora may not work on Raspbian, and vice versa. The options available to `cmdline.txt` depend on what kernel the distribution is using and what features were included when the kernel was built.

If you're a kernel developer, you can use `cmdline.txt` to pass parameters for enabling or disabling new functionality that you've compiled into the kernel. As with `config.txt`, any changes require a reboot to take effect.

Part II

Building a Media Centre, Productivity Machine or Web Server

Chapter 8
The Pi as a Home Theatre PC

ONE OF THE most popular tasks for a Pi to carry out is that of a home theatre PC, or HTPC. The Broadcom BCM2835 at the Pi's heart is specifically designed as a multimedia power-house, originally developed for use in HTPCs.

The graphics portion of the BCM2835 system-on-chip (SoC) design, a Broadcom VideoCore IV module, is capable of full-speed high-definition video playback using the popular H.264 format. The chip is also able to play back audio files in a variety of formats, both through the analogue 3.5 mm audio output and digitally via the HDMI port.

The small size, low power draw and silent operation combine to make the Pi a tempting device for home theatre enthusiasts. A variety of distributions and software packages designed to turn the Pi into a user-friendly home theatre PC have appeared since its launch, but you don't necessarily need to give up your existing operating system to get started.

Playing Music at the Console

If you're a developer, you will likely spend most of your time at the Pi's console. With the majority of music playback software being aimed at desktop use, it can be a quiet experience—but it doesn't have to be.

The Pi supports a powerful text-based music playback package called moc (which stands for *music on console*). Unlike other tools (such as LXMusic), moc can be installed and used even when there is no graphical user interface (GUI) installed on the Pi.

To get started, install the moc package from your distribution's repositories. For the Raspbian distribution, this is as simple as typing the following command at the console or in a terminal window:

```
sudo apt-get install moc
```

| TIP | Some distributions already have another tool called moc, which has nothing to do with audio playback. If you find that installing moc doesn't give you the result you're expecting, try substituting mocp as the package name. |

If you spend a lot of time outside of the graphical user interface and working at the console, moc is a great choice for music playback. Unlike other tools, it runs in the background, meaning there's no interruption to your music if you start doing something else.

To load moc, the command is mocp rather than moc. The reason for this is that there's another tool which uses the command moc, so a different name was chosen to prevent the operating system from getting confused between the two packages.

To get started, just enter the console—or a terminal window if you're using a desktop environment—and type the following:

mocp

The standard mocp interface is split into two panes (see Figure 8-1). The left pane is a file browser, which allows you to look for music to play. The cursor keys scroll up and down the list, while the Enter key starts playback from the currently highlighted song. If you press Enter on a directory name, the browser will enter that directory, while pressing it at the ../ entry at the top of the list goes back one directory level. The right pane shows the current playlist.

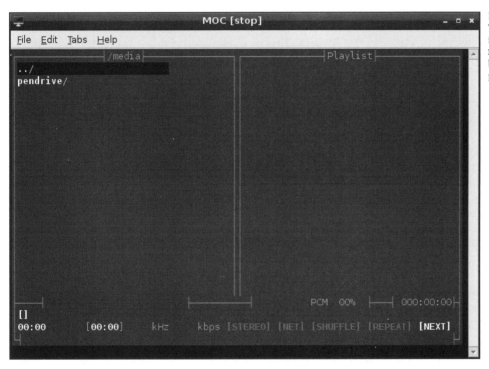

FIGURE 8-1:
The standard interface of the mocp console-based music player

Where the power of mocp becomes apparent is when you exit the application by pressing the Q key. If mocp is in the middle of playing back music, it will continue to do so even as you use the console or terminal window for other tasks. Running the mocp command again will restore the interface, allowing you to change songs, pause or stop playback. You can also control mocp directly from the terminal, without having to use the interface. Running the mocp command with flags—the options that follow a command, prefixed with a hyphen character—allow you to start, stop, pause, skip and otherwise change the playback without having to go into the software.

The most commonly used mocp flags are the following:

- **-s**—Stop the current playback
- **-G**—Pause playback, or resume playback if currently paused
- **-f**—Skip to the next song in the directory or playlist
- **-r**—Return to the previous song in the directory or playlist
- **-i**—Print information on the current song to the terminal or console
- **-x**—Stop playback and quit mocp altogether

For more information on controlling mocp, type man mocp.

Dedicated HTPC with Raspbmc

Being able to play music on the Raspberry Pi is one thing, but the BCM2835 can do much more than that. Using its VideoCore IV GPU, it can decode and play back Full HD 1080p H.264 video, making the Pi a powerful media centre machine in a tiny package and with incredibly low power demands.

To get the most from the Pi as a home theatre PC, however, some additional software is required. This software can be installed in the Raspbian distribution, but there's an easier way to get started: switching to the *Raspbmc* distribution.

Raspbmc, created by Sam Nazarko, is a distribution aimed specifically at turning the Raspberry Pi into a fully featured media centre system, complete with video and music playback, photo viewing and Internet streaming capabilities. It's based on the popular Xbmc distribution, which has been chosen by several device manufacturers to power their commercial set-top box systems.

If you're planning on making use of the Pi's high-definition video output and H.264 decoding capabilities in your home theatre setup, Raspbmc is an excellent choice and no more complicated to get up and running on the Pi than any other Linux distribution. First, download the installer from the official website at http://www.raspbmc.com/download/. This is the easiest way to get Raspbmc up and running. Installers for Linux, OS X and Windows are provided which automatically download the image file for Raspbmc and write it to an SD card connected to the system. Although you can also download an image file and use the instructions from Chapter 1, "Meet the Raspberry Pi", it's not necessary to do so.

WARNING   If you already have an SD card you use with the Pi, be aware that installing Raspbmc on it will delete the contents of the card. Back up any files you want to keep, or if you want to be able to switch between the two distributions, buy a second SD card specifically for Raspbmc use or install it alongside Raspbian using the NOOBS tool described in Chapter 2, "Getting Startedwith the Raspberry Pi".

When the Raspbmc installer has finished, insert the SD card into the Pi and re-connect the power supply—but make sure the Ethernet cable is connected as well, because Raspbmc needs to download some data from the Internet when it first loads. The initial load of Raspbmc can take 10 or 15 minutes to complete as it downloads updates and partitions the SD card, but subsequent loads are significantly faster. Don't panic if the first boot hangs at the Formatting Partitions stage—a long pause here is normal.

When loaded, Raspbmc automatically starts the Xbmc service (see Figure 8-2). This provides a custom user interface specifically designed for living-room use. Everything is accessible through the keyboard or mouse, with large and easily readable text and categorised menus to make it easier to find things. You can also purchase infrared remote controls, which come with a receiver that plugs into the Pi's USB port and a transmitter that allows for a true home theatre experience with no bulky keyboard or trailing wires.

FIGURE 8-2:
The Xbmc home
screen, loaded
by Raspbmc

Streaming Internet Media

By default, Xbmc is configured to play only files it can find on the Raspberry Pi itself. If you choose Add-ons from beneath the Video menu, you'll be able to add some impressive Internet streaming capabilities to the device, including access to various TV channels and Internet-only streaming services. After clicking Add-ons, choose Get More to access the full list of compatible plug-ins (see Figure 8-3).

FIGURE 8-3:
Adding new
video add-ons in
Raspbmc

Scroll through the list with the mouse or cursor keys, and click on an entry or press the Enter key to access more information. To install an add-on, just click Install from the pop-up information box that appears when you click on an entry in the list. This will download the add-on from the Internet and automatically install it into Xbmc. Watch out for add-ons listed as Broken—these have been reported as not working correctly, and should not be installed until the problem is fixed by the add-on developer.

After you finish choosing and installing video add-ons, click the Home button in the bottom-right corner of the screen to return to the main Xbmc interface. Now click on the word Video in the centre of the screen or press Enter, and then choose Video Add-ons from the options that appear. This provides access to your installed add-ons. Click on one to download a list of files for viewing. If an add-on has various categories, it will download those categories first—in this case, click on an individual category to see the files it contains (see Figure 8-4).

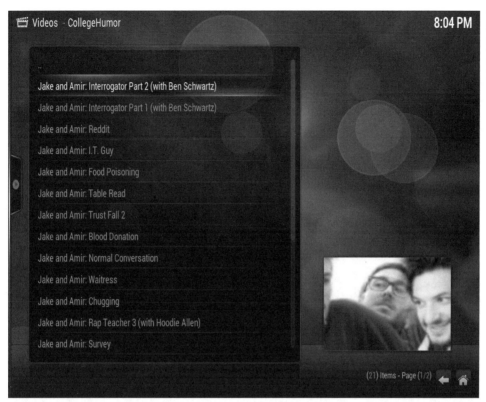

FIGURE 8-4: A
list of videos
available
through the
CollegeHumor
Xbmc add-on

Similar add-ons are available under the Music and Video menus, and operate in the same
way. Using these add-ons, you can view picture content and stream audio content from sites
such as Flickr, Picasa, The Big Picture, Grooveshark, Sky.fm and SoundCloud.

Streaming Local Network Media

The Xbmc software supports the *Universal Plug and Play (UPnP)* media streaming standard,
allowing it to connect to a range of devices on your home network. UPnP support is included
in most modern mobile phones, games consoles and *network-attached storage (NAS)* devices
for sharing and streaming videos, music and pictures. Many laptops and desktops also come
with support for UPnP or the closely linked *Digital Living Network Alliance (DLNA)* standard—check your documentation to find out how to enable this feature on your own devices.

Xbmc isn't just limited to UPnP connections, however—the software can also connect to
network servers running the *Network File System (NFS)* standard common to Unix-based systems, the *Server Message Block (SMB)* standard common to Windows servers and the *Zeroconf*
standard common to OS X devices. No matter what network-attached device you use to store
your media content, it's likely that Xbmc will support at least one way of connecting to it.

To configure Xbmc to connect to a server on your home network, choose the media type—
Video, Music or Pictures—and click the Add Source option. In the window that appears,
choose Browse to retrieve a list of source types (see Figure 8-5). These source types include
local drives connected to the Raspberry Pi, which are highlighted with a blue icon, as well as
network devices, which are highlighted with a red icon. Choose the type of server you're trying to connect to from the list, and then click on the server that appears.

FIGURE 8-5:
Choosing a
network source
in Xbmc

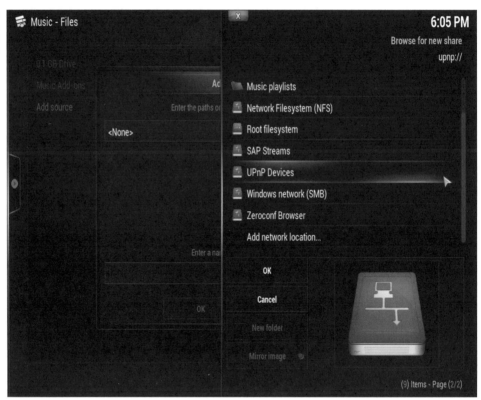

If the server you select has multiple folders available—such as folders for different genres,
artists, albums or file types—select the folder you want Xbmc to connect to and click the OK
button. This will return you to the Add Source screen (see Figure 8-6) with the required information filled in. If additional details are required—such as a user name and password for a
protected server—you'll need to fill these in before clicking OK.

FIGURE 8-6:
Adding a UPnP
music source to
Xbmc

You can also use the same menu to add an external hard drive as a source to Xbmc by selecting its entry in the initial list. Most external drives will appear automatically, and do not need to be added explicitly—you only need to add a drive as a source if its contents do not appear in Xbmc's menus.

Configuring Raspbmc

The Programs menu on the home screen provides access to the Raspbmc Settings menu (shown in Figure 8-7) where network settings, software upgrade settings and various system settings can be adjusted. Normally, this menu can be ignored—however, if you're having problems connecting to the Internet or the Raspbmc system is continuously crashing, the Programs menu can provide important tools for resolving the issue.

Clicking the Raspbmc Settings option under the Programs menu will open a window with three tabs. The first tab allows you to adjust the network settings, including disabling DHCP and setting a manual network configuration (see Chapter 5, "Network Configuration", for more details). If you needed to set the Raspberry Pi to use a manual network configuration in other distributions, this is the place to do the same in Raspbmc.

The second tab, marked XBMC, allows you to install the *nightly* build of the XBMC software. The nightly build is so called because it is created from the program's source code automatically every night, and contains the latest changes made by the software's developers. As a result, it can have fixes for any bugs you may encounter—but it can also have untested changes that may make matters worse. This same screen allows you to switch between different versions of XMBC, making it easy to test the nightly build and return to the default version if a problem is found.

Finally, the System tab allows you to set a new password for the *pi* user account to secure Raspbmc for network access. As with the general-purpose Raspbian distribution, this password is set to *raspberry* by default. The System tab also allows you to disable automatic upgrading of the Raspbmc software. This should be left enabled where possible, as it will ensure you get the latest security and bug fixes delivered automatically, but if you're on a per-megabyte metered Internet connection, you can disable the feature.

Chapter **9**
The Pi as a Productivity Machine

THE FLEXIBILITY OF the Raspberry Pi makes it a good choice as a low-power general-purpose desktop computer. Although it will never reach the same levels of performance as a standard desktop or laptop, its low cost and environmentally friendly power consumption help to make up for any problems with occasionally sluggish performance.

Although the Raspberry Pi-specific Raspbian distribution provided on the official website doesn't include any of the usual productivity software you might expect of a general-purpose PC—such as a word processor, spreadsheet or image editing—this software can be installed via the apt-get command. You can also skip the local installation and use cloud-based software through the web browser, which can offer improved performance over locally installed packages at the cost of flexibility and advanced functionality.

Using either of the methods described in this chapter—locally installed applications or cloud-based services—the Pi can be used as a day-to-day machine for office and school work, while not harming its usability as a platform for programming and experimentation.

TIP   If you're planning to use the Pi as a pure productivity machine, it's a good idea to reserve more of the memory for general-purpose use and less for the graphics processor. To learn how to change this split, see Chapter 6, "The Raspberry Pi Software Configuration Tool".

Using Cloud-Based Apps

If you use your Pi connected to the Internet the majority of the time, either through the Model B's integrated Ethernet port or a USB wired or wireless adapter on the Model A, *cloud-based* software offers a powerful yet lightweight means of using office-centric software on the Pi.

Cloud-based software is so called because it doesn't live locally on your computer like a regular piece of software. Instead, it's stored on powerful servers located in data centres throughout the world and accessed over the Internet using a web browser. By tapping into the processing and storage capabilities of a far more powerful remote server, it's possible for the Pi to work on more complicated documents and tasks without slowing down.

Cloud-based software has other advantages over locally installed applications, too. Any given cloud-based application will look the same on any given device, and many of these applications include mobile-oriented versions designed for access from smartphones and tablets. Files are also stored on the remote servers, making them accessible from any device without taking up any room on the Pi's SD card.

Cloud-based applications aren't perfect, however. They typically lag behind their locally installed counterparts in functionality, and often lack advanced features or support fewer file formats. They are also inaccessible when no Internet connection is available, making them a poor choice for users with unreliable connections.

If you think that the improved performance and saved space on your Pi's SD card is worth the trade-off, continue reading. If not, skip to the next section of this chapter to learn how to install LibreOffice.org, an open-source office suite equivalent to Microsoft Office.

The most popular cloud-based office suites are the following:

- **Google Drive**—Run by the search and advertising giant Google, Google Drive (formerly known as Google Docs) includes a word processor, a spreadsheet and a presentation tool (see Figure 9-1). Corporate users can also sign up for a Google Apps account, which provides improved functionality. If you have a Gmail web-based email account, it will automatically work for Google Drive. You can access the service at `http://docs.google.com`.

- **Zoho**—With five million registered users, Zoho is another popular choice. As with Google Drive, a word processor, a spreadsheet and a presentation package are included, but Zoho also offers enhanced business-centric features like a wiki-based knowledge base system, web conferencing, financial management and even customer relationship management. Many of the advanced features, however, require a paid account. You can access the service at `http://www.zoho.com`.

- **Office 365**—If you're a Microsoft Office user, Office 365 is a great choice. Based on the same user interface as the current editions of the Microsoft Office suite for desktops, Office 365 is powerful and flexible. Unlike Zoho and Google Drive, Office 365 has no free user level and requires a monthly subscription. Additionally, some features won't work when the software is accessed from a Linux computer. You can subscribe to the service at `http://office365.microsoft.com`.

- **ThinkFree Online**—A web-based interface to the Hancom ThinkFree Office software, ThinkFree Online offers word processing, spreadsheet and presentation software for free, with 1 GB of storage. The system also ties in to ThinkFree Mobile for tablets and smartphones, as well as the enterprise-targeted ThinkFree Server software. You can subscribe to the service at `http://online.thinkfree.com`.

Unfortunately, many of these web-based services require a browser more capable than Midori, which is provided as the default with the recommended Raspbian distribution. As a result, you'll have to install a different browser in order to make use of any of these packages. The following instructions are for installing the Chromium browser, which is an open-source project on which Google's Chrome browser is based. Its relatively lightweight memory usage makes Chromium a good choice for the Pi. If you're running the Pidora distribution, which comes with Mozilla Firefox as its default browser, you can skip these instructions and proceed to the next section.

FIGURE 9-1:
Google Drive
running in
Chromium on
the Raspberry Pi

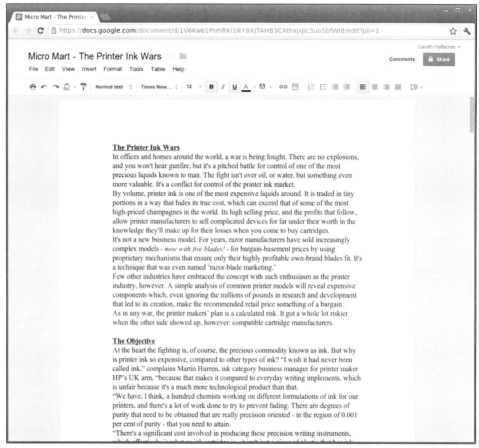

To install the Chromium browser under Raspbian, open a terminal and type the following:

```
sudo apt-get install chromium-browser
```

TIP   Make sure you install the `chromium-browser` package, and not the `chromium` package—the latter is a top-down shoot-'em-up arcade game, and although it's fun, it won't help you in your quest to use cloud-based office suites on your Pi!

With Chromium installed, using a cloud-based office suite is as simple as visiting the site, signing up for an account—providing your credit card details in the case of premium services like Microsoft Office 365—and logging in. If you find performance slow, changing the memory partitioning to give the ARM processor a larger share can help. Chapter 6, "The Raspberry Pi Software Configuration Tool", has full instructions for how to do this.

Using LibreOffice

If you would prefer not to use a cloud-based service, the alternative is to install LibreOffice. Designed as an open-source, cross-platform alternative to the popular Microsoft Office suite and based on the OpenOffice.org project, LibreOffice is powerful and offers just as much functionality as its closed-source inspiration.

That functionality comes at a cost, however. The LibreOffice package is large, taking up nearly 400 MB of space on the Pi's SD card once all the dependencies are included. That can be a problem: in its default setup, the recommended Raspbian distribution has less free space available on the SD card than LibreOffice requires. (For more information on the partition layout of the Raspbian distribution, see the "File System Layout" section in Chapter 3, "Linux System Administration".)

If you want to install LibreOffice, you'll need a 4 GB or larger SD card. You'll also need to resize the root filesystem to make use of the SD card's free space. For instructions on doing this, see Chapter 6, "The Raspberry Pi Software Configuration Tool". Make sure you perform this task before continuing with this chapter, or you'll find your Pi's SD card running out of space before you can use LibreOffice.

With enough free space on the SD card, installing LibreOffice is no more complex than installing any other package. Although it comes bundled with a great deal of additional packages, a single *metapackage* takes care of everything and installs the software with a single command. Open a terminal window and type the following:

```
sudo apt-get install libreoffice
```

If you receive error messages saying files are missing when you're installing software like LibreOffice, the package cache is likely out of date. Run the command `sudo apt-get update` to refresh the cache, and then try again. (See Chapter 3, "Linux System Administration", for more details.)

TIP

When installed, LibreOffice will appear as a series of entries in the Applications Menu in the Pi's desktop environment. These entries are as follows:

- **LibreOffice**—The main application, which provides links to the individual sections of the suite

- **LibreOffice Calc**—The spreadsheet application, equivalent to Microsoft Excel

- **LibreOffice Draw**—A vector illustration application, designed for drawing high-quality scalable images for use as clipart in other LibreOffice programs

- **LibreOffice Impress**—The presentation application, equivalent to Microsoft PowerPoint

- **LibreOffice Math**—A small yet powerful package designed to make it easy to create and edit scientific formulae and equations for embedding in other LibreOffice programs

- **LibreOffice Writer**—The word processor application, equivalent to Microsoft Word (see Figure 9-2)

FIGURE 9-2:
LibreOffice
Writer running
on the
Raspberry Pi

By default, LibreOffice saves and loads files in a format known as the *Open Document Format (ODF)*. This is a standards-based, royalty-free file format supported by the majority of office suite packages—including newer versions of Microsoft Office.

When saving a file in LibreOffice, you can change the format using a drop-down menu in the Save As dialogue. Under File Type, you can select a variety of formats, including several that are fully compatible with older versions of Microsoft Office. When you're sharing files created on the Pi in LibreOffice with users of older software, remember to change the format to ensure that everyone can open the files. Alternatively, you could convince them to install LibreOffice themselves, which is available free for Linux, Windows and OS X.

Image Editing with The Gimp

LibreOffice is a powerful piece of software, but one area where it lacks is in image editing. Although LibreOffice Draw is a powerful tool for illustrative work, unfortunately, you can't use it to touch up digital photographs. These are known as *bitmapped images*, and are very different to the vector images Draw is designed to edit.

For image editing, one of the most powerful tools available for Linux is the GNU Image Manipulation Program, usually referred to as The Gimp. The Gimp is one of the most popular projects in open source, because it offers powerful features for editing bitmapped images with a user interface that is similar to the interface that's used by the commercial Adobe Photoshop package (see Figure 9-3).

FIGURE 9-3: The Gimp running on the Raspberry Pi

The Gimp is not installed by default in most Raspberry Pi distributions, so you'll have to connect your Pi to the Internet and install it through the package management system (see Chapter 3, "Linux System Administration", for details). The Gimp takes up quite a lot of space on the SD card—although not as much as LibreOffice—so make sure you have enough free space before installing it.

To install The Gimp, open a terminal window and type the following:

```
sudo apt-get install gimp
```

The Gimp can take a little while to get used to, because its user interface uses three different windows rather than just one. By default, the window on the left contains the Toolbox; the window on the right displays the Layers, Channels and Gradients options; and the middle window displays the image you're currently editing. If you open more than one image, you'll get more than one main window—but still only one each of the Toolbox and the Layers, Channels and Gradients windows.

By default, *The Gimp User Manual* is not installed. For the Pi, this is a good thing: the Gimp is a powerful tool, and its user manual takes up a not inconsiderable amount of space on the SD card. If you try to access the manual by pressing the F1 key or choosing Help from the Help menu, you'll be prompted to read an online, web-based version instead. Click the Read Online button to open the user manual in your browser.

The Gimp is a very powerful utility and uses a lot of memory. As a result, it runs relatively slowly on the Raspberry Pi—although it is definitely usable. Be patient with it, especially if you're opening large photographs from a digital camera. It may help to increase the amount of system memory available (see Chapter 6, "The Raspberry Pi Software Configuration Tool", for more details on how this is achieved).

When saving files in The Gimp, you can use a variety of file formats. If you're planning on coming back to the file and doing more editing, you should use The Gimp's default XCF file format. This keeps important *metadata* intact, uses lossless compression to maximise image quality and supports images comprised of multiple layers.

If you're planning on uploading your image to the Internet or otherwise sharing it with others, a more portable format like JPG or PNG is recommended. To change the format of the file, choose the Export option from the File menu rather than the Save option (see Figure 9-4). This allows you to choose the file format from a wide variety of file types.

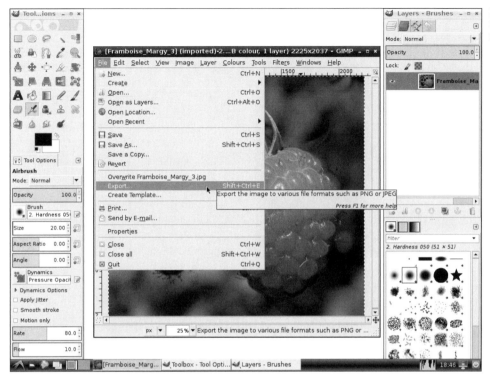

FIGURE 9-4:
Exporting a file
from The Gimp

Chapter 10
The Pi as a Web Server

ALTHOUGH THE PI is significantly less powerful than most devices you would find in a data centre, that doesn't mean that it can't act as a useful server in a home or business environment. Despite a small amount of memory and relatively underpowered processor, the Pi's low power draw and silent running makes it a great choice for serving low-traffic simple pages to a local network or even out onto the Internet.

A large proportion of modern web servers run a combination of Linux, Apache, MySQL and PHP—commonly referred to as a *LAMP stack*. Linux provides the underlying operating system; MySQL the database back-end; Apache the web server; and PHP a scripting language for dynamic pages. Using a LAMP-based server, you can run some quite complex packages ranging from content management systems like WordPress to interactive forums like phpBB. All of this is possible with the Raspberry Pi, so long as you don't expect performance similar to that of a powerful commercial server.

TIP   Web servers work best with plenty of memory. To ensure maximum performance, switch the Pi's memory partitioning to reserve just 16 MB or 32 MB for the GPU (see Chapter 6, "The Raspberry Pi Software Configuration Tool") and don't run a *graphical user interface (GUI)* at the same time.

Installing a LAMP Stack

If you're running the recommended Raspbian distribution for the Raspberry Pi, you're already one-quarter of the way to having a fully operational LAMP stack—specifically, you've already got the Linux portion installed. The next step is to install the missing components: Apache, MySQL and PHP. At the terminal or console, type the following commands to install these packages:

```
sudo apt-get update
sudo apt-get install apache2 php5 php5-mysql mysql-server
```

This will prompt the `apt` package manager (see Chapter 3, "Linux System Administration") to find a number of dependencies required to get a fully functional LAMP stack running (see Figure 10-1). These packages and their dependencies take up a lot of room on the Pi's SD card—around 113 MB in total—so if you haven't resized the root partition on the SD card, turn to Chapter 6, "The Raspberry Pi Software Configuration Tool", for instructions on how to expand the root partition.

Installation of the full LAMP stack can take quite some time on the Pi. Don't panic if the system appears to freeze for a minute or two; the installation should continue normally after. Partway through the installation process, MySQL will prompt you for a password (see Figure 10-2). Make sure you pick a secure password, as this protects the MySQL database—which, depending on what your web server is designed to do, can store user names, payment details and other personally identifiable information. Also make sure you pick a password you can remember! You'll be asked to confirm the password—to check for typing errors—and then the installation will continue.

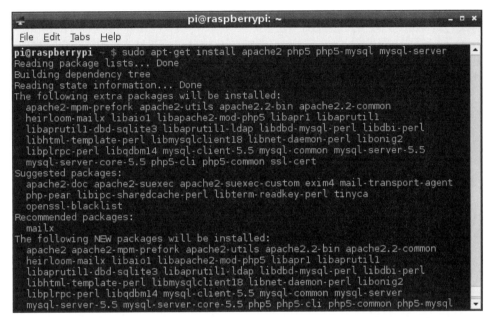

FIGURE 10-1:
Installing the
LAMP stack on
Raspbian

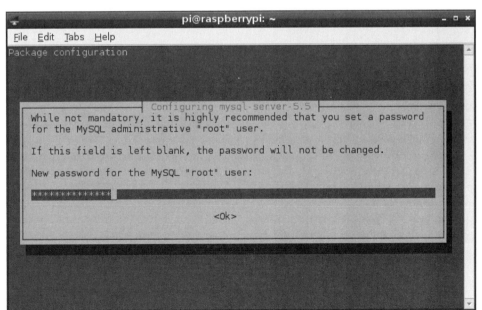

FIGURE 10-2:
Choosing a
password for
MySQL

When the software installation has finished, both the MySQL and Apache servers—known in Linux parlance as *daemons*—will be running in the background. To check that the server is working correctly, use another computer on the network to connect to the Raspberry Pi using a web browser. In the address bar, type the IP address of the Pi to display the default Apache installation page (see Figure 10-3). If you're not sure what IP address the Pi is using, type `ifconfig` at the terminal and look for the IP address listed in the `eth0` section, or the section corresponding to the network adapter in use on your Pi if you're not using the Model B's built-in Ethernet port. For more information on checking and adjusting network settings on the Pi, see Chapter 5, "Network Configuration".

FIGURE 10-3:
Connecting to
the Pi's Apache
server using a
web browser

The final step is to confirm that the PHP scripting module is loaded correctly in Apache. This module is important: because it allows the Apache web server to run PHP scripts to serve dynamic content. Without a working PHP module—or an alternative module for another scripting language like Python—Apache is only able to serve static pages. To test the Apache PHP module, create a new PHP script file using the following command, typed as a single line:

```
sudo sh -c 'echo "<?php phpinfo(); ?>" > ↵
  /var/www/phptest.php'
```

This command creates a new file called `phptest.php` in the `/var/www` directory. This file tells PHP to create an information page for diagnostic purposes. Visit this using either a browser on another computer by typing `http://ipaddress/phptest.php` (replacing *ipaddress* with the IP address of the Raspberry Pi) or on the Pi itself by typing `http://localhost/phptest.php` into the address bar (see Figure 10-4).

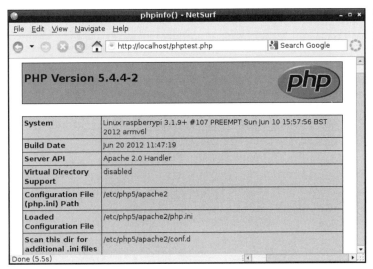

FIGURE 10-4:
Testing Apache's
PHP module on
the Raspberry Pi

When you've finished testing, remove the `phptest.php` file with the following command:

```
sudo rm /var/www/phptest.php
```

Although Apache is the most common web server, there are others. If you find the performance of Apache too slow, experiment with lighttpd—a lightweight web server designed to use less memory than Apache. It can be installed under Raspbian with the command `sudo apt-get install lighttpd`.

TIP

With the LAMP stack installed and working, you can now create your own websites that will be served by the Pi. As long as the sites aren't too complex, and don't receive too many simultaneous users, the Pi should be able to cope with the task admirably—and the device's small size and extremely low power draw more than make up for any slowdown should your site become popular.

By default, files for the web server are stored in the `/var/www` folder, which is writeable only by the *root* user. To adjust where Apache looks for its files—to move the website onto more capacious external storage, for example—edit the text file `000-default` found in the folder `/etc/apache2/sites-enabled`. For more information on configuring Apache, PHP and MySQL, type the following commands at the terminal or console:

```
man apache2
man php5
man mysql
```

Installing WordPress

One of the most popular blogging platforms around, WordPress is an open-source project that aims to give users a simple yet powerful platform to create attractive, interactive websites. WordPress is built on a base of PHP and JavaScript, and offers an attractive web-based interface for creating rich websites. For example, some of the most popular news sites in the world are built on a customised WordPress platform.

To install WordPress on the Raspberry Pi, type the following command at the terminal or console:

```
sudo apt-get install wordpress
```

Like the LAMP stack, WordPress comes with a selection of dependencies (see Figure 10-5). You'll need to make sure you have around 37 MB of free space on the Pi's SD card for the full installation, in addition to the 113 MB required for the LAMP stack. If you have enough free space, type Y to continue the installation process.

When WordPress has finished installing, its default installation directory—`/usr/share/wordpress`—needs to be *linked* into the `/var/www` directory in order for Apache to see the files. Type the following command at the terminal:

```
sudo ln -s /usr/share/wordpress /var/www/wordpress
```

Linking a file or directory is different to moving: the files for WordPress now exist in both `/usr/share` and `/var/www` simultaneously, without taking up any extra space on the Pi's SD card. If you've told Apache to use a different directory for the default website, change the linking command accordingly. Next, run the WordPress MySQL configuration script using the following command, typed as a single line:

```
sudo bash /usr/share/doc/wordpress/examples/setup-mysql ⏎
 -n wordpress localhost
```

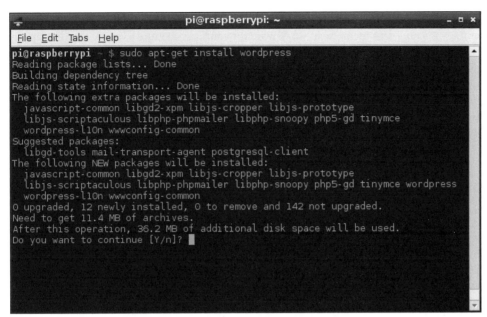

FIGURE 10-5:
Installing
WordPress on
the Raspberry Pi

This adds a new database into MySQL, installed as part of the LAMP stack, for WordPress to use. This database stores your user accounts, posts, comments and other details. Once this script has completed, you'll be told to visit http://localhost in a browser on the Raspberry Pi to continue the installation. This instruction is slightly incorrect: the address you need to visit to finish the WordPress installation is http://localhost/wordpress (see Figure 10-6).

FIGURE 10-6:
Configuring
WordPress in
the NetSurf web
browser

Fill in the form that loads in the web browser, picking a descriptive name for your site and setting a secure—but memorable—password for your user. Be sure to change the Username field from admin to something else in order to make it more secure. When you have filled in all the fields, click the Install WordPress button at the bottom of the page.

The installation process will take a minute or two to complete, and then a new page confirming the successful installation of WordPress will load in the browser. To start using WordPress, click the Log In button at the bottom of this page to log into WordPress with the user name and password you chose at the earlier screen (see Figure 10-7).

FIGURE 10-7:
Logging in to
WordPress on
the Raspberry Pi

Before you can access WordPress from another computer, you'll need to create an additional configuration file. This is created by linking the existing configuration file—set up for local access—using the following command, typed as a single line:

```
sudo ln -s /etc/wordpress/config-localhost.php ⏎
  /etc/wordpress/config-ipaddress.php
```

Replace *ipaddress* in this code with the IP address of your Raspberry Pi. If you've given the Raspberry Pi a hostname in DNS, you can also create a configuration file for that hostname using the same command, but replacing *ipaddress* with the chosen hostname. If you do not have a hostname, simply use the Pi's IP address. For example, the command for a Pi on IP address 192.168.0.115 would be as follows:

```
sudo ln -s /etc/wordpress/config-localhost.php ↵
  /etc/wordpress/config-192.168.0.115.php
```

To complete configuration for external access, choose General from the Settings menu that's located on the left side of the WordPress Dashboard, and change the URL to match either the IP address of the Pi or the chosen hostname (see Figure 10-8).

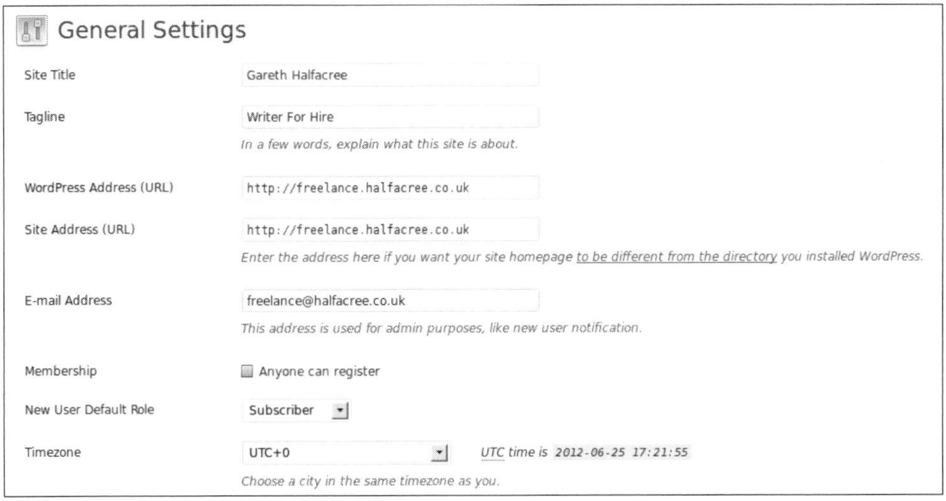

FIGURE 10-8: Altering the URL in the WordPress General Settings menu

WordPress is very memory intensive. For best results, use the Pi as a *headless server*, which is a system that runs without a graphical user interface loaded. Then use a web browser on another computer connected to the network to access the WordPress Dashboard at http:// *ipaddress*/wordpress/wp-login.php. Accessing the WordPress Dashboard directly on the Pi can result in a very long wait!

TIP

The WordPress software includes an automatic update feature, which ensures that your installation is running the latest version. Because of its popularity, WordPress is often the target of malware attacks, and frequent updates are released to patch security holes or add new features. However, when installed via APT, WordPress lacks the permissions required to keep itself up-to-date. To correct this, type the following command at the terminal:

```
sudo chown -R www-data /usr/share/wordpress
```

This gives the www-data user—the account used by the Apache web server—the rights to change files located in the /usr/share/wordpress folder. This will allow automatic upgrading to operate when chosen from the WordPress Dashboard.

For more information on using WordPress, visit the official website at http://www.wordpress.org.

Part III

Programming with the Raspberry Pi

Chapter 11
An Introduction to Scratch

SO FAR IN this book, you've learned a lot about how to use programs that other people have written on your Raspberry Pi. The chief goal of the Raspberry Pi project is to get people writing their own programs, however—and not just adults. The Raspberry Pi Foundation is working to get the device adopted as an educational tool for all age ranges.

A key requirement for reaching that goal is ensuring that young children can experience the joy of creating their own software, rather than just consuming other people's code. The secret to this is *Scratch*.

Introducing Scratch

Created by the Lifelong Kindergarten group at the Massachusetts Institute of Technology Media Lab in 2006 as an offshoot of the Squeak and Smalltalk languages, Scratch takes the core concepts of programming and makes them accessible to all. Long-winded typing—tiring and dull for younger children—is replaced with a simple jigsaw-like drag-and-drop environment, which nevertheless encourages programmatic thinking and introduces the core concepts used by all programming languages.

Officially considered a program for ages eight and above, but accessible to even younger programmers with a little help and guidance, Scratch is deceptively powerful. Behind its colourful and mouse-driven user interface is a programming language that includes impressive multimedia functionality. It should come as no surprise then that, of the more than two-and-a-half million Scratch projects shared by users of the software on the official website, the majority are games.

Encouraging children to learn how to make their own games can be a great way of sneaking a little learning into their playtimes. Scratch's friendly user interface and excellent handling of core concepts mean that children are unlikely to get frustrated by a sudden steep learning curve. Better still, the concepts learned in Scratch offer an excellent foundation for progression to a more flexible language like Python (see Chapter 12, "An Introduction to Python").

Even before moving on to another language, Scratch offers more than just a framework for games. It can be used to create interactive presentations and cartoons, as well as interfaces with external sensors and motors through the use of add-on hardware such as the PicoBoard and the LEGO WeDo robotics kit.

The recommended Raspbian distribution for the Raspberry Pi comes with the latest version of the Scratch development environment pre-loaded, so if you've been following the recommendations throughout this book you're ready to start. If you're using a different operating system, visit the official Scratch website at `http://scratch.mit.edu` to download the software—and you can find versions for Windows and Apple's OS X in the same place.

Example 1: Hello World

When learning a new programming language, it's traditional to start with a very basic program: one that displays a single line of text. This is typically referred to as a Hello World program, and it's the first step towards learning how to create your own programs.

Unlike a traditional programming language, Scratch doesn't expect the user to memorise the names of instructions like `print` or `inkey$`. Instead, almost everything is done by dragging and dropping blocks of code and arranging them into a logical pattern.

To begin, load Scratch by double-clicking its icon on the desktop or clicking on its entry in the Programming menu. After a few seconds, the main Scratch interface will appear (see Figure 11-1). If it's off-centre or small, click the Maximise button—the middle of the three window control buttons on the right side of the top title bar—to fill the screen.

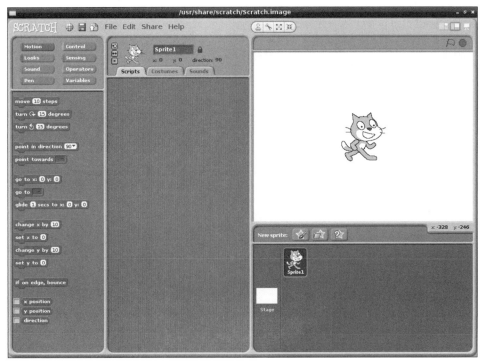

FIGURE 11-1:
The main Scratch interface, shown running on the Raspberry Pi

The Scratch interface is split into multiple panes. At the left is the *block palette*, which holds all the different code blocks you can use to create a program. A list of objects in the program, known as *sprites*, appears at the bottom-right along with a control for the *stage* on which the sprites appear. The stage itself is at the top-right of the window, which is where you will see the program running. Finally, the middle of the window is where the program itself is constructed.

To get the user started, a new Scratch project already includes a blank stage and a single sprite. What it lacks is a program, so clicking the green flag icon at the top-right of the window achieves nothing, because Scratch doesn't yet know what you want it to do.

For the Hello World program, you'll need to change the blocks palette at the left of the screen to the Looks mode by clicking on its button. Partway down the list of Looks blocks is one that reads say Hello!—click this block and drag it into the empty space in the middle of the window labelled Scripts. To obey the decades of tradition behind this type of program, you can also click on the block where it says Hello! and customise it to read Hello World! if you so desire (see Figure 11-2).

FIGURE 11-2:
The first block
placed in a
Scratch program

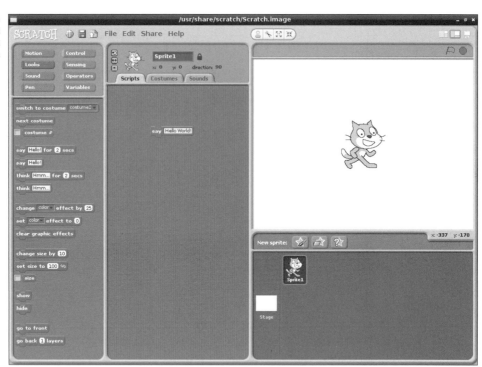

If you click the green flag again, the program still does nothing. That's because although Scratch knows that it is supposed to make the cat sprite say something, it doesn't know when. The event requires a *trigger block*, which can be found in the Control section of the block palette.

Enter this section now by clicking Control, and then drag the top entry—marked when [flag icon] clicked—and place it just above the purple say brick (see Figure 11-3). If you drop it close enough, it should automatically join to the existing brick like a jigsaw piece.

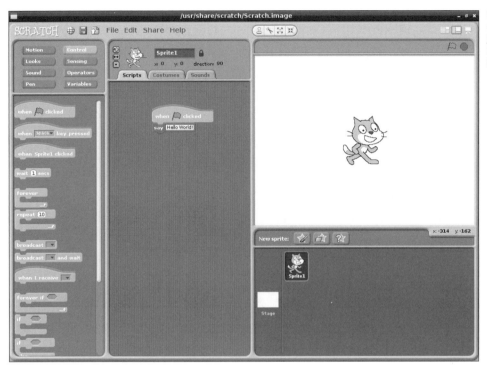

FIGURE 11-3: A Control block joined to a Looks block in Scratch

This concept of connecting multiple bricks together is the heart of Scratch. If you look at the Control brick you just placed, you'll see there's no connecting hole at the top. This means that you can't stack another brick on top, because this Control brick is designed to trigger a series of other bricks directly and must come at the start of a stack. The bottom of the say brick, meanwhile, has a connector that fits into the top of other bricks, which indicates that more bricks can be placed underneath.

With the two bricks in place, click the green flag icon at the top-right of the screen again. This time, a speech bubble will appear from the cat's mouth (see Figure 11-4), and the Hello World program is complete.

Before moving on to the next example, take the time to save your work using the File menu. Scratch is designed to have a single project open at a time, so if you create a new blank file, the current file will be closed to make room. Don't worry if you forget about this when you go to create a new file—if there are unsaved changes in the existing file, Scratch will prompt you to save these changes before closing it.

FIGURE 11-4:
The Hello World
program
executing in
Scratch

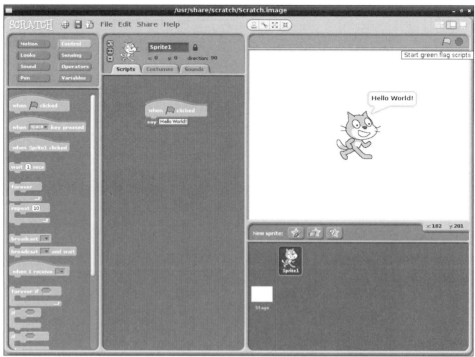

Example 2: Animation and Sound

While Hello World is a very traditional example, it's not particularly interesting. It also fails to show off the true power of Scratch, which lies in its impressive multimedia capabilities and sprite-handling system. This system is particularly well suited to simple animations, which can form the basis of an interactive game.

To begin, start a new project in Scratch by either loading the program afresh or choosing New from the File menu. As with any starter project, Scratch will provide a default sprite—it's this sprite that you will be controlling.

To control a simple animation in Scratch, you use the Motion section of the blocks palette. When you start a new project, this is the default palette. Drag the block labelled move 10 steps to the Scripts area. As its name suggests, this block tells the selected sprite to move 10 steps in the direction it is currently facing. The default sprite in Scratch is always started facing directly to the right—thus, the move 10 steps block will move the sprite 10 steps to the right.

Ten steps isn't a very large value, so click on the value 10 and change it to 30. The block should then read move 30 steps. An animation of a cat moving to the right of the stage isn't that interesting, however, so switch to the Sound block palette and drag the play sound meow block to the Scripts area and link it beneath the existing move block. To keep the cat in this position for a while, add in a wait 1 secs block from the Control block palette. Without this, the sprite will appear to flick quickly between its starting position and the target position.

To make it so the program can be run multiple times without the cat sprite disappearing off the edge of the stage, add another move 10 steps block beneath the play sound block and modify it to read move -30 steps. Scratch will happily allow you to use negative figures like this: if a value of 30 makes the sprite move a certain distance to the right, -30 will make it move the exact same distance in the opposite direction.

Finally, add the when [flag icon] clicked block from the Control block palette to the top of the Script area's stack of blocks to complete the program as shown in Figure 11-5. Clicking the green flag icon on the top-right of the screen will trigger the program—make sure you've got speakers or headphones connected to the Pi for the full effect!

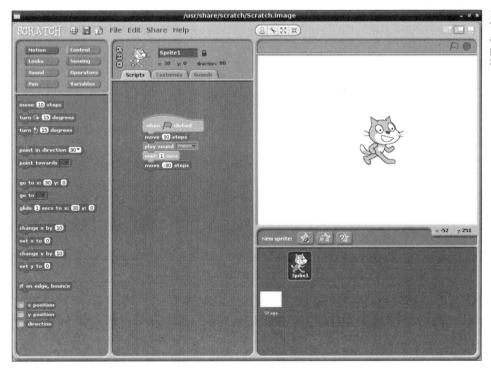

FIGURE 11-5:
The completed animation program in Scratch

This simple animation program can be extended in a variety of ways. Using the New Sprite option just below the stage on the right side of the Scratch window allows the programmer to add more sprites that can move and play sounds independently. Adding in the say block from the first example—or the similar think block, which creates a thought bubble rather than a speech bubble—allows for the creation of an animated comic strip.

More importantly, even this simple example teaches important programming concepts: despite being a mere five blocks long, it covers sprite movement in positive and negative distances, sound playback and the concept of *delays* in a program. To introduce yet another concept—at the risk of driving yourself insane with repetitive noises—try adding a for-ever block from the Control block palette (see Figure 11-6). This adds a *loop* to the program, causing it to run through its list forever—or at least until the noise becomes too much and you click the red stop button at the top of the stage!

FIGURE 11-6:
Adding an
infinite loop to
the simple
Scratch
animation

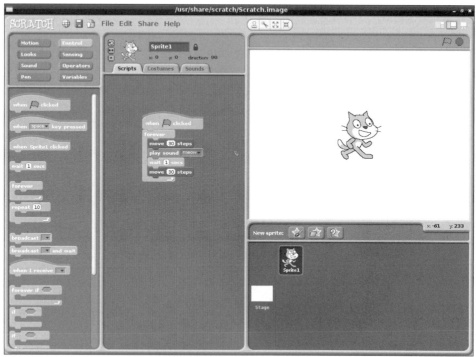

Example 3: A Simple Game

Using Scratch for simple animation is one thing, but the software also allows users to read inputs from the keyboard to introduce interactivity. By combining some simple animation controls to the previously described program, you can create a simple game—and, at the same time, introduce the concepts of *sprite collision, if statements* and *input.*

For this example, start a new Scratch project—remembering to save the previous example, if you haven't already done so—and begin by dragging a move 10 steps block to the Scripts area. This time, rather than telling the code blocks to execute when the flag icon is clicked, go to the Control block palette and drag a when space key pressed block above the move block.

As the name suggests, the when space key pressed block looks for input from the user—in this instance, the spacebar being pressed—and uses that as the trigger for executing a list of blocks. The block works at any time—if you press the spacebar now, the sprite will obey its instructions and move 10 steps to the right.

The when space key pressed block also differs from the when [flag icon] clicked block in another important way: it can be customised. Click the down-arrow button next to the word space to see a list of all the keys the block can watch, and then select right arrow from the list to change the block into a when right arrow key pressed block.

A game in which the player can move in only one direction isn't much fun, so drag a new when space key pressed block into the Scripts area. This can't link to the existing block list—you can only have a single trigger block—so start a new list somewhere further down. As before, use the down-arrow button next to the word space to customise the block, turning it into a when left arrow key pressed block. Finally, switch the block palette back to Motion mode and connect a move 10 steps block beneath the new when left arrow key pressed block before changing it to read move -10 steps.

If you press the left and right arrow keys now, you'll see that the cat moves according to your input (see Figure 11-7): pressing the left arrow moves the cat 10 steps to the left (although, as far as Scratch is concerned, it's moving minus 10 steps to the right), and pressing the right arrow moves the cat 10 steps to the right.

Now that the sprite can be moved by the player, it's time to give the sprite something to do. As this is just a very simple game, the goal should also be simple: to collect some food. Click the Choose New Sprite From File button, found in the middle of the three buttons above the Sprite palette at the bottom-right of the Scratch window.

FIGURE 11-7:
Using input
blocks to control
the motion of a
sprite in Scratch

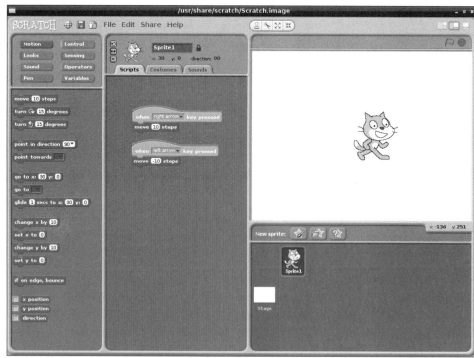

A dialogue box will appear asking you to pick a sprite: double-click on the Things folder, and then double-click on the Cheesy-Puffs sprite (shown in Figure 11-8). This will place the sprite as a new entry in the Sprite palette, giving you a new object to control in the game.

TIP   The Scratch language is naturally *multi-threaded* and partially *object-oriented*. This means that each object in the program, including sprites, can have its own code attached, and that each section of code runs simultaneously and independently of any other block. Used properly, these features enable you to create some quite complex programs.

By default, any sprite added into a Scratch project will appear in the dead centre of the stage. As a result, this obscures the existing cat sprite. Click on the new sprite and drag it to the right of the cat to fix the problem.

With the bowl of Cheesy-Puffs moved, it's still too large for our anthropomorphic two-legged cat to eat. Click the Shrink Sprite button, which is located at the top-right of the stage area and looks like four arrows pointing inwards. If you're not sure which one it is, hover the mouse pointer over each icon for a short description of what it does.

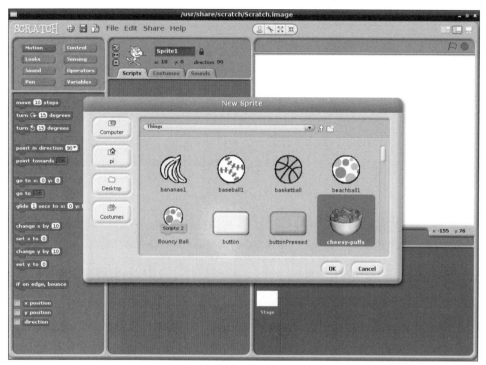

FIGURE 11-8:
Adding the
Cheesy-Puffs
sprite to the
Scratch game
project

Clicking the Shrink Sprite button—or the Grow Sprite button, which does exactly the opposite—changes the mouse cursor into a duplicate of the button's icon. Using this new cursor, click on the Cheesy-Puffs sprite to shrink it. Keep clicking, and the sprite will continue to shrink. Once it's a sensible-looking size, click anywhere outside of the stage area to return the mouse cursor to normal. You can then drag the bowl closer to the right edge of the stage, if you so choose.

Try using the arrow keys on the keyboard to move the cat sprite towards the Cheesy-Puffs sprite now. As you can see, when the two sprites meet, nothing happens. That's because the program doesn't contain any instructions for what to do when the two sprites overlap—known as a *sprite collision*—so it doesn't do anything. This can be rectified with a new type of block: a *Sensing* block.

With the Cheesy-Puffs sprite currently active (its image should appear at the top of the Scripts pane, but if it doesn't, just double-click the sprite on the stage), switch the Blocks palette into Sensing mode by clicking the Sensing button. From the Sensing palette, drag a `touching ?` block into the Scripts pane.

Like the `when space key pressed` block used to control the cat sprite's motion, the `touching ?` block can be customised. Click the down-arrow button next to the question mark, and choose Sprite1 (the cat sprite) from the list. This block will now be activated when the two sprites collide.

TIP	You can name a sprite by clicking on the box next to its image in the Scripts pane and typing in a name. Giving the sprites sensible names—such as `Cat`, `CheesyPuffs`, and so forth—makes it significantly easier to track what's going on in the program.

Look at the shape of the `touching Sprite1?` block. As you can see, it has no jigsaw-like connectors on the top or the bottom, and it's shaped like a diamond—the same shape used for a decision point in a flowchart. That's no accident: the majority of the Sensing blocks need to be embedded in a Control block in order to operate.

Switch the Blocks palette to Control mode, and look for the `if` block—it's shaped like a squished and bumpy letter C. Note that the `if` block has a diamond-shaped indentation—the same shape as the `touching Sprite1?` block. Drag the `if` block onto the Scripts pane, and then drag the `touching Sprite1?` block onto its diamond-shaped indentation. The result is a two-coloured block that now reads `if touching Sprite1?`.

This represents an *if conditional* in the program: when this point is reached, any code located within its confines will be executed if and only if the *condition* is met. In this case, the condition is that Sprite2 is being touched by Sprite1. With the use of `and`, `or` and `not` logic blocks from the Operators block palette, some quite complex scenarios can be accommodated.

Boolean Logic

Named for George Boole, Boolean logic or Boolean algebra is a key concept to understanding how computers work. In Scratch, Boolean logic is implemented in three Operators bricks: `and`, `or` and `not`.

The `and` operator requires that two inputs—in Scratch's case, Sensing blocks—are both true before its own output will be true. If either or both of its inputs is false, its own output will be false; only when both inputs are true will the output be true. You can use this operator to check to see if a sprite is touching two other sprites, as an example.

The `or` operator requires that one or the other of its two inputs are true. If either input is true, the operator's output will also be true. This is a handy way of re-using code: if you have multiple sprites that are lethal to the player sprite, a single block of code can be used with the `or` operator to trigger when any of the enemy sprites are touched.

Finally, the `not` operator is known as an *inverter*: whatever its single input is, it outputs the opposite. If its input is false, then the output is true; if the input is true, then the output is false.

From the Looks block palette, drag a say Hello! For 2 secs block into the centre of the if touching Sprite1? conditional. Change the text to read Don't eat me!, and then add a wait 1 secs Control block, changing the value to 2. Add a when space key pressed block to the top, changing the value to read when right arrow key pressed. Finally, drag a hide block from the Looks palette to the bottom of the loop to end up with the block list that's shown in Figure 11-9.

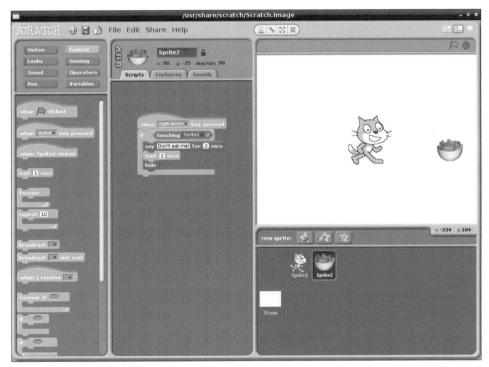

FIGURE 11-9: Controlling the Cheesy-Puffs with a Scratch if block

Double-click the cat sprite on the stage to return to editing its scripts. The script you created for the Cheesy-Puffs sprite will disappear, but don't worry—it's still saved but only appears when you're editing that particular sprite.

Drag another if block from the Control palette along with another touching ? sensing block, and this time, change the Sensing block so both blocks together read if touching Sprite2?. Into this block, insert a wait 1 secs Control block with the value changed to 2 and a say Hello! for 2 secs Looks block with the message changed to read Yum-yum-yum!. Finally, drag the whole stacked block up so it connects to the bottom of the existing when right arrow key pressed block, beneath the move 10 steps block. The final code for the cat sprite should look like the blocks in Figure 11-10.

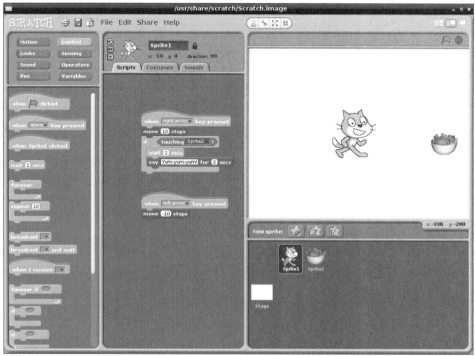

If you move the cat towards the Cheesy-Puffs with the right-arrow key on the keyboard, the game starts. When the cat reaches the Cheesy-Puffs, the dialogue exchange takes place and the bowl should disappear.

Although this example is effective for introducing some important programming concepts, it's hardly the best way the game could be coded. Scratch includes a *message broadcast* system that allows code attached to one object to communicate with code attached to another, which enables you to create much neater collision results that don't rely on carefully timed pauses in order to make sense.

To experiment with broadcasting, try using the broadcast and when I receive blocks from the Control palette. A message created for a broadcast block in any object can trigger code in any other object using the when I receive flag, meaning you can use it to link multiple objects and their code together.

Robotics and Sensors

In addition to purely software-based inputs and outputs, it's also possible to tie Scratch into external hardware using sensor boards and robotics systems. Thanks to its multithreaded nature and powerful inter-process messaging system, Scratch can be used to create a surprisingly advanced robotics engine and is by far the easiest way to place a Raspberry Pi at the heart of a simple robot.

Unlike Python, which is a more powerful but significantly more complex programming language, Scratch can't make use of the Raspberry Pi's GPIO port to communicate with external hardware. As a result, it needs some additional equipment before it can interact with the physical world.

Sensing with the PicoBoard

Designed by the SparkFun electronics company, the PicoBoard is an add-on module that connects to a computer running Scratch and provides a variable slider input, a light sensor, a button, a sound sensor and four pairs of alligator clips that can be used to monitor external electrical devices.

There are currently two types of PicoBoard: the original model, which uses a serial connection, and its replacement, which uses a USB connection. The latter is supported by the Raspberry Pi. Simply connect it to a free USB port or a port on a USB hub connected to the Pi, restart Scratch, and you'll be able to use its various functions within the Scratch interface.

Details on the PicoBoard can be found at `http://www.sparkfun.com/products/10311`.

Robotics with LEGO

In addition to add-in sensor modules, it's possible to control an external robotics system through Scratch. The LEGO Education WeDo robotics kit is designed to connect motors, distance sensors and speed sensors to a computer—all of which can be controlled using specialised blocks found in Scratch.

For children, the WeDo kit is an excellent way to get started with robotics: the components clip together just like regular LEGOs, and there are no risks of receiving an electric shock should anything be badly connected. The WeDo kit boasts compatibility with regular LEGO and LEGO Technik kits, too, meaning it's possible to build large projects quickly and easily.

More information on using a LEGO Education WeDo kit with Scratch can be found at `http://info.scratch.mit.edu/WeDo`.

Further Reading

Although this chapter serves as a brief introduction to Scratch, it's far from exhaustive. It's also a little verbose for younger readers, who tend to learn more quickly when their lessons are accompanied by lots of colour pictures.

The Support section of the official Scratch website, hosted by MIT at `http://info.scratch.mit.edu/support`, includes a link to a Getting Started Guide in PDF format. The guide describes how to work with Scratch in a colourful, child-friendly manner, and is a great educational tool. This learning experience can be enhanced even further when combined with Scratch Cards, which are downloadable flash cards containing explanations for each of the block types found in Scratch.

MIT also runs a user forum for Scratch, allowing enthusiasts of the software to learn together and share solutions for common problems. Membership is free, and the site works well using the Midori web browser included in the Raspbian distribution for the Raspberry Pi. The forums can be accessed at `http://scratch.mit.edu/discuss/`.

The easiest way to advance your Scratch skills, however, is to play. The name Scratch has its roots in turntablism: when a DJ spins a record, the needle creates a scratching sound. Just as DJs remix existing songs into something new, Scratch enthusiasts are encouraged to submit their creations to the official website for others to download, examine, modify and remix. The official Scratch site currently hosts more than 2.5 million Scratch programs, making it a perfect source for learning how Scratch is being used to create projects and for sharing your own ideas with others. A list of the most recently shared projects can be found at `http://scratch.mit.edu/explore/`.

Chapter 12

An Introduction to Python

THE RASPBERRY PI gets the first half of its name from a long-standing tradition of using fruit to name new computing systems—from classic microcomputers like the Acorn, Apricot and Tangerine to more recognisably modern brands including Apple and BlackBerry—but the second half comes courtesy of the *Python* programming language.

Introducing Python

Flexible and powerful, Python was originally developed in the late 1980s at the National Research Institute for Mathematics and Computer Science by Guido van Rossum as a successor to the ABC language. Since its introduction, Python has grown in popularity thanks to what is seen as a clear and expressive syntax developed with a focus on ensuring that code is readable.

Python is a *high-level language*. This means that Python code is written in largely recognisable English, providing the Pi with commands in a manner that is quick to learn and easy to follow. This is in marked contrast to *low-level languages*, like assembler, which are closer to how the computer "thinks" but almost impossible for a human to follow without experience. The high-level nature and clear syntax of Python make it a valuable tool for anyone who wants to learn to program. It is also the language that is recommended by the Raspberry Pi Foundation for those looking to progress from the simple Scratch (described in Chapter 11, "An Introduction to Scratch") to more "hands-on" programming.

Python is published under an open-source licence, and is freely available for Linux, OS X and Windows computer systems. This cross-platform support means that software written using Python on the Pi can be used on computers running almost any other operating system as well—except where the program makes use of Pi-specific hardware such as the GPIO Port. To learn how Python can be used to address this port, see Chapter 13, "Learning to Hack Hardware".

Example 1: Hello World

As you learned in Chapter 11, "An Introduction to Scratch", the easiest way to learn a new programming language is to create a project that prints "Hello World!" on the screen. In Scratch, you just had to drag and drop bricks of prewritten code, but in Python, you need to write this program entirely by hand.

A Python project is, at heart, nothing more than a text file containing written instructions for the computer to follow. This file can be created using any text editor. For example, if you enjoy working at the console or in a terminal window, you can use nano; if you prefer a graphical user interface (GUI), you can use Leafpad. Another alternative is to use an integrated development environment (IDE) such as IDLE, which provides Python-specific functionality that's missing from a standard text editor, including syntax checking, debugging facilities and the ability to run your program without having to leave the editor. This chapter gives you instructions on how to create Python files using IDLE, but of course, the IDE program that you choose to use for programming is up to you. The chapter also includes instructions for running your created files directly from the terminal, which can be used in conjunction with any text editor or other IDE.

To begin the Hello World project, open IDLE from the Programming menu in the Raspbian distribution's desktop environment. If you're not using IDLE, create a blank document in your favourite text editor and skip the rest of this paragraph. By default, IDLE opens up in *Python shell* mode (see Figure 12-1), so anything you type in the initial window will be immediately executed. To open a new Python project which can be executed later, click on the File menu and choose New Window to open a blank file.

FIGURE 12-1:
The IDLE
Python Shell
window

It's good practice to start all Python programs with a line known as a *shebang*, which gets its name from the # and ! characters at the beginning of the line. This line tells the operating system where it should look for the Python files. Although this is not entirely necessary for programs that will be run from within IDLE or will call Python explicitly at the terminal, it *is* required for programs that are run directly by calling the program's filename.

To ensure the program runs regardless of where the Python executable is installed, the first line of your program should read as follows:

```
#!/usr/bin/env python
```

This line tells the operating system to look at the *$PATH* environment variable—which is where Linux stores the location of files that can be executed as programs—for the location of Python, which should work on any Linux distribution used on the Pi. The *$PATH* variable contains a list of directories where executable files are stored and is used to find programs when you type their name at the console or in a terminal window.

To achieve the goal of printing out a message, you should use Python's `print` command. As its name suggests, this command prints text to an output device—by default, to the console or terminal window from which the program is being executed. Its usage is simple: any text following the word `print` and placed between quotation marks will be printed to the standard output device. Enter the following line in your new project:

```
print "Hello, World!"
```

The final program should look like this:

```
#!/usr/bin/env python
print "Hello, World!"
```

If you're creating the example program in IDLE rather than a plain text editor, you'll notice that the text is multicoloured (see Figure 12-2, where colours are represented as differing shades of grey in the print edition). This is a feature known as *syntax highlighting* and is a feature of IDEs and the more-advanced text editing tools. Syntax highlighting changes the colour of sections of the text according to their function in order to make the program easier to understand at a glance. It also makes it easy to spot so-called *syntax errors* caused by forgetting to put an end-quote in a `print` command or forgetting to comment out a remark. For this short example, syntax highlighting isn't necessary—but in larger programs, it can be an invaluable tool for finding errors.

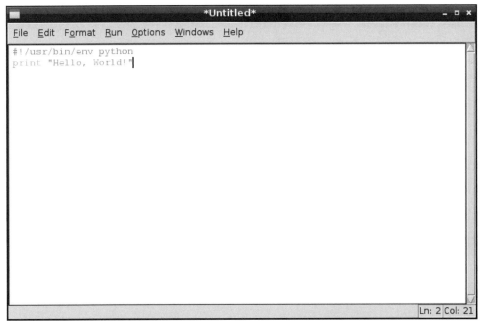

FIGURE 12-2: Syntax highlighting in IDLE

Before you run your program, save it as `helloworld.py` using the File menu. If you're using IDLE, the file will be given the extension `.py` automatically. If you're using a text editor, be sure to type `.py` at the end of the filename (not `.txt`) when you save it. This extension indicates that the file contains Python code—although Python is clever enough to run the program even if it's saved with a different file extension.

How you run the file will depend on whether you're using IDLE or a text editor. In IDLE, simply choose Run Module from the Run menu, or press the F5 key on the keyboard. This will switch IDLE back to the Python shell window and run the program. You should then see the message `Hello, World!` appear onscreen in blue (see Figure 12-3). If not, check your syntax—in particular, check that you have quotation marks at both the beginning and end of the message on the `print` line.

If you created the `helloworld.py` program in a text editor, you'll need to open a terminal window from the Accessories menu on the desktop. If you saved the file anywhere except your home directory, you'll also have to use the `cd` command to change to that directory (see Chapter 3, "Linux System Administration"). Once you're in the right directory, you can run your program by typing the following:

```
python helloworld.py
```

FIGURE 12-3:
Running
helloworld.
py in IDLE

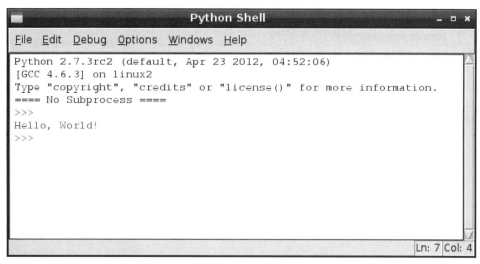

This tells the operating system to run Python and then load the helloworld.py file for execution. Unlike the Python shell in IDLE, Python will quit when it reaches the end of the file and return you to the terminal. The result, however, is the same: the message Hello, World! is printed to the standard output (see Figure 12-4).

FIGURE 12-4:
Running
helloworld.
py at the
terminal

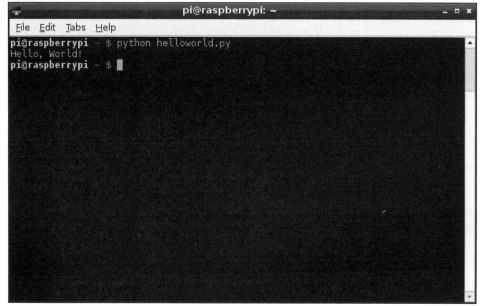

Making Python Programs Executable

Normally, the only way to run a Python program is to tell the Python software to open the file. With the shebang line at the top of the file, however, it's possible to execute the file directly without having to call Python first. This can be a useful way of making your own tools that can be executed at the terminal: once copied into a location in the system's $PATH environment variable, the Python program can be called simply by typing its name.

First, you need to tell Linux that the Python file should be marked as executable—an attribute that means the file is a program. To protect the system from malware being downloaded from the Internet this attribute isn't automatically set, since only files that are marked as executable will run. To make the helloworld.py file executable, use the chmod command (described in detail in Chapter 3, "Linux System Administration") by typing the following:

```
chmod +x helloworld.py
```

Now try running the program directly by typing the following:

```
./helloworld.py
```

Despite the fact that you didn't call the Python program, the helloworld.py program should run just the same as if you'd typed python helloworld.py. The program can only be run by calling it with its full location—/home/pi/helloworld.py—or from the current directory by using ./ as the location. To make the file accessible in the same way as any other terminal command, it needs to be copied to /usr/local/bin with the following command:

```
sudo cp helloworld.py /usr/local/bin/
```

The sudo prefix is required because, for security reasons, non-privileged users cannot write to the /usr/local/bin directory. With the helloworld.py file located in /usr/local/bin, which is included in the $PATH variable, it can be executed from any directory by simply typing its name. Try changing to a different directory, and then run the program by typing the following:

```
helloworld.py
```

To make your custom-made programs seem more like native utilities, you can rename them to remove the .py file extension. To change the helloworld.py program in this way, just type the following line at the terminal as a single line:

```
sudo mv /usr/local/bin/helloworld.py ↵

 /usr/local/bin/helloworld
```

Once renamed, the program can be run simply by typing helloworld at the terminal or console.

Example 2: Comments, Inputs, Variables and Loops

Although the Hello World program is a useful, gentle introduction to a language, it's not terribly exciting. By its nature, it covers only the basics and fails to introduce some of the concepts required for creating useful or interesting programs. The next example, however, uses some of the basic tools required to make interactive programs in Python.

As in Example 1, begin by opening a new blank document in IDLE or your text editor, and then start the program with the following shebang line:

```
#!/usr/bin/env python
```

As previously discussed, this line isn't strictly necessary unless the program is going to be made executable, but it does no harm and is a good habit to develop.

Next, add a comment to the program to provide context if you need to open the file at a later date. Note that this needs to be entered as a single line, as with all code lines that end in a ↵ symbol:

```
# Example 2: A Python program from the ↵
 Raspberry Pi User Guide
```

In Python, anything following a hash symbol—with the exception of the shebang line—is treated as a comment. When a comment is found, Python ignores it and skips to the next line. Commenting your code is good practice: although you might know what a particular section of code does now, things might not be so clear when you open the file again six months down the line. Comments also help make code more maintainable, and if you decide to share your code with other people, your comments help them understand what each section is supposed to do. For simple programs, it's not strictly necessary to include comments—but as with adding the shebang line, it's a very good habit to get in to. Comments can be on their own line, as with the preceding comment, or at the end of a line, in which case Python will run the code line up until it reaches the hash symbol.

Next, ask the user for his or her name using the following line:

```
userName = raw_input("What is your name?  ")
```

This small line actually achieves quite a lot. The first part, `userName =`, tells Python to create a new *variable*—a location for storing a piece of information—called `userName`. The equals symbol tells Python that the variable should be set to whatever follows. However, in this case what follows isn't just a piece of information, but another command: `raw_input`. This is a tool designed to accept *string* (text) input from the keyboard, and allows for a message to be printed to the default output so the user knows what to type. This helps keep the program simple—without the ability to print a prompt telling the user what to type, a second line with a `print` command would be required. Remember to leave a space at the end of the prompt; otherwise, the user's input will begin immediately after the question mark.

When asking the user to type in text, always use `raw_input`. This provides security that the **WARNING** `input` command alone does not—if you just use `input`, a user may *inject* his or her own code into your program and have it crash or work contrary to your intentions.

With the user's name now stored safely in the `userName` variable, the program can begin to get clever. Welcome the user using the following line:

```
print "Welcome to the program,", userName
```

This line demonstrates a secondary function of the `print` command introduced in Example 1: the ability to print out the contents of variables. This `print` command is split into two: the first section prints everything between the two quotation marks, and the second comma tells `print` that more should be printed to the same line. Simply typing the variable name `userName` is enough for Python to know that it should print the contents of that variable, resulting in a message customised to the user's own name.

This example program is going to take the form of a simple but friendly calculator. Unlike Example 1, it will continue to run until the user tells it otherwise. This is achieved using a loop, just as in Scratch. Begin the loop by typing the following two lines:

```
goAgain = 1
while goAgain == 1:
```

The first line creates a new variable called `goAgain` and sets it to 1. The second line begins the loop, and tells Python that `while` the `goAgain` variable is equal to 1, it should continue to loop through the following code. As the next few lines are written, they will need to be *indented* by inserting four spaces at the start of each line. These spaces tell Python which lines are part of the loop and which lines are outside the loop. If you're using IDLE, the spaces will be inserted automatically; if you're using a text editor, remember to insert the spaces manually.

Why ==?

Previously, you've been using a single equals symbol to set the value of variables. The `while` loop, however, uses two. Using two equals symbols next to each other performs an *evaluation*, which compares a variable's value to whatever follows. A single equals symbol instead sets the variable to the value that follows.

There are other evaluations as well as the double-equals, which is only true if the variable matches the given value exactly: > means greater than, < means less than, >= means greater than or equal to, <= means less than or equal to, and != means not equal to.

Using these evaluation symbols, you can control the flow of a program according to the rules of Boolean logic. For more information on Boolean logic, see Chapter 11, "An Introduction to Scratch".

In its most basic form, a calculator takes two numbers as input and performs a mathematical operation on them. To make your calculator work, first take the two numbers from the user with the following lines:

```
firstNumber = int(raw_input("Type the first number: "))
secondNumber = int(raw_input("Type the second number: "))
```

These lines not only use the `raw_input` instruction to ask for two numbers, but they also use `int`. Short for *integer*, the `int` instruction tells Python to treat input as a number rather than a string. Obviously, this is important for a calculator program since it won't be calculating words.

With the two numbers stored as variables, the program can perform its calculations. Type the following lines, which add, subtract and multiply the two numbers and send the output to the user:

```
print firstNumber, "added to", secondNumber, "equals", ↵
firstNumber + secondNumber
print firstNumber, "minus", secondNumber, "equals", ↵
firstNumber - secondNumber
print firstNumber, "multiplied by", secondNumber, "equals", ↵
firstNumber * secondNumber
```

Notice that while the addition and subtraction operations use the expected plus and minus symbols, multiplication uses the * symbol. Also notice that there are no formatting spaces between the quotation marks. This is because Python automatically adds spaces where required when it prints integers and strings together. Finally, note that there is no division operation (which would be indicated with the / symbol). This is because the example calculator program uses *integers*, which can only be whole numbers, with no decimal places or fractions allowed.

Although the calculation part of the program is now complete, it will run forever because there is currently nothing to tell Python when it's time to exit the loop. To provide the user with a way to exit the program, add the following line:

```
goAgain = int(raw_input("Type 1 to enter more numbers, ↵
or any other number to quit: "))
```

This allows the user to change the goAgain variable, which controls the while loop. If the user enters the number 1, the goAgain variable is still equal to 1 and the loop will run again. However, if the user enters any other number, the evaluation is no longer true (goAgain is no longer equal to 1), and the loop will end.

The finished program should look like this, remembering that anything marked with ↵ should be entered onto a single line:

```
#!/usr/bin/env python
# Example 2: A Python program from the Raspberry Pi User Guide
userName = raw_input("What is your name?  ")
print "Welcome to the program,", userName
goAgain = 1
while goAgain == 1:
    firstNumber = int(raw_input("Type the first number: "))
    secondNumber = int(raw_input("Type the second number: "))
    print firstNumber, "added to", secondNumber, "equals", ↵
    firstNumber + secondNumber
    print firstNumber, "minus", secondNumber, "equals", ↵
    firstNumber - secondNumber
    print firstNumber, "multiplied by", secondNumber, "equals", ↵
    firstNumber * secondNumber
    goAgain = int(raw_input("Type 1 to enter more numbers, or ↵
    any other number to quit: "))
```

Save the program as calculator.py, and run it by choosing Run Module from the Run menu in IDLE or by typing python calculator.py at the terminal. Enter your user name when prompted, and then provide the numbers that you want to calculate (see Figure 12-5) until you get bored and then type anything other than 1 to exit the program.

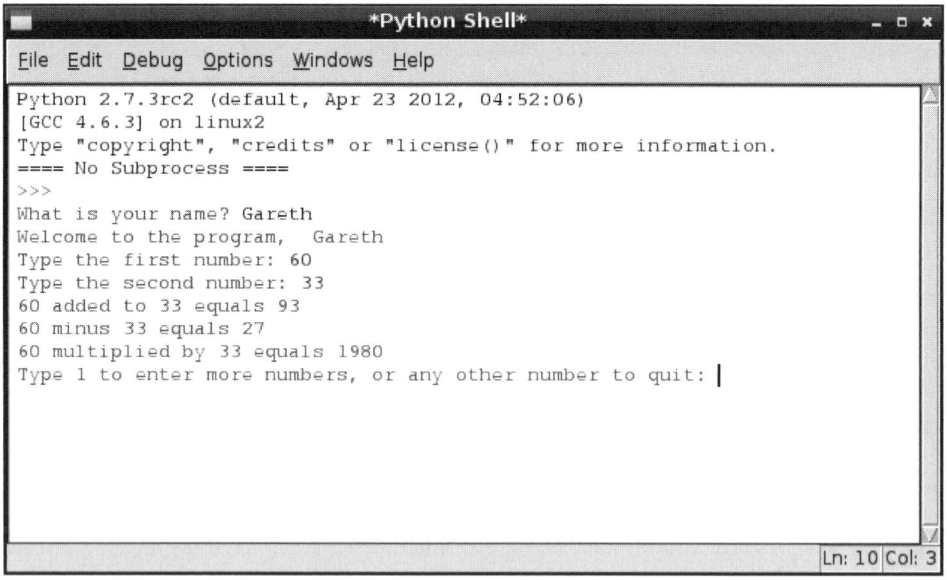

FIGURE 12-5:
Running
calculator.
py in IDLE

```
*Python Shell*                                        _ □ ✕

File  Edit  Debug  Options  Windows  Help

Python 2.7.3rc2 (default, Apr 23 2012, 04:52:06)
[GCC 4.6.3] on linux2
Type "copyright", "credits" or "license()" for more information.
==== No Subprocess ====
>>>
What is your name? Gareth
Welcome to the program,  Gareth
Type the first number: 60
Type the second number: 33
60 added to 33 equals 93
60 minus 33 equals 27
60 multiplied by 33 equals 1980
Type 1 to enter more numbers, or any other number to quit: |

                                                   Ln: 10 Col: 3
```

For more short programs that introduce important Python concepts, visit the official Python Simple Programs wiki page at http://wiki.python.org/moin/SimplePrograms.

Example 3: Gaming with pygame

To illustrate the power of Python, this example creates a fully functional arcade game based on the classic game of Snake or Nibbles. To accomplish this, it uses an external Python library called *pygame*.

Originally written by Pete Shinners, pygame is a collection of python *modules* designed to add new functionality to the language—functionality specifically designed to make it easy to write a game in Python. Each pygame module provides a function required by a modern game, including sound, graphics and even networking support. Although it's possible to write a game in Python without using pygame, it's a lot easier if you take advantage of the code already written in the pygame library.

Before you can write a pygame program, you need to install the pygame library. If you're using the recommended Raspbian distribution, this is as simple as typing the following at the console or terminal:

```
sudo apt-get install python-pygame
```

For other distributions, the pygame source files can be downloaded from the official pygame website at `http://www.pygame.org/download.shtml`. Instructions for installation are provided on the same page.

Starting a pygame program is the same as starting any other Python project. Open a new blank document in either IDLE or a text editor, and add the following shebang line to the top:

```
#!/usr/bin/env python
```

Next you need to tell Python that this program uses the pygame modules. To do this, you use an `import` instruction, which tells Python to load an external module (another Python file) and make it accessible from the current program. Type the following two lines to import the necessary modules into your new project:

```
import pygame, sys, time, random
from pygame.locals import *
```

The first line imports the main `pygame` module along with the Python modules `sys`, `time` and `random`, which will also be used in this program. Typically, a module must then be called by typing its name followed by a full stop and the name of the instruction from within the module, but the second line in the preceding code tells Python to load all the instructions from the `pygame.locals` module as though they're native instructions. As a result, you will need to do less typing when using these instructions. Other module names—such as `pygame.clock`, which is separate to `pygame.locals`—will still need to be typed in full.

Enter the next two lines to set up pygame so it's ready to use in the example program:

```
pygame.init()
fpsClock = pygame.time.Clock()
```

The first line tells pygame to initialise itself, and the second line sets up a new variable called `fpsClock`, which will be used to control the speed of the game. Next, set up a new pygame display surface—the canvas onto which in-game objects will be drawn—with the following two lines:

```
playSurface = pygame.display.set_mode((640, 480))
pygame.display.set_caption('Raspberry Snake')
```

Next, you should define some colours for the program to use. Although this step isn't strictly necessary, it again saves on typing: if you want to set a particular object to be red, you can simply use the `redColour` variable rather than having to call the `pygame.Color` instruction and remember the three colour values for red, green and blue. To define the colours for this example program, type the following lines:

```
redColour = pygame.Color(255, 0, 0)
blackColour = pygame.Color(0, 0, 0)
whiteColour = pygame.Color(255, 255, 255)
greyColour = pygame.Color(150, 150, 150)
```

The next few lines initialise some of the game's variables so they're ready for use. This is an important step, because if these variables are left blank when the game begins, Python won't know what to do. Don't worry about what each variable does for now—just type in the following lines:

```
snakePosition = [100,100]
snakeSegments = [[100,100],[80,100],[60,100]]
raspberryPosition = [300,300]
raspberrySpawned = 1
direction = 'right'
changeDirection = direction
```

Notice that three of the variables—snakePosition, snakeSegments and raspberry-Position—are set to a list of comma-separated values. This causes Python to create the variables as *lists*—a number of different values stored in a single variable name. Later, you'll see how you can access individual values stored in a list.

Next, you need to define a new function—a fragment of Python code which can be called upon later in the program. Functions are useful for avoiding code repetition and making the program easier to understand. If you have a particular set of instructions that are needed at multiple points in the same program, using def to create a function means you'll only have to type them once—and only have to change them in a single place if you alter the program later. Type the following lines to define the gameOver function:

```
def gameOver():
    gameOverFont = pygame.font.Font ↵
    ('freesansbold.ttf', 72)
    gameOverSurf = gameOverFont.render ↵
    ('Game Over', True, greyColour)
    gameOverRect = gameOverSurf.get_rect()
    gameOverRect.midtop = (320, 10)
    playSurface.blit(gameOverSurf, gameOverRect)
    pygame.display.flip()
    time.sleep(5)
    pygame.quit()
    sys.exit()
```

As with loops, the code for a function should be indented. Every line after the `def` instruction should have four spaces at the start—if you're using IDLE, these spaces will be inserted automatically, but if you're using a text editor, you will need to insert the spaces yourself. After the final line of the function—`sys.exit()`—you can stop indenting.

The `gameOver` function uses a selection of pygame's commands to perform a simple task: write the words `Game Over` to the screen in a large font, pause for 5 seconds, and then quit both pygame and Python itself. It may seem strange to set up the instructions for quitting the game before the game has even begun, but functions should always be defined before they are called. Python won't execute these instructions until it is told to do so using the newly created `gameOver` instruction.

With the beginning of the program complete, it's time to start the main section. This takes place in an infinite loop—a `while` loop that never exits. This is so that the game can continue to run until the player dies by hitting a wall or eating his or her own tail. Begin the main loop with the following line:

```
while True:
```

Without anything to evaluate, Python will check to see if `True` is true. Because that's always the case, the loop will continue to run forever—or, at least until you tell Python to quit out of the loop by calling the `gameOver` function.

Continue the program with the following lines, paying attention to the indentation levels:

```
for event in pygame.event.get():
    if event.type == QUIT:
        pygame.quit()
        sys.exit()
    elif event.type == KEYDOWN:
```

The first line, which comes right after the `while` loop begins, should be indented four spaces—but it's a loop of its own, using a `for` instruction to check for pygame events like key presses. As a result, the line under that needs to be indented an additional four spaces for a total of eight—but that line, too, is a loop, using an `if` instruction to check whether the user has pressed a key. As a result, the next line—`pygame.quit()`—is indented an additional four spaces for a total of 12 spaces. This logical progression of indentation tells Python where each loop begins and ends, which is important: if the wrong number of spaces is used, the program won't work correctly. This is why using a development environment like IDLE, which attempts to automatically indent code where required, can be easier than using a plain text editor to create Python programs.

An `if` loop tells Python to check to see if a particular evaluation is true. The first check, `if event.type == QUIT`, tells Python to execute the indented code below if pygame reports a QUIT message (which happens when the user presses the Escape key). The two lines beneath that should be familiar from the gameOver function: they tell pygame and Python to close down and exit.

The line beginning elif is used to extend if loops. Short for *else if*, an elif instruction is evaluated when a previous if instruction was found to be false. In this case, the elif instruction is used to see if pygame is reporting a KEYDOWN event, which is returned when the user is pressing a key on the keyboard. As with the if instruction, code to be executed when an elif is true should be indented by an additional four spaces plus whatever indentation the elif instruction itself has. Type the following lines to give the elif instruction something to do when the user presses a key:

```
if event.key == K_RIGHT or event.key == ord('d'):
    changeDirection = 'right'
if event.key == K_LEFT or event.key == ord('a'):
    changeDirection = 'left'
if event.key == K_UP or event.key == ord('w'):
    changeDirection = 'up'
if event.key == K_DOWN or event.key == ord('s'):
    changeDirection = 'down'
if event.key == K_ESCAPE:
    pygame.event.post(pygame.event.Event(QUIT))
```

These instructions modify the value of the changeDirection variable, used to control the direction the player's snake is travelling during the game. Using or with an if statement allows more than one evaluation to be made. In this case, it provides two ways of controlling the snake: the player can use the cursor keys, or the W, A, S and D keys to make the snake go up, right, down or left. Until a key is pressed, the snake travels to the right according to the value set for changeDirection at the start of the program.

If you look back at the variables you initialised at the start of the program, you'll see that there's another variable called direction. This is used alongside changeDirection to see if the instruction the user has given is valid. The snake should not be allowed to turn immediately back on itself—if it does, the snake dies and the game is over. To prevent this from happening, the direction requested by the player—stored in changeDirection—is compared to the current direction in which the snake is travelling—stored in direction. If they are opposite directions, the instruction is ignored and the snake continues in the same direction as before. Type the following lines to set up the comparisons:

```
if changeDirection == 'right' and not direction == 'left':
    direction = changeDirection
```

```
if changeDirection == 'left' and not direction == 'right':
    direction = changeDirection
if changeDirection == 'up' and not direction == 'down':
    direction = changeDirection
if changeDirection == 'down' and not direction == 'up':
    direction = changeDirection
```

With the user's input checked to make sure it makes sense, the snake—which appears on the screen as a series of blocks—can be moved. During each turn, the snake moves a distance equal to the size of one of its blocky segments. With each segment measuring 20 pixels, you can tell pygame to move the snake a single segment in any direction. Type in the following code:

```
if direction == 'right':
    snakePosition[0] += 20
if direction == 'left':
    snakePosition[0] -= 20
if direction == 'up':
    snakePosition[1] -= 20
if direction == 'down':
    snakePosition[1] += 20
```

The += and -= operators are used to change the value of a variable by a certain amount: += sets the variable to its previous value plus the new value, while -= sets the variable to its previous value minus the new value. By way of example, snakePosition[0] += 20 is a shorthand way of writing snakePosition[0] = snakePosition[0] + 20. The number in square brackets following the snakePosition variable name is the position in the list being affected: the first value in the snakePosition list stores the snake's position along the X axis, while the second value stores the position along the Y axis. Python begins counting at zero, so the X axis is controlled with snakePosition[0] and the Y axis with snakePosition[1]. If the list were longer, additional entries could be affected by increasing the number: [2], [3] and so on.

Although the snakePosition list is always two values long, another list created at the start of the program is not: snakeSegments. This list stores the location of the snake's body, behind the head. As the snake eats raspberries and grows longer, this list increases in size and provides the difficulty in the game: as the player progresses, it becomes harder to avoid hitting the body of the snake with the head. If the head hits the body, the snake dies and the game is over. Type the following line to make the snake's body grow:

```
snakeSegments.insert(0,list(snakePosition))
```

This uses the `insert` instruction to insert a new value into the `snakeSegments` list: the current position of the snake. Each time Python reaches this line, it will increase the length of the snake's body by one segment, and locate that segment at the current position of the snake's head. To the player, it will look as though the snake is growing. However, you only want this to happen when the snake eats a raspberry—otherwise the snake will just grow and grow. Type the following lines:

```
if snakePosition[0] == raspberryPosition[0] ↵
and snakePosition[1] == raspberryPosition[1]:
    raspberrySpawned = 0
else:
    snakeSegments.pop()
```

The first instruction checks the X and Y coordinates of the snake's head to see if it matches the X and Y coordinates of the raspberry—the target the player is chasing. If the values match, the raspberry is considered to have been eaten by the snake—and the `raspberrySpawned` variable is set to 0. The `else` instruction tells Python what to do if the raspberry has not been eaten: pop the earliest value from the `snakeSegments` list.

The pop instruction is simple but clever: it returns the oldest value from the list but also removes it, making the list one item shorter. In the case of the `snakeSegment` list, it tells Python to delete the portion of the snake's body farthest away from the head. To the player, it will look as though the entire snake has moved without growing—in reality, it grew at one end and shrank at the other. Because of the `else` statement, the pop instruction only runs when a raspberry has not been eaten. If a raspberry has been eaten, the last entry in the list doesn't get deleted—so the snake grows in size by one segment.

At this point in the program, it's possible that the player has eaten a raspberry. A game in which only a single raspberry is available is boring, so type the following lines to add a new raspberry back to the playing surface if the player has eaten the existing raspberry:

```
if raspberrySpawned == 0:
    x = random.randrange(1,32)
    y = random.randrange(1,24)
    raspberryPosition = [int(x*20),int(y*20)]
raspberrySpawned = 1
```

This section of code checks to see if the raspberry has been eaten by testing if the `raspberrySpawned` variable is set to 0, and if so, the code picks a random location on the playing surface using the `random` module you imported at the start of the program. This location is then multiplied by the size of a snake's segment—20 pixels wide and 20 pixels tall—to give

Python a place on the playing field to position the new raspberry. It's important that the location of the raspberry is set randomly: this prevents the player from learning where the raspberry will appear next. Finally, the raspberrySpawned variable is set back to 1, to make sure that there will only be a single raspberry on the playing surface at any given time.

Now you have the code required to make the snake move and grow, and cause raspberries to be eaten and created—a process known in gaming as *respawning*. However, nothing is being drawn to the screen. Type the following lines:

```
playSurface.fill(blackColour)
for position in snakeSegments:
    pygame.draw.rect(playSurface,whiteColour,Rect ↵
    (position[0], position[1], 20, 20)) ↵
    pygame.draw.rect(playSurface,redColour,Rect ↵
    (raspberryPosition[0], raspberryPosition[1], 20, 20))
pygame.display.flip()
```

These lines tell pygame to fill in the background of the playing surface in black, draw the snake's head and body segments in white, and finally, draw a raspberry in red. The last line, pygame.display.flip(), tells pygame to update the screen—without this instruction, items will be invisible to the player. Every time you finish drawing objects onto the screen, remember to use pygame.display.flip() so the user can see the changes.

Currently, it's impossible for the snake to die. A game where the player can never die would rapidly get boring, so enter the following lines to set up some scenarios for the snake's death:

```
if snakePosition[0] > 620 or snakePosition[0] < 0:
    gameOver()
if snakePosition[1] > 460 or snakePosition[1] < 0:
    gameOver()
```

The first if statement checks to see if the snake has gone off the playing surface vertically, while the second if statement checks if the snake has gone off the playing surface horizontally. In either case, it's bad news for the snake: the gameOver function, defined earlier in the program, is called to print a message to the screen and quit the game. The snake should also die if its head hits any portion of its body, so add the following lines:

```
for snakeBody in snakeSegments[1:]:
    if snakePosition[0] == snakeBody[0] and ↵
    snakePosition[1] == snakeBody[1]:
        gameOver()
```

The `for` statement runs through each of the snake segments' locations, from the second list entry to the end of the list, and compares it to the current position of the snake's head. It's important to start the comparison at the second entry using `snakeSegments[1:]` and not the first. The first entry is always set to the position of the head, and starting the comparison here would result in instant death for the snake as soon as the game begins.

Finally, all that is required for the game to be complete is to control the speed using the `fpsClock` variable. Without the variable, which you created at the start of the program, the game would run too quickly to play. Type in the following line to finish the program:

```
fpsClock.tick(20)
```

If you think the game is too easy or too slow, you can increase this number; or if the game is too hard or too fast, decrease the number. Save the program as `raspberrysnake.py`, and run it either by using IDLE's Run Module option in the Run menu or from the terminal by typing `python raspberrysnake.py`. The game will start as soon as it has loaded (see Figure 12-6), so make sure you're ready!

FIGURE 12-6:
Playing
Raspberry Snake
on the
Raspberry Pi

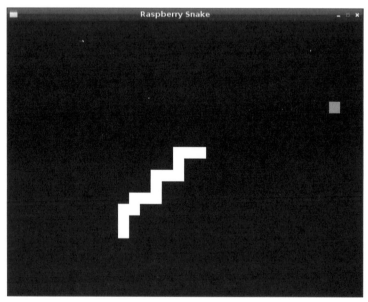

A full copy of the program listing for Raspberry Snake is included in Appendix A, "Python Recipes", and on the Raspberry Pi User Guide website at www.wiley.com/go/raspber-rypiuserguide2e. Downloading the source code from the website will save you some typing, but entering the code by hand is a good way of ensuring that you understand what each section does. In addition to the functions used in Raspberry Snake, pygame provides lots of features not used in this program, including audio playback, sprite handling for better graphics and mouse control. The best place to learn about pygame's more-advanced functions is on the official website, `http://www.pygame.org/wiki/tutorials`, where you can download tutorials and example programs to get a handle on how things work.

Example 4: Python and Networking

So far, you have learned how Python can be used to create standalone programs, but the language can also be used to create programs that communicate with the outside world over a computer's network connection. This next example, written by Tom Hudson, offers a brief glimpse of these possibilities with a tool for monitoring the users connected to an Internet Relay Chat (IRC) channel.

As usual, create a new project in IDLE or a text editor and enter the shebang line along with a comment describing the purpose of the program:

```
#!/usr/bin/env python
# IRC Channel Checker, written for the ↵
Raspberry Pi User Guide by Tom Hudson
```

Next, import the modules required by the program—`sys`, `socket` and `time`—with the following line:

```
import sys, socket, time
```

You used the `sys` and `time` modules previously in the Raspberry Snake program, but you have not yet used `socket`. The `socket` module provides Python with the ability to open, close, read from and write to network sockets—giving Python programs rudimentary networking capabilities. It's the `socket` module that provides this example with its ability to connect to a remote IRC server.

There are some *constants* needed for this program to operate. Constants are like variables in that they can have values assigned to them—but unlike variables, the value in a constant shouldn't change. To help differentiate a constant from a variable, it's good practice to use all-capital letters for their names—that way it's easy to see at glance whether a particular section of the code is using a constant or a variable. Type the following two lines into the program:

```
RPL_NAMREPLY = '353'
RPL_ENDOFNAMES = '366'
```

These are IRC *status codes*, provided by the server to indicate when particular operations have completed. These are used by the program to know when it has received the required list of names from the IRC server. Next, set up the variables for the server connection by entering the following lines:

```
irc = {
    'host' : 'chat.freenode.net',
    'port' : 6667,
    'channel' : '#raspiuserguide',
    'namesinterval' : 5
}
```

The first line tells Python to create a *dict* data type. Short for dictionary, this allows multiple variables to be stored in a single master variable—in this case, `irc`. These individual variables can then be recalled later in the program. Although you could write this program without using dicts to store variables, it would make the program significantly more difficult to read. The dict begins with the opening curly brace, and ends with the closing curly brace on the final line.

The `host` variable should be set to the fully qualified domain name (FQDN) of the IRC server to which the program will connect. In this example, `chat.freenode.net` is used, but if you want to customise the program to use a different server, change the domain name here. The `port` variable tells the program which network port IRC is running on, which will usually be 6667. The `channel` variable tells Python which channel to join in order to monitor the users, while `namesinterval` controls how long the program waits to refresh the list of users, measured in seconds.

Set up a second dict to store the user-specific variables by typing in the following lines:

```
user = {
    'nick' : 'botnick',
    'username' : 'botuser',
    'hostname' : 'localhost',
    'servername' : 'localhost',
    'realname' : 'Raspberry Pi Names Bot'
}
```

As with `irc`, all these variables are stored within a dict called `user` to make it clear which variables pertain to which section. The `nick` variable should be set to the IRC nickname the program will use. Don't use your usual nickname if you're planning to connect to the IRC server at the same time; instead, try appending -bot to the end of your name to make it clear that the user is a program rather than a real person. Do the same with username, and fill in the realname variable with a descriptive message about whom the bot belongs to. The hostname and servername variables can be left set to localhost, or altered to match your Internet address.

The socket module requires the user to create a socket *object*. This object provides network connectivity to the rest of the program. Create the socket object by typing in the following line:

```
s = socket.socket(socket.AF_INET, socket.SOCK_STREAM)
```

Next, you need to tell the program to try connecting to the IRC server specified in the variables at the start of the program. Type the following lines:

```
print 'Connecting to %(host)s:%(port)s...' % irc
try:
    s.connect((irc['host'], irc['port']))
except socket.error:
    print 'Error connecting to IRC server ↵
    %(host)s:%(port)s' % irc
    sys.exit(1)
```

The try and except commands are included in this code for *error handling*. If the system fails to connect to the server—because the Pi isn't connected to the Internet, for example, or because the server is down for maintenance—the program will print an error message and gracefully exit. The s.connect line tells the socket module to try connecting to the IRC server, using the host and port variables held in the irc dict.

If the program doesn't quit from the exception, it has successfully connected to the IRC server. Before you can get a list of names in a channel, however, you need to identify yourself to the server and issue some commands using the send function of the socket module. Type the following lines into the program:

```
s.send('NICK %(nick)s\r\n' % user)
s.send('USER %(username)s %(hostname)s ↵
 %(servername)s :%(realname)s\r\n' % user)
s.send('JOIN %(channel)s\r\n' % irc)
s.send('NAMES %(channel)s\r\n' % irc)
```

The send function works in almost exactly the same way as the print function, except that instead of printing to the standard output—usually the terminal window or console—it sends the output through the network connection. In this case, the program is sending strings of text to the IRC server and telling it to register the program using the nickname held in the `nick` variable and the user details held in the `username`, `hostname`, `server-name` and `realname` variables. Next, the program sends the command to join the channel specified in the `channel` variable, and finally, it sends the command to receive the list of users in that channel. Although this example is tailored to IRC, the same basic principle can be used to issue commands to any network service—with modifications, this program could be used to list the files on an FTP server, or unread emails on a POP3 server.

Receiving data from the socket is a little more complicated. First, you need to create an empty string variable that will act as the *receive buffer*, holding data from the server as it's received until it can be processed. Initialise the buffer by typing in the following line:

```
read_buffer = ''
```

Note that there are two single quotes after the equals sign, not one double quote.

Next, create an empty list, which will be used to store the names of users, by typing the following line:

```
names = []
```

The list data type is the same as you used to store the locations in the Raspberry Snake game. Unlike a normal variable, it can store multiple values—in this case, the names of users present in the IRC channel.

The next step is to create an infinite loop, during which the program will continuously query the server for user names and print them to the screen. Start the loop by typing:

```
while True:
    read_buffer += s.recv(1024)
```

The first line of the loop, following `while True:`, tells the `socket` module to receive 1,024 bytes (1 KB) of data from the IRC server and place it into the `read_buffer` variable. Because the `+=` operator is used, rather than just `=`, the received data will be appended to anything already in the buffer. The value of 1024 bytes is more or less arbitrary.

The next step is to split the buffer into individual lines of text, using the following program lines:

```
lines = read_buffer.split('\r\n')
read_buffer = lines.pop();
```

The first line sets the `lines` variable to a full line of text from the receive buffer by using the `split` function to find *end of line* characters—signified by `\r\n`. These characters only occur at the end of a line, so when the buffer has been split in this way you know that `lines` contains only full-line responses from the server. The pop instruction in the second line makes sure that only full lines are removed from the `read_buffer`: because responses from the server are read in 1 KB chunks, it's likely that at any given time the buffer will contain only fractions of a line. When that's the case, the fraction is left in the buffer ready to receive the remainder of the line the next time the loop runs and the next 1 KB chunk is received from the server.

At this point, the `lines` variable contains a list of full responses—full lines—received from the server. Type the following to process these lines and find the names of channel participants:

```
for line in lines:
    response = line.rstrip().split(' ', 3)
    response_code = response[1]
    if response_code == RPL_NAMREPLY:
        names_list = response[3].split(':')[1]
        names += names_list.split(' ')
```

This runs through every line found in the `lines` variable, and looks for the numerical IRC response code provided by the server. Although there are plenty of different response codes, this program is only interested in the two defined as constants at the start of the program: `353`, which means a list of names follows, and `366`, which means the list has ended. The `if` statement looks for the first of these responses, and then uses the `split` function to retrieve these names and add them to the names list.

Now, the names list contains all the names received from the server in response to the program's query. This may not be all the names, however: until the `366` response, which signals the end of the member names, is received, the list is incomplete. That is why the last line— `names += names_list.split(' ')`—is appending the newly received names to the existing list, rather than blanking it out entirely: each time that section of the code runs, the program is only likely to have received a sub-section of the entire member list. To tell Python what to do when the full list has been received, enter the following lines:

```
    if response_code == RPL_ENDOFNAMES:
        # Display the names
        print '\r\nUsers in %(channel)s:' % irc
        for name in names:
            print name
        names = []
```

This tells Python that when the 366 response has been received, it should print out the now-complete list of names to the standard output before blanking the names list again. This last line—names = []—is important: without it, each time the loop runs it will add users' names to the list even though they already exist from an earlier run.

Finally, finish the program by entering the following lines:

```
time.sleep(irc['namesinterval'])
s.send('NAMES %(channel)s\r\n' % irc)
```

This tells Python to wait the namesinterval number of seconds before sending another request for user names and beginning the loop again. Be careful to set namesinterval to a reasonable value—if the IRC server receives too many requests in too short a space of time, it may forcibly disconnect you for *flooding*.

Save the program as ircuserlist.py, and run it either by using IDLE's Run Module option in the Run menu or from the terminal by typing python ircuserlist.py. When the program first runs, it may take a while to connect to the server; once connected, however, the list of names (see Figure 12-7) should refresh quickly. To quit the program, press CRTL + C.

FIGURE 12-7:
Using Python to
list users in an
IRC channel

A full copy of the program listing for the IRC user list is included in Appendix A, "Python Recipes", and on the Raspberry Pi User Guide website at www.wiley.com/go/ raspberrypiuserguide2e. Downloading the source code from the website will save you some typing, but entering the code by hand is a good way of ensuring that you understand what each section does.

Further Reading

I hope this chapter has given you a taste of what you can do with Python. It's far from exhaustive—to do the language full justice would take a considerably larger book. However, there are plenty of resources out there for learning more about the Python language, including the following:

○ The official *Beginner's Guide to Python*, which you can access at http://wiki. python.org/moin/BeginnersGuide.

○ A free, interactive tutorial that runs entirely in your browser is available for download at http://www.learnpython.org/.

○ Zed A. Shaw's *Learn Python The Hard Way* (Shavian Publishing, 2012) offers great insight into best-practice coding for Python, and despite the name, it's suitable for beginners. This book is commercially available, or you can read it for free at http:// learnpythonthehardway.org/.

○ Although somewhat outdated and since replaced by *Dive Into Python 3* (APRESS, 2009), *Dive Into Python* by Mark Pilgrim (APRESS, 2004) does a good job of addressing the basics of writing programs in Python. It's available for free download at http://www. diveintopython.net/ or for purchase in printed format from all good booksellers.

○ If you prefer hands-on learning with other interested individuals, a list of local Python User Groups—sometimes called PIGgies—can be found at http://wiki.python. org/moin/LocalUserGroups.

○ For learning pygame, Al Sweigart's book *Making Games with Python & Pygame* (CreateSpace, 2012) is a great introduction with practical examples. You can purchase the hardcopy book or downloaded it for free at http://inventwithpython.com/.

Part IV

Hardware Hacking

Chapter 13
Learning to Hack Hardware

IN EARLIER CHAPTERS, you learned how the Raspberry Pi can be turned into a flexible platform for running a variety of software. In this, it's not alone: any desktop or laptop can run the same software, and in many cases run it far faster than the Pi's low-power processor can manage.

The Pi has another trick up its sleeve, though, which places it above and beyond the capabilities of the average PC: its 26-pin *general-purpose input-output (GPIO)* port, located on the top-left of the Pi's printed circuit board.

The GPIO enables the Pi to communicate with other components and circuits, and allows it to act as a controller in a larger electronic circuit. Through the GPIO port, it's possible to have the Pi sense temperatures, move servos and talk to other computing devices using a variety of different *protocols* including *Serial Peripheral Interface (SPI)* and *Inter-Integrated Circuit (I²C)*. Chapter 14, "The GPIO Port", provides details on working with the GPIO pins.

Before you can get begin building circuits to use with the Pi's GPIO port, however, you're going to need some additional equipment and to understand some of the language surrounding the world of electronics.

Electronic Equipment

To start building circuits that can be controlled by the Pi's GPIO port, you'll need various components and tools. The following list provides a sample shopping list for getting started with electronics:

- **Breadboard**—An electronic breadboard provides a grid of holes spaced at 2.54 mm intervals into which components can be inserted and removed. Below each grid is a series of electrical contacts, which allow components in the same row to be connected together without wires. A breadboard is a valuable tool for electronics work, because it allows you to quickly make mock-up circuits that can be modified without needing to be soldered or desoldered.

- **Wires**—While a breadboard allows some components to be joined without wiring, you'll still need wires to connect one row to another. These are known as *jumper wires*, and if you're working on a breadboard, it's a good idea to get solid-core wire rather than stranded-core wire. Solid-core wire is easier to insert into the breadboard's holes compared to stranded. It's also helpful to get various colours, so you can colour-code each connection according to its purpose.

- **Resistors**—The vast majority of electrical circuits make use of components called *resistors*, and the example projects in this chapter are no exception. Resistors are measured in *ohms*, written as the symbol Ω. Always try to have a handful each of a variety of common values: 2.2 KΩ, 10 KΩ, and 68Ω are good values to start with. Some retailers carry *resistor kits,* which include a wide range of useful values.

○ **Push-buttons**—A very common input component, a *push-button* completes an electrical circuit when pushed. At the most basic level, a keyboard is little more than a collection of push-buttons. If you're designing a circuit to provide a simple input to the Pi, pick the button labelled *momentary switch*.

○ **LEDs**—*Light-emitting diodes* (LEDs) are the most common output device in existence. An LED lights up when voltage is applied, giving you visual feedback on whether a pin on the Pi's GPIO port is high or low. When you're buying LEDs for use with the Pi, opt for low-power ones. The GPIO port isn't that powerful, and high-current LEDs—such as bright-white or bright-blue models—will require an external power supply and an extra component known as a *transistor*.

Additionally, if you're planning on making something more permanent once you've finished your breadboard prototype (which you'll learn about later in this chapter), you'll also need the following:

○ **Stripboard**—This can be thought of as a single-use breadboard. As with breadboards, holes are arranged in a 2.54 mm grid. Unlike breadboards, the components need to be soldered into place—after which you've got a permanent electronic circuit.

○ **Soldering iron**—When you need to connect a component permanently into a circuit, you need to solder it. You don't have to spend a fortune on a soldering iron, but if your budget stretches to a temperature-controlled model, it's a wise investment. Make sure any soldering iron you buy has a small, pointed tip—chisel-tip irons aren't suitable for delicate electronic work.

○ **Solder**—Your soldering iron needs solder. Solder is a mixture of conductive metals mixed with a cleaning substance known as flux. Make sure the solder you buy is suitable for electronics work—thick, plumbing solder is cheap but may damage delicate circuits, because it requires too much heat to melt.

○ **Stand and sponge**—It's important to have somewhere to put the hot soldering iron when it's not in use, and a way of cleaning the tip of the iron while you're using it. Some soldering irons come with a stand with a built-in cleaning sponge—if yours didn't, buy a separate stand-and-sponge set.

○ **Side cutters**—Through-hole components have long legs, which are left sticking out after you've soldered them in place. *Side cutters* allow you to cleanly and quickly trim these excess legs without damaging the solder joint.

○ **Tweezers**—Electronics components can be small and fiddly, and a good pair of tweezers is invaluable. If you're thinking of using surface-mount components, instead of the easier-to-solder through-hole components, tweezers are an absolute necessity—without tweezers, you'll burn your fingers if you try to hold the component and solder it at the same time!

○ **Work stand**—Commonly referred to as *helping hands*, these are weighted stands with clamps or clips that hold the item to be soldered in place. Some work stands include an integrated magnifying glass for delicate work, while the most expensive work stands add a light to help illuminate the work area.

○ **Multimeter**—Multimeters are test meters that have multiple functions including voltage, resistance and capacitance measurement, along with continuity testing for finding breaks in circuits. Although a multimeter is not an absolute necessity, it can be extremely useful for diagnosing issues with circuits. Professional multimeter units can be quite expensive, but a simple model is fairly inexpensive and is a sound investment for anyone getting started in electronics.

○ **Desoldering wick**—Mistakes happen, but they don't have to be permanent. A desoldering wick is a braided metal tape that can be placed over a solder joint and heated, pulling the solder away from the component and into the wick. With practice, it's possible to use a desoldering wick to salvage components from discarded electronic equipment—a handy way to gather common components cheaply.

Reading Resistor Colour Codes

Most electronic components are clearly labelled. For example, *capacitors* will have their *capacitance*, measured in *farads*, printed directly on them, while *crystals* will have their *frequency* likewise marked.

The major exception is a resistor, which typically has no writing on its surface. Instead, the resistance value in ohms is calculated from the colour bands that adorn the resistor's surface. Learning to decode these bands is an important skill for a hardware hacker to learn, because once a resister is removed from its packaging, the only way to figure out its value is to use a multimeter, which is an awkward and slow measuring tool for this particular job.

Thankfully, the resistor colour codes follow a logical pattern. Figure 13-1 shows a typical four-band resistor. A high-resolution colour version of this diagram is available on the *Raspberry Pi User Guide* website at `www.wiley.com/go/raspberrypiuserguide2e`. The first two bands are assigned a colour that equates to a resistance value in ohms. The third band is the *multiplier,* by which the first two numbers are multiplied to arrive at the actual resistance value. The final band indicates the *tolerance* of the resistor, or how accurate it is. A resistor with a lower tolerance will be closer to its marked value than a resistor with a higher tolerance, but you'll pay more for the component.

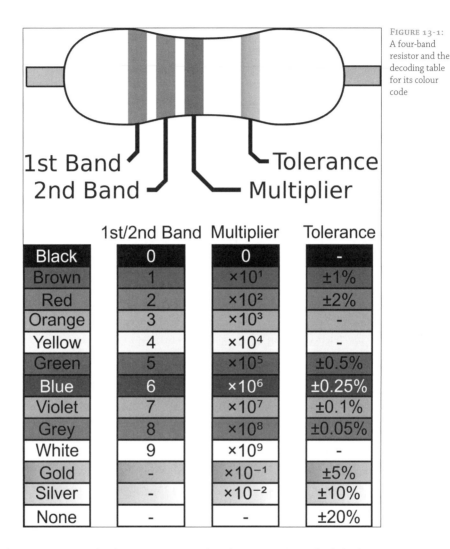

FIGURE 13-1:
A four-band
resistor and the
decoding table
for its colour
code

To read the example resistor, first take the two resistance bands starting from the left: these are coloured red and red. Red, on the table included in Figure 13-1, equates to the value 2, so the initial reading is 22. The next band is green, which is the multiplier and equates to 10^5 or 100,000 (10 followed by five zeros). Multiplying 22 by 100,000 equals 2,200,000, which is the resistance value in ohms: 2,200,000 Ω.

There are 1,000 ohms in a *kiloohm*, and 1,000 kiloohms in a *megaohm*. Thus, 2,200,000 Ω would typically be written as 2,2 MΩ. The final band, located on the right side of the resistor, is gold and details the tolerance, or accuracy, of the resistor, which is plus or minus 5 percent in the example shown in Figure 13-1.

There are also five-band resistors. You read these in the same way as a four-band resistor, except that the first three bands offer resistance figures, the fourth the multiplier, and the fifth the tolerance.

Sourcing Components

If you haven't dabbled in electronics before, it can be difficult to find components and tools. Thankfully, there are plenty of online and offline sources that specialise in the hard-to-find components you might need to complete your project.

Online Sources

Two of the largest retailers of electronic components and tools in the world are *RS Components* and *Farnell*. Both operate offices and warehouses across the world, and both have a substantial selection of hardware from which to choose. Chances are you're familiar with at least one of the two retailers. At the time of this writing, RS Components and Farnell were the only two companies licensed to produce the Raspberry Pi hardware by the Raspberry Pi Foundation, so unless you're reading this book while considering the purchase of a Raspberry Pi, you'll have ordered the device from one of the two.

Both RS Components and Farnell focus on *business-to-business* transactions, meaning that their main source of income is from electronics companies buying large quantities of components. However, both will happily allow consumers to register with their respective web stores and place orders as small as individual components.

When you're placing small orders, be aware that there may be additional charges incurred. RS Components charges for its next-day delivery service, and while the charge is quite reasonable for larger orders, it can cost significantly more than the components being purchased for smaller orders. On the other hand, Farnell doesn't charge for next-day delivery but does mandate a minimum total value for orders placed through its website.

Depending on where you live, you may be able to reserve items for collection at one of RS Components' or Farnell's trade counters. This saves on the cost of postage and gets you the goods faster, but it may not be an option at your location. The websites for both retailers can be found here:

RS Components: `http://www.rs-online.com`

Farnell: `http://www.farnell.com`

Offline Sources

You may find that you need a component immediately, and even next-day delivery would not be soon enough. Or you may only need a single resistor or a small length of wire and can't justify a high delivery cost or minimum order value for one of the online retailers. Thankfully, there are brick-and-mortar stores that specialise in electronic components. Although there are not as many of these types of stores as in previous decades, most major towns and cities will include at least one physical shop that stocks the most commonly required tools and components.

In the UK, the most popular chain of electronic component shops is Maplin Electronics. Established in Essex in 1972, the company has grown from a small mail-order outlet to include 187 stores across the UK. Inhabitants of most cities will find themselves within reach of a Maplin Electronics store, which can be a handy source of hardware if you're running low on common parts.

Maplin Electronics also offers a mail-order and click-and-reserve service through its website, but beware its *business-to-consumer* focus. Many components are significantly more expensive when ordered from Maplin than from RS Components or Premier Farnell, because the company relies on mark-up rather than high-volume trade to make a profit.

In the US and other countries, Radio Shack remains the most popular chain of electronics stores. Founded in 1921 and boasting over 7,150 stores across the world, the company stocks a wide selection of common electronic components and tools that can be purchased in person or ordered for delivery through its website.

As with Maplin Electronics in the UK, Radio Shack is a *business-to-consumer* operation. As a result, buyers can expect to pay more for components purchased at Radio Shack than the same parts ordered from RS Components or Farnell. However, the large number of Radio Shack stores make it a convenient choice for buyers who are in a hurry or who are looking for one-off items.

Both Maplin and Radio Shack also have the advantage of being staffed by people to whom you can speak. Many employees of both companies have significant knowledge in electronics, and are happy to offer advice and assistance if you're unsure of what parts you need for a given project. The websites for both retailers can be found here:

Maplin Electronics: `http://www.maplin.co.uk`

Radio Shack: `http://www.radioshack.com`

Hobby Specialists

In addition to the major chains, there are smaller companies that specialise in working with hobbyists. Although their selection is dwarfed by those of the larger chains, it's typically hand-picked and comes with the personal recommendation of the people behind the company.

Many of these hobby shops sprang up in the wake of the Arduino, an open-source project to create an educational-friendly microcontroller prototyping platform. With the Raspberry Pi appealing to much the same audience as the Arduino—albeit for very different tasks—the majority are investigating support for the Pi in addition to their existing product lines.

Buying from a hobby specialist has several advantages. If the products are sold as working with the Pi, then they've been tested for that specific reason—taking much of the guesswork out of the equation. Several companies also design their own add-on hardware for various platforms, with the Pi being no exception. These devices, designed to address a need in the community, may include additional ports and/or extra hardware, or can otherwise extend the functionality of the target device.

In the UK, one of the most popular hobby specialists is oomlout. Founded by open-source enthusiasts working with Arduino hardware, it's an excellent source of add-on kits as well as common components including push-buttons, displays and transistors. Unlike the larger retailers, oomlout equips its components with all necessary extras—such as pull-up resistors for the push-buttons—and a circuit schematic for easy assembly. Where possible, sample source code is also provided to get you up and running as quickly as possible.

In the US, Adafruit offers a similar service. Founded with the intention of making open-source add-ons for the Arduino boards, Adafruit offers a wide selection of components and kits—including one of the first add-on boards designed specifically for the Raspberry Pi (see Chapter 16, "Add-on Boards", for more details).

The websites for both retailers can be found here:

oomlout: `http://oomlout.co.uk/`

Adafruit: `http://www.adafruit.com`

Moving Up From the Breadboard

As the previous examples in this chapter have shown, breadboards are excellent for quickly creating prototype circuits for experimentation. They're fast and reusable, and they don't damage components.

However, breadboards also have some disadvantages. They're bulky, expensive, and prone to loose connections—which can result in critical components falling out, especially while the breadboard is being transported from place to place. Figure 13-2 demonstrates this perfectly: despite best efforts, the push-button component is only loosely secured in the breadboard, and is likely to fall out if the circuit is handled roughly.

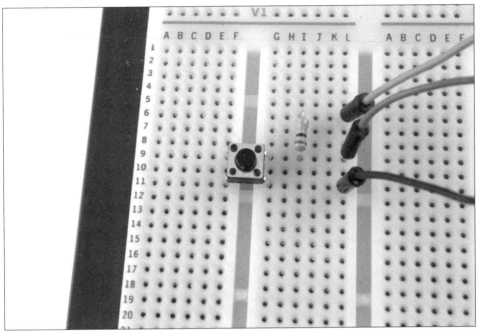

FIGURE 13-2:
A sample
breadboard
circuit, with
loose-fitting
components

This, among other reasons, is why the Raspberry Pi itself is built on a *printed circuit board (PCB)* rather than a breadboard—although the breadboard method was certainly used in the early days of prototyping the device. It's possible to print and etch your own PCBs at home, but there is a simpler intermediate step you can take: using *stripboard* to create permanent stand-alone circuits.

At first glance, stripboard looks similar to breadboard, because its surface is covered in small holes at 2.54 mm spacing. Unlike a breadboard, however, there's no clever mechanism for ensuring that electronic components placed into these holes stay in place—instead, you'll have to solder them onto the stripboard. Stripboard is often referred to by the trade name *Veroboard,* which is a trademark of Vero Technologies in the UK and Pixel Print in Canada.

Creating a stripboard circuit has many advantages over using a breadboard. A sheet of stripboard is significantly cheaper than an equivalently sized breadboard, and it can be snapped to size for smaller circuits. This also allows a single, large piece of stripboard to be used in the creation of several smaller, independent circuits.

Because components are soldered onto stripboard, it's also significantly more robust than a breadboard prototype. A stripboard circuit can be carried around from place to place with little risk that one of its components will become dislodged and lost. Figure 13-3 shows a piece of stripboard flipped to show the copper tracks on its underside.

FIGURE 13-3:
The copper
tracks on the
underside of a
piece of
stripboard

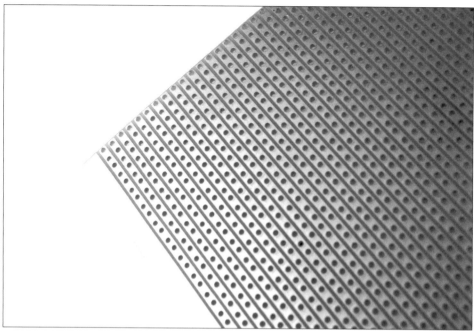

Stripboard is extremely easy to use, which makes it a great stepping-stone to custom circuit board design and manufacturing. However, you should be aware of the following before you buy stripboard:

○ There are different types of stripboard. Some stripboards have copper tracks on the underside, which go all the way across a row or down a column, while other stripboards are split into two separate rows with a gap in the middle like a breadboard. Yet another type of stripboard, often called a *project board*, has no copper tracks at all and requires the use of wires to join components together electrically.

○ Stripboard can be made in different thicknesses and with different materials, and one type of stripboard may be more suited to a particular project than another. For example, a heatproof stripboard is good for a circuit that is going to be in a high-temperature environment, while thicker stripboard should be used for circuits that may be exposed to rough handling.

○ To make the component layout on a stripboard neater, it's possible to break the tracks on the underside to separate components electrically. This avoids wasted board space and is an absolute necessity in more complex circuits—but to achieve the neatest results, you'll need a small hand-held tool called a *track cutter*. Remember to add that to your shopping list if you're planning on using stripboard, although a small drill bit can also be used.

There are also some tricks to handling stripboard that, if ignored, can make things harder than they have any reason to be:

○ The copper tracks on the underside of stripboard are not usually coated in any way. As you touch the tracks, you will tarnish the copper and make it difficult to solder. Avoid touching the underside of stripboard unless you're going to use it immediately; if it's too late, get some steel wool and give the copper a gentle brush to remove the corrosion before attempting to solder.

○ Unlike a printed circuit board, stripboard has no *solder mask*—a substance that prevents solder from going anywhere it isn't supposed to. As a result, soldering is somewhat trickier than it is on a PCB—it's all too easy to accidentally join tracks together with too-large a blob of solder. If this happens, use your desoldering wick to remove the excess solder and try again.

○ The holes in stripboard make it easy to snap into custom sizes, but leave the edges ragged. After snapping stripboard, take the time to file down the edges before assembling your circuit. Make sure you wear a face-mask when doing this, because the dust from stripboard isn't particularly healthy to breathe.

A Brief Guide to Soldering

Having a soldering iron is one thing, but you also need to know how to use it. Soldering, like any skill, takes practice to become proficient. If you follow the tips in this section and keep practising, you'll be creating clean, tidy solder joins in no time.

This may seem obvious, but it's worth pointing out: soldering irons get extremely hot during use. Make sure you don't touch any exposed metal surface, even away from the tip, and be careful where you put the iron down. If possible, buy an iron with a stand, or obtain a separate heatproof stand. Never leave a hot iron unattended, and if you drop an iron, don't be tempted to try to catch it!   **WARNING**

Soldering works by melting a small quantity of metal to form a join between two components. If you turn the Raspberry Pi over, you'll see plenty of evidence of this. All the larger components are connected using what's called *through-hole soldering*, where the components' leads are passed through holes in the printed circuit board and then soldered into place. Smaller components are attached via *surface-mount soldering*.

Solder isn't pure metal—it also contains a substance called *flux*, which is designed to etch away any tarnish on the surfaces to be soldered in order to ensure as clean a join as possible. Most electronic solder includes three to five *cores* of flux. You can also buy flux separately as a paste or in liquid form, although for most hobby soldering, this isn't necessary.

When you're starting a soldering project, make sure you have a clean, well-lit workspace. Also make sure the area is well ventilated. Solder fumes aren't very healthy, and while they're extremely unlikely to build up to dangerous levels in low-volume hobby soldering, it's still a good idea to keep exposure to a minimum.

In addition, you should protect the work surface in some way. It's not uncommon for small blobs of molten solder to fall, which can burn and mark tables. You can purchase an anti-static workmat (see Figure 13-4 for an example), but a glossy magazine works just as well. Don't be tempted to use a few sheets of cheap newspaper—solder can burn through thin paper before it cools.

FIGURE 13-4:
An example
soldering work
area, with a
protective
antistatic
workmat

If you're doing delicate, close-up work, you should wear protective glasses. Sometimes the boiling flux inside the solder can cause it to spit upwards, and if it hits you in the eye, you'll be in for a world of pain.

Don't let these warnings put you off soldering, however. Although solder is extremely hot, it cools quickly and burns are not only rare but nearly always inconsequential. Respect the equipment, but don't fear it.

With your work surface chosen and protected, lay out your equipment. The iron should be placed on the side of your dominant hand, and positioned so that the cable isn't trailing across your work area. Make sure you can move the iron freely before plugging it in. If the cable gets caught on something, you may end up burning yourself.

Dampen your soldering sponge with water—it should be damp, but not dripping wet. This is important: the damp sponge will be used to clean the iron, and if it's dry, it will burn and may damage the iron's delicate tip.

It will take a few minutes for the soldering iron to reach its operating temperature. If you've purchased a temperature-controlled iron, this will normally be indicated either by a light that switches on or off to indicate the temperature has been reached or by a numerical temperature read-out. (See the operating manual that came with your soldering iron to find out how temperatures are indicated on it.)

Once the operating temperature has been reached, it's time to prepare the soldering iron using a process known as *tinning*. Follow these steps:

1. Push the tip of the solder against the tip of the iron, allowing a small amount to melt onto the iron. Be careful not to melt too much onto the iron: not only is this a waste of solder, but it can cause excess solder to fall onto the work area.

2. Wipe the tip of the iron onto the sponge. If it hisses and spits, the sponge is too wet; allow it to cool, then remove it from the stand and wring it out.

3. Keep wiping the tip of the iron until it is coated in a silver layer of solder (see Figure 13-5). If necessary, apply more solder to the tip.

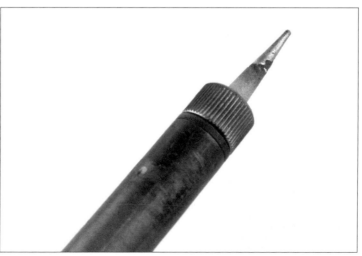

FIGURE 13-5:
A soldering iron tip that is in the process of being tinned with solder

This process of tinning the tip protects it against damage and ensures that it will efficiently transfer heat onto the surfaces to be soldered. Failure to properly tin the iron's tip is one of the most common causes of bad solder joints. You may need to repeat this process more than once if you're soldering a lot of connections, and you'll need to do it again at the end of the soldering session. In general, if the tip of the soldering iron loses its shiny coating, repeat the tinning process.

With the iron prepared, it's time to start soldering. Place the items to be soldered—such as a printed circuit board and the legs of a component—into the work stand, and ensure that you've got a good view. Extend a length of solder from the container or reel, and begin to solder the components using these basic steps:

1. If you're soldering through-hole components into a printed circuit board, stripboard or similar through-hole board, place the legs of the component through the holes and bend them outwards so the component doesn't fall out when the board is flipped over.

2. With the board secured in the work stand, push the tip of the iron against both the component and the copper contact on the board. It's important that the iron touches both items: if the iron is only in contact with one, the finished joint will be bad.

3. It takes only a few seconds for the area to heat up. Count to three, and then push the solder against the component and copper contact (see Figure 13-6). If the solder doesn't melt, withdraw it, count a couple of seconds more, and then try again. If it still doesn't melt, try repositioning the soldering iron.

4. As the solder flows, you'll see it drawn down into the hole in the board. This is an indication that the area is hot enough for a good solder join. If the solder floats, it indicates that the area is not yet hot enough.

5. Remove the solder from the join first, followed by the iron. (If you remove the iron first, the solder will harden and leave your spool of solder stuck to the contact!)

If all went well, you'll be left with a solid solder join that will last for many years. If not, don't be disheartened—just press the iron against the join to reflow the solder, and use the desoldering wick if you need to clean up a spill or any excess. A perfect solder joint should have a shape somewhat like a volcano, rising up from the surface of the board to meet the leg of the component.

Never leave the iron in contact with the parts for more than a few seconds. This is especially important when soldering heat-sensitive components like integrated circuits, which can be damaged by prolonged contact with a hot soldering iron. If you're using a temperature-controlled solder station, make sure the temperature is set to an appropriate level for the solder being used (check the solder's packaging or data sheet for details).

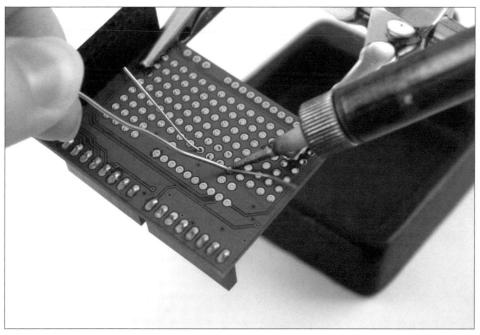

FIGURE 13-6:
Soldering a
through-hole
component into
a printed circuit
board

When you've finished, remember to re-tin the tip of the iron. If you don't, the tip may corrode in storage and need to be replaced significantly sooner than would otherwise be the case.

Remember to heat both surfaces with the iron. Heating only one surface results in what is known as a *dry joint* or *cold joint,* where the solder is not properly mated to one surface. Over time, these joints will fail and need to be re-soldered.

TIP

As with any skill, soldering takes practice. Many electronics shops sell kits that include a printed circuit board and a selection of components, which you can use to practice soldering through-hole components. Some add-on boards for the Raspberry Pi are also provided in kit form and require soldering, including the Slice of Pi from Ciseco. You'll learn about these in Chapter 16, "Add-on Boards".

Chapter 14
The GPIO Port

THE RASPBERRY PI'S *general-purpose input-output (GPIO)* port is located on the top-left of the printed circuit board, labelled P1. It's a 26-pin port, fitted with two rows of 13 *male 2.54 mm headers* at the factory. The spacing of these headers is particularly important: 2.54 mm pin spacing (0.1 inches in imperial measurements) is a very common sight in electronics and is the standard spacing for prototyping platforms that include stripboards and breadboards.

Identifying Your Board Revision

The pin layout of the Raspberry Pi's GPIO port differs slightly depending on what revision of the board you own. All Model As and recent Model Bs have a common pin layout; the original Model B, however, has a slightly different layout.

Before using the GPIO port for a hardware project, be sure you know which model of Raspberry Pi you have. If you have a Model A, you can use the first diagram in this chapter; if you have a Model B, you will need to use the first diagram—unless it's an original Revision 1 model.

The easiest way to spot a Model B Revision 1 board is to look at the top side of the board, just underneath the GPIO pins themselves: where a Revision 2 board has two rows of four copper-plated holes, the Revision 1 is solid. Another method is to see how much memory is available: the Model B Revision 1 had just 256 MB of memory, compared to 512MB on Revision 2 boards.

For more details on the board revisions and how to tell them apart, see Chapter 1, "Meet the Raspberry Pi".

GPIO Pinout Diagrams

Each pin of the GPIO port has its own purpose, with several pins working together to form particular circuits. The layout of the GPIO port can be seen in Figure 14-1.

The GPIO port is the same across both the Raspberry Pi Model A and the Model B Revision 2. If you have one of the original Raspberry Pi Model B Revision 1 boards—and if you do, congratulations on having a collector's item—then the pins available on the GPIO port are subtly different. These details can be seen in Figure 14-2.

TIP   If you're not sure which revision of the Raspberry Pi you have, and thus which pinout applies to your board, load IDLE and type `import RPi.GPIO as GPIO` followed by `GPIO.RPI_ REVISION` to return the revision number.

Pin numbers for the GPIO port are split into two rows, with the bottom row taking the odd numbers and the top row the even numbers. It's important to keep this in mind when working with the Pi's GPIO port: most other devices use a different system for numbering pins, and because there are no markings on the Pi itself, it's easy to get confused as to which pin is which.

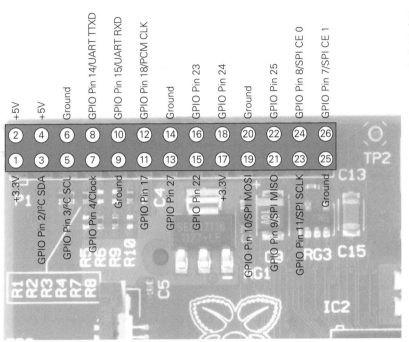

FIGURE 14-1:
The Raspberry
Pi's GPIO port
and its pin
definitions

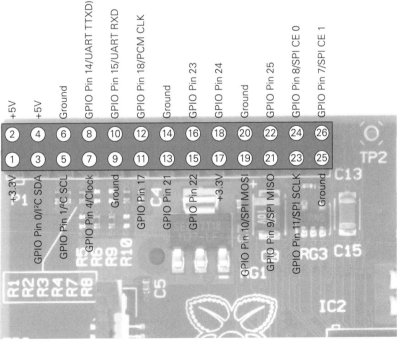

FIGURE 14-2:
The original
Raspberry Pi
Model B
Revision 1 GPIO
pinout

Although the Pi's GPIO port provides a 5 V power supply, tapped from the incoming power on the micro-USB hub, on Pin 2, the Pi's internal workings are based on 3.3 V logic. This means that the components on the Pi work from a 3.3 V power supply. If you're planning on creating a circuit that will interface with the Pi through its GPIO port, make sure you are using components compatible with 3.3 V logic or are passing the circuit through a *voltage regulator* before it reaches the Pi.

WARNING   Connecting a 5 V supply to any pin on the Raspberry Pi's GPIO port, or directly shorting either of the power supply pins (Pin 1 and Pin 2) to any other pin will result in damage to the Pi. Because the port is wired directly to pins on the Broadcom BCM2835 SoC processor, you will not be able to repair any damage you do to it. Always be extra careful when working around the GPIO port.

GPIO Features

The GPIO port provides eight pins for general-purpose use by default: Pin 7, Pin 11, Pin 12, Pin 13, Pin 15, Pin 16, Pin 18 and Pin 22. These pins can be toggled between two states: *high*, where they are providing a positive voltage of 3.3 V; and *low*, where they are equal to ground or 0 V. This equates to the 1 and 0 of binary logic, and can be used to turn other components on or off. You'll learn more about this later in the chapter.

WARNING   The Pi's internal logic operates at 3.3 V. This is in contrast to many common microcontroller devices, such as the popular Arduino and its variants, which typically operate at 5 V. Devices designed for the Arduino may not work with the Pi unless a *level translator* or *optical isolator* is used between the two. Likewise, connecting pins on a 5 V microcontroller directly to the Raspberry Pi's GPIO port will not work and may permanently damage the Pi.

In addition to these general-purpose pins, the GPIO port has pins dedicated to particular *buses*. These buses are described in the following subsections.

UART Serial Bus

The *Universal Asynchronous Receiver/Transmitter (UART) serial bus* provides a simple two-wire serial interface. When a serial port is configured in the `cmdline.txt` file (as described in Chapter 7, "Advanced Raspberry Pi Configuration"), it's this serial bus that is used as the port for the messages. Connecting the Pi's UART serial bus to a device capable of displaying the data will reveal messages from the Linux kernel. If you're having trouble getting the Pi to boot, this can be a handy diagnostic tool—especially if nothing is showing on the display.

The UART serial bus can be accessed on Pins 8 and 10, with Pin 8 carrying the *transmit* signal and Pin 10 carrying the *receive* signal. The speed can be set in the `cmdline.txt` file, and is usually 115,200 bits per second (bps).

I²C Bus

As the name suggests, the *Inter-Integrated Circuit (I²C) bus* is designed to provide communications between multiple *integrated circuits (ICs)*. In the case of the Pi, one of those integrated circuits is the Broadcom BCM2835 SoC processor at the heart of the system. These pins include access to *pull-up resistors* located on the Pi, meaning no external resistors are required to access the I²C functionality.

The I²C bus can be accessed on Pins 3 and 5, with Pin 3 providing the *Serial Data Line (SDA)* signal and Pin 5 providing the *Serial Clock (SCL)* signal. The I²C bus available on these pins is actually only one of two provided by the BCM2835 chip itself, and is known as I²C0. The second, I²C1, is terminated at resistors on the Raspberry Pi circuit board itself and is not available for general-purpose use.

SPI Bus

The *Serial Peripheral Interface (SPI) bus* is a synchronous serial bus designed primarily for *in-system programming (ISP)* of microcontrollers and other devices. Unlike the UART and I²C buses, it's a four-wire bus with multiple *Chip Select* lines, which allow it to communicate with more than one target device.

The Pi's SPI bus is available on Pins 19, 21 and 23, with a pair of Chip Select lines on Pin 24 and Pin 26. Pin 19 provides the *SPI Master Output, Slave Input (MOSI)* signal; Pin 21 provides the *SPI Master Input, Slave Output (MISO)* signal; Pin 23 provides the *Serial Clock (SLCK)* used to synchronise communication; and Pins 24 and 26 provide the *Chip Select* signals for up to two independent slave devices.

Although additional buses are present in the Raspberry Pi's BCM2835 SoC processor, they are not brought out to the GPIO port and are thus unavailable for use.

Using the GPIO Port in Python

With the theory out of the way, it's time to get practical. In this section, you'll l learn how to construct and program two simple electronic circuits that demonstrate how to use the GPIO port for input and output.

As you saw in Chapter 12, "An Introduction to Python", Python is a friendly yet powerful programming language. It's not, however, the perfect choice for every scenario. Although it works fine for the simple circuits you'll be creating in this chapter, it does not offer what is known as *deterministic real-time operation*. For the majority of users, this doesn't matter; if you're planning on using the Pi at the heart of a nuclear reactor or a complex robotics platform, however, you may want to investigate a lower-level language such as *C++* or even *assembler* running on a dedicated real-time microcontroller.

If true real-time operation is required for your project, the Pi may be a bad choice. Instead, consider using a microcontroller platform such as the popular open-source Arduino, or one of the MSP430 family of microcontrollers from Texas Instruments. Both of these devices can interface with the Pi either through the GPIO header or over USB, and provide a specialised real-time environment for control and sensing.

GPIO Output: Flashing an LED

For the first example, you'll need to build a simple circuit consisting of an LED and a resistor. The LED will provide visual confirmation that the Pi's GPIO port is doing what your Python program tells it to do, and the resistor will limit the current drawn by the LED to protect it from burning out.

Calculating Limiting Resistor Values

An LED needs a *current limiting resistor* to protect it from burning out. Without a resistor, an LED will likely only work for a short time before failing and needing to be replaced. Knowing a resistor is required is one thing, but it's also important to pick the right resistor for the job. Too high a value and the LED will be extremely dim or fail to light at all; too low a value and it will burn out.

To calculate the resistor value required, you will need to know the *forward current* of your LED. This is the maximum current the LED can draw before being damaged, and is measured in milliamps (mA). You'll also need to know the *forward voltage* of the LED. This latter value, measured in volts, should be 3.3 V or lower—any higher, and the LED will require an external power supply and a switching device known as a *transistor* before it will work with the Pi.

The easiest way to work out how large a resistor is required is with the formula $R=(V-F)/I$, where R is resistance in ohms, V is the voltage applied to the LED, F is the forward voltage of the LED and I is the maximum forward current of the LED in amps (with a thousand mA to the amp).

Taking a typical red LED with a forward current of 25 mA and a forward voltage of 1.7 V, and powering it using the 3.3 V supplied by the Pi's GPIO port, you can calculate the resistor needed as $(3.3 - 1.7) / 0.025 = 64$. Thus, a resistor of 64 Ω or higher will protect the LED. These figures rarely come out to match the common resistor values as sold, so when you're choosing a resistor, always round up to ensure the LED is protected. The nearest commonly available value is 68 Ω, which will adequately protect the LED.

If you don't know the forward voltage and forward current of your LEDs (for example, if the LEDs did not come with documentation or were salvaged from scrap electronics), err on the side of caution and fit a reasonably large resistor. If the LED is too dim, you can revise downwards—but it's impossible to repair an LED that has been blown.

To assemble the circuit, you'll need a breadboard, two jumper wires, an LED and an appropriate current-limiting resistor (as described in the "Calculating Limiting Resistor Values" sidebar). Although it's possible to assemble the circuit without a breadboard by twisting wires together, a breadboard is a sound investment and makes assembling and disassembling prototype circuits straightforward.

Assuming the use of a breadboard, assemble the circuit in the following manner to match Figure 14-3:

1. Insert the LED into the breadboard so that the long leg (the *anode*) is in one row and the shorter leg (the *cathode*) is in another. If you put the LED's legs into the same row, it won't work.

2. Insert one leg of the resistor into the same row as the LED's shorter leg, and the other resistor leg into an empty row. The direction in which the resistor's legs are placed doesn't matter, as a resistor is a *non-polarised* (direction-insensitive) device.

3. Using a jumper wire, connect Pin 11 of the Raspberry Pi's GPIO port (or the corresponding pin on an interface board connected to the GPIO port) to the same row as the long leg of the LED.

4. Using another jumper wire, connect Pin 6 of the Raspberry Pi's GPIO port (or the corresponding pin on an interface board connected to the GPIO port) to the row that contains only one leg of the resistor and none of the LED's legs.

Be very careful when connecting wires to the Raspberry Pi's GPIO port. As discussed earlier in the chapter, you may do serious damage to the Pi if you connect the wrong pins. **WARNING**

At this point, nothing will happen. That's perfectly normal: by default, the Raspberry Pi's GPIO pins are switched off. If you want to check your circuit immediately, move the wire from Pin 11 to Pin 1 to make the LED light up. Be careful not to connect it to Pin 2, though: a current-limiting resistor suitable for a 3.3 V power supply will be inadequate to protect the LED when connected to 5 V. Remember to move the wire back to Pin 11 before continuing.

To make the LED do something useful, start a new Python project. As with the projects in Chapter 12, "An Introduction to Python", you can use a plain text editor or the IDLE software included in the recommended Raspbian distribution for this project as well.

Before you can use the Raspberry Pi GPIO port from Python, you'll need to import a library into your Python project. Accordingly, start the file with the following line:

```
import RPi.GPIO as GPIO
```

FIGURE 14-3:
A breadboard
circuit for a
simple LED
output

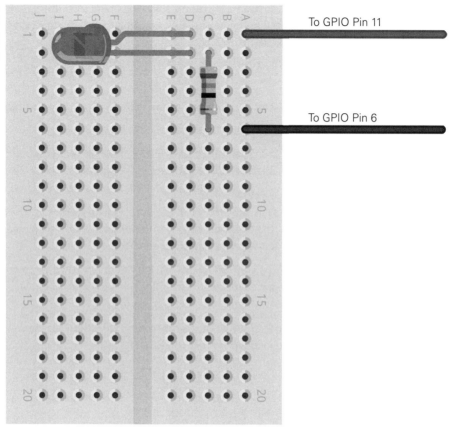

To GPIO Pin 11

To GPIO Pin 6

Remember that Python is case-sensitive, so be sure to type `RPi.GPIO` exactly as it appears. To allow Python to understand the concept of time (in other words, to make the LED blink, rather than just turning it on and off), you'll also need to import the time module. Add the following line to the project:

```
import time
```

With the libraries imported, it's time to address the GPIO ports. The GPIO library makes it easy to address the general-purpose ports through the instructions `GPIO.output` and `GPIO.input`, but before you can use them, you'll need to set the GPIO library in board mode—which numbers the pins according to their physical position on the Raspberry Pi—and initialise the pins as either inputs or outputs. In this example, Pin 11 is an output, so add the following line to the project:

```
GPIO.setmode(GPIO.BOARD)
GPIO.setup(11, GPIO.OUT)
```

The last line tells the GPIO library that Pin 11 on the Raspberry Pi's GPIO port should be set up as an output. If you were controlling additional devices, you could add more `GPIO.setup` lines into the project. For now, however, one will suffice.

With the pin configured as an output, you can switch its 3.3 V supply on and off in a simple demonstration of binary logic. The instruction `GPIO.output(11, True)` will turn the pin on, while `GPIO.output(11, False)` switches it off again. The pin will remember its last state, so if you only give the command to turn the pin on and then exit your Python program, the pin will remain on until told otherwise.

Although you could just add `GPIO.output(11, True)` to the Python project to switch the pin on, it's more interesting to make it blink. First, add the following line to create an infinite loop in the program:

```
while True:
```

Next, add the following lines to switch the pin on, wait two seconds, and then switch it off again before waiting another two seconds. Make sure each line starts with four spaces, to signify that it is part of the infinite `while` loop:

```
    GPIO.output(11, True)
    time.sleep(2)
    GPIO.output(11, False)
    time.sleep(2)
```

The finished program should look like this (see Figure 14-4):

```
import RPi.GPIO as GPIO
import time
GPIO.setmode(GPIO.BOARD)
GPIO.setup(11, GPIO.OUT)
while True:
    GPIO.output(11, True)
    time.sleep(2)
    GPIO.output(11, False)
    time.sleep(2)
```

Save the file as `gpiooutput.py`. If you're using a Python development environment such as SPE, don't try to run the program from within the editor. Most Raspberry Pi Linux distributions restrict the use of the GPIO port to the *root* user, so the program will need to be run using the command `sudo python gpiooutput.py` at the terminal to get it started. If all has gone well, you should see the LED begin to blink on and off at regular intervals—and you've created your first home-made output device for the Pi.

FIGURE 14-4:
The
gpiooutput.
py program,
being edited in
nano, and
waiting for its
final line

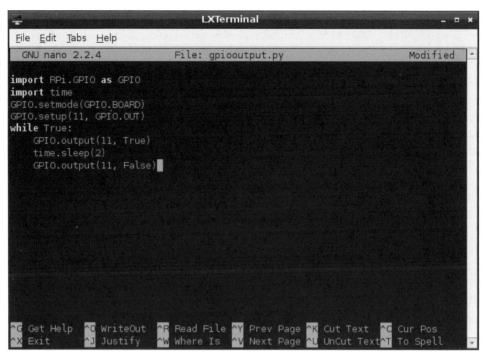

If things don't work, don't panic. First, check all your connections. The holes in a breadboard are quite small, and it's easy to think you've inserted a component into one row only to find it's actually in another. Next, check that you've connected the circuit to the right pins on the GPIO port—with no labelling on the Pi itself, mistakes are unfortunately easy to make. Finally, double-check your components—if the forward voltage of your LED is higher than 3.3 V or if your current limiting resistor is too large, the LED won't light up.

Although this example is basic, it's a good demonstration of some fundamental concepts. To extend its functionality, the LED could be replaced with a buzzer to make an audible alert, or a servo or motor as part of a robotics platform. The code used to activate and deactivate the GPIO pin can be integrated into other programs, causing an LED to come on when new email arrives or a flag to be raised when a friend has joined an IRC channel.

GPIO Input: Reading a Button

Being able to use the GPIO as an output is undeniably useful, but it becomes significantly more so when you can combine that with one or more inputs. In the following example, you'll see how to connect a push-button switch to another pin on the GPIO port and read its status in Python.

If you've already built the GPIO output example, you can either disconnect that from your Pi or leave it connected—this example uses different pins, so both can co-exist quite happily. If you do leave the previous example connected, make sure to use different rows on the breadboard for the new components or you'll find things don't work quite as planned.

Build the circuit as follows, matching Figure 14-5:

1. Insert the push-button switch into the breadboard. Most switches have either two or four legs. You only need worry about two of the legs in the circuit. If the button has four legs, they'll be set up in in pairs: check the push-button's data sheet to find out which legs are paired together.

2. Connect a 10 KΩ resistor to the same row as one of the push-button's legs and an unused row. This is a pull-up resistor, and will provide the Pi with a reference voltage so it knows when the button has been pressed.

3. Connect the unused leg of the pull-up resistor to Pin 1 of the Raspberry Pi's GPIO port. This provides the 3.3 V reference voltage.

4. Connect the unused leg of the push-button switch to Pin 6 of the Raspberry Pi's GPIO port. This provides the ground connection.

5. Finally, connect Pin 12 of the Raspberry Pi's GPIO port to the other leg of the push-button switch in the same row as the 10 KΩ resistor. Your breadboard should now look like Figure 14-5.

The circuit you just built creates a situation whereby the input pin, which in this instance is Pin 12 of the Raspberry Pi's GPIO port, is constantly *high* thanks to the pull-up resistor connected to a 3.3 V supply. When the push-button is pressed, the circuit is grounded and becomes *low*, providing the cue for your Python program to know that the button has been activated.

You may wonder why the resistor is required at all, and why the switch does not simply connect Pin 12 to Pin 6 or Pin 1 directly. While this is possible, it creates what is known as a *floating* pin, which is a pin that doesn't know whether it's high or low. As a result, the circuit will act as though the button is being pressed even when it isn't, and may fail to detect the button being pressed even when it is.

Open a new Python file, either in a text editor or using one of the Python integrated development environments (IDEs) available on the Raspberry Pi. To begin, you will need to import the same GPIO library as in the previous GPIO output example:

```
import RPi.GPIO as GPIO
```

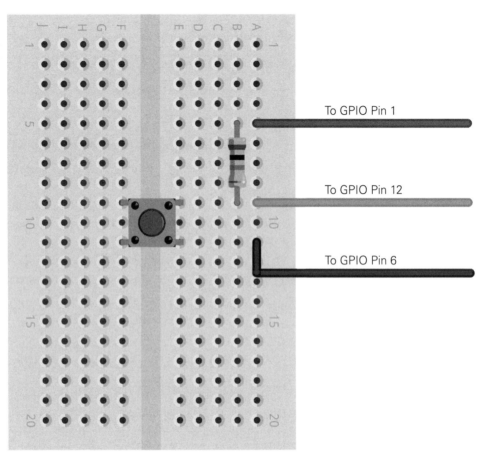

FIGURE 14-5:
The example
breadboard
layout for a
simple push-
button input

To GPIO Pin 1

To GPIO Pin 12

To GPIO Pin 6

You don't need to import the time library, because this example doesn't need any timing instructions. Instead, you can get right to enabling board mode and setting up Pin 12 as an input. This is done in the same way as setting a pin as an output, with just the final part of the instruction changed accordingly:

```
GPIO.setmode(GPIO.BOARD)
GPIO.setup(12, GPIO.IN)
```

If you're not using Pin 12 for this, make sure you change the pin number in the preceding instruction.

As with the previous example, the next step is to create an infinite loop that constantly checks the input pin to see if it's been brought low (in other words, if it's been pressed). Begin the loop with the following code line:

```
while True:
```

Reading the status of an input pin is very similar to setting the status of an output pin, with one exception: before you can do anything useful with the resulting value, you'll need to store it in a variable. The following instruction tells Python to create a new variable called input_value (as described in Chapter 12, "An Introduction to Python") and set it to the current value of Pin 12:

```
input_value = GPIO.input(12)
```

Although the program could be executed now and work, it doesn't do anything useful. To make sure you know what's going on, add the following print instruction to get feedback:

```
if input_value == False:
    print("The button has been pressed.")
    while input_value == False:
        input_value = GPIO.input(12)
```

The last two lines—the second while and the second input_value, an *embedded loop*—are important. Even on the Raspberry Pi's processor, which is relatively underpowered when compared to high-performance desktop and laptop processors, Python runs very quickly. This embedded loop tells Python to keep checking the status of Pin 12 until it's no longer low, at which point it knows the button has been released. Without this loop, the program will loop while the button is being pressed—and no matter how quick your reflexes, you'll see the message printed to the screen multiple times, which is misleading.

The final program should look like this:

```
import RPi.GPIO as GPIO
GPIO.setmode(GPIO.BOARD)
GPIO.setup(12, GPIO.IN)
while True:
    input_value = GPIO.input(12)
    if input_value == False:
        print("The button has been pressed.")
        while input_value == False:
            input_value = GPIO.input(12)
```

Save the file as `gpioinput.py`, and then execute it from the terminal with `sudo python gpioinput.py`. At first, nothing will happen—but if you press the push-button switch, the program will print the message from line seven to the terminal (see Figure 14-6). Release the button and press it again, and the message will be repeated.

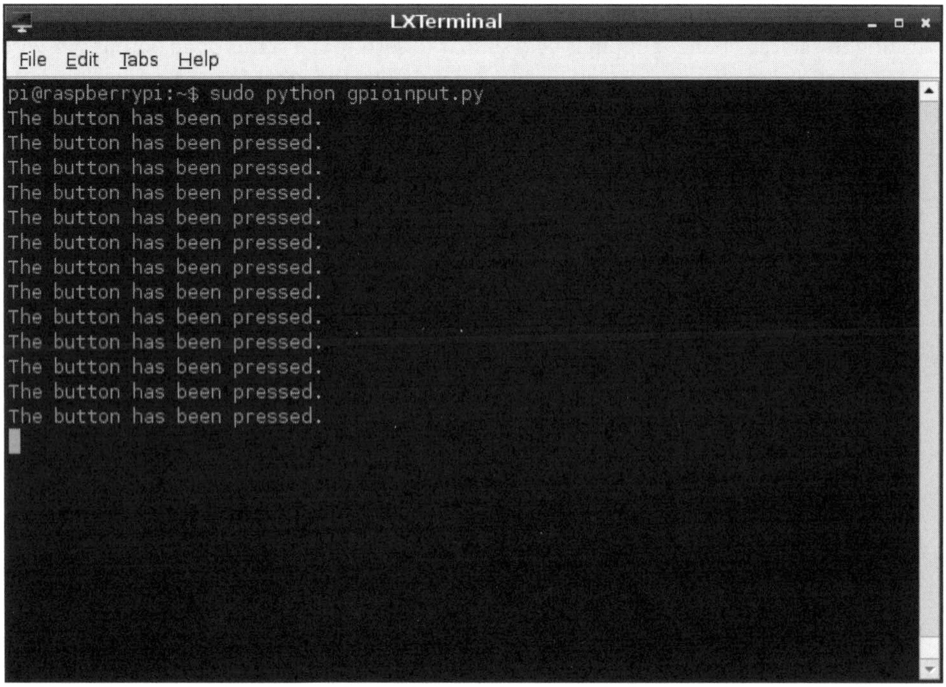

FIGURE 14-6:
The output
of the
gpioinput.
py program

```
pi@raspberrypi:~$ sudo python gpioinput.py
The button has been pressed.
The button has been pressed.
The button has been pressed.
The button has been pressed.
The button has been pressed.
The button has been pressed.
The button has been pressed.
The button has been pressed.
The button has been pressed.
The button has been pressed.
The button has been pressed.
The button has been pressed.
The button has been pressed.
```

As with the previous input example, this is a deceptively simple program that can be used for many purposes. In addition to being able to read when a switch is pressed, the same code can be used to read when the pins of a separate device—such as a sensor or external microcontroller—have been pulled high or low.

By extending the code to look for multiple push-buttons, each on an individual GPIO pin, you could even create a simple four-button game controller. For example, you could combine the preceding code with the Raspberry Snake game from Chapter 12, "An Introduction to Python", to turn the Raspberry Pi into a simple games console. You can also combine both input and output examples into a single program, which waits for the button to be pushed and then turns on the LED by sending the output pin high. To ensure that you've understood the concepts in this section, try creating that combined program now. If you get stuck, or you want to check your method, turn to Appendix A, "Python Recipes", for a sample solution.

Chapter 15

The Raspberry Pi Camera Module

DESIGNED BY ENGINEERS working for the Raspberry Pi Foundation, the Raspberry Pi Camera Module is the most compact way of adding the ability to record still images and video to your project. Designed to connect to the *Camera Serial Interface (CSI)* of the Raspberry Pi, the Camera Module measures just 25 mm on its longest edge and weighs just 3 grammes (see Figure 15-1).

FIGURE 15-1:
The Raspberry Pi
Camera Module,
pictured without
its ribbon cable

Since its release, the Camera Module has found a place in projects ranging from simple home security systems to more complex computer vision experiments that track a user's face or hand gestures. The module has even reached near-space, as the result of photography projects that tether a Raspberry Pi to a weather balloon and release it to gather high-altitude images.

The camera module is built around a five-megapixel sensor of a type commonly used in smartphones, located behind a fixed-focus lens. The module works in tandem with the Raspberry Pi's graphics processor to ensure that high-resolution video and stills can be captured smoothly without overloading the Pi's main processor or requiring too much memory.

Why Use the Camera Module?

If you have no need to capture images or video, you don't need the Camera Module. It's an optional extra, and the Pi works just fine without one. It's also possible to add vision to your Pi using alternative products, such as webcams, that connect to a free USB port.

The Pi has only a limited number of USB ports, however, and these are often used for more critical functions such as a keyboard, mouse or wireless network adapter. This is particularly important in the Raspberry Pi Model A, which has just one USB port available for use.

The official Camera Module has other advantages over a traditional webcam: it draws considerably less power, meaning it doesn't strain the Raspberry Pi's power supply or drain the batteries in a portable or solar-powered project; it offers image capture at a resolution of up to five megapixels, and video capture at a Full HD resolution and 30 frames per second; and it is considerably smaller than USB-connected cameras.

The Camera Module is compatible with all models and revisions of Raspberry Pi, so if you haven't decided whether you'll need a camera in your project, don't worry; you can pick up any Pi model now and add the Camera Module at a later date.

Installing the Camera Module

The Raspberry Pi Camera Module, like the Raspberry Pi itself, is supplied as a bare circuit board. Although this is reasonably robust, you must take care when handling it so as not to damage any of its components, particularly the plastic lens located over the camera sensor itself.

The Camera Module connects to the Pi through a *ribbon cable*, a thin, semi-rigid cable that should be inserted into the Raspberry Pi's CSI connector. When you receive the camera, one end of the cable will already be inserted into the module itself; one side of the other end is coloured blue and the other side has visible silver contacts. These contacts connect to pins in the Pi's CSI connector, transferring power and data between the Pi and the Camera Module.

The CSI connector is labelled S5 and is located towards the right-hand side of the board, near where the USB ports are located (see Figure 15-2). The CSI connector of a Raspberry Pi Model B is located just to the left of the Ethernet port; on a Model A, it is found in the same place, just to the left of the gap on the board below the USB ports. Some models may have the CSI connector covered by a protective piece of plastic film; you should peel this off before you try to install the camera.

There's a similar-looking connector located to the left side of the Raspberry Pi. This is the *Display Serial Interface (DSI)* connector, and is designed for connecting the Pi to liquid crystal display panels. The two ports aren't interchangeable; if you connect the camera to the DSI port rather than the CSI port, it won't work.

Before inserting the cable, small *lugs* on either side of the connector must be gently lifted. This can be done with your fingernails without needing any tool, but be careful: they should lift easily and stop moving once they're a couple of millimetres above the rest of the CSI connector (see Figure 15-3).

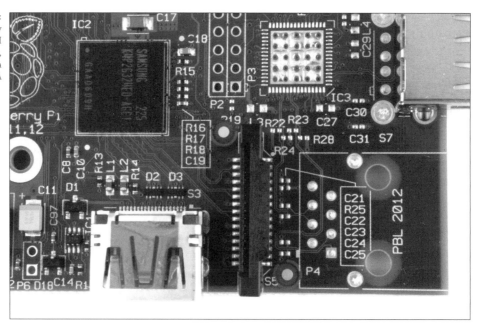

Insert the free end of the ribbon cable into the CSI port, making sure that the silver contacts are facing towards the left of the Pi and the blue portion of the cable to the right. Gently push the cable home, making sure not to bend it, and then push the lugs back down to secure it in place (see Figure 15-4). When properly inserted, the cable should be coming out of the connector perfectly straight and should withstand a gentle tug; don't pull it too hard while testing this, however, as it can be damaged.

FIGURE 15-4:
The Camera Module's ribbon cable, securely inserted into the CSI connector

---

The ribbon cable included with the Raspberry Pi Camera Module is reasonably robust and will prove reliable even in daily use. It is, however, susceptible to damage if folded. When inserting the cable or moving the camera, be sure not to fold the ribbon cable back on itself. If you do damage your ribbon cable, replacements are available from most Pi stockists.

WARNING

When using the Camera Module with a Raspberry Pi case, it is usually necessary to thread the ribbon cable through a thin slot or in between layers of plastic. Some cases are not directly compatible with the Camera Module; in these cases, you may need to leave the lid of the case off in order to route the ribbon cable. Position the Camera Module with the ribbon cable at the bottom; if this isn't possible, a software option to flip the captured image upside down is described later in this chapter.

The final step in the camera's physical installation is to remove the small, protective piece of plastic film found over the lens. This can simply be peeled off and discarded by pulling gently upwards on the tab that extends out from the lens. Although it's tempting to leave it in place to protect the lens, this will give everything you capture an unpleasant blue hue.

Enabling Camera Mode

The software to drive the Raspberry Pi Camera Module is included in the Raspbian distribution by default. If you're using a particularly old release, you may find that the files are missing; if so, update your system using the following command at the terminal or console (see Chapter 3, "Linux System Administration" for details):

```
sudo apt-get update && sudo apt-get upgrade
```

You will need to change some system settings in order for the Camera Module to work correctly, however. In particular, recording video requires that the graphics processing portion of the Pi's BCM2835 processor has at least 128MB of memory available; with any less than that, still image capturing will work but video recording will fail. For details on how to change this split, see Chapter 6, "The Raspberry Pi Software Configuration Tool".

The easiest way of ensuring that your Pi is camera-ready is to use the Raspberry Pi Software Configuration Tool `raspi-config`. At the terminal, type the following command to load the tool:

```
sudo raspi-config
```

In the menu that appears, select option 5—Enable Camera—using the cursor keys and Enter. Choose Enable in the screen that appears and press Enter again (see Figure 15-5). If Camera Mode was disabled previously, you will be prompted to reboot the Pi; confirm this by pressing Enter.

FIGURE 15-5:
Enabling
Camera Mode in
the Raspberry Pi
Software
Configuration
Tool `raspi-config`

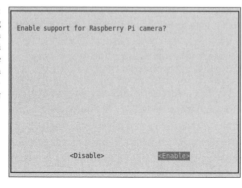

If you can't find a camera option in `raspi-config`, you may be running an outdated version. Use the `sudo apt-get update && sudo apt-get upgrade` command to update your software, then reboot the Pi and try running `raspi-config` again.   **TIP**

Once the Pi has rebooted, your Camera Module will be ready to use.

An optional final step, if you would like to view captured images from the Raspbian console without having to load the graphical user interface, is to install the *framebuffer image viewer* `fbi`. To do this, type the following command:

```
sudo apt-get install fbi
```

To view images using the tool (see Figure 15-6) simply type the command followed by the name of the image:

```
fbi imagename.jpg
```

FIGURE 15-6:
Viewing captured images using the `fbi` package

To quit `fbi`, press the Q or Escape key.

Capturing Stills

The best way to test that the camera is working correctly is to try capturing an image. The Camera Module uses a custom software package called `raspistill` to capture still images, which are saved, by default, in the *Joint Photographers Expert Group (JPEG)* file format—the same format used by most digital cameras and smartphones.

The software for the Raspberry Pi camera is run from the terminal or console. For best results, run the software at the console without using the `startx` command to load the graphical user interface (see Chapter 3, "Linux System Administration" for details).

The `raspistill` command accepts a number of optional arguments that control settings such as the horizontal and vertical resolution of the captured image, the exposure mode of the camera, the file type saved, and the level of compression applied to the final image. If these options are left out of the command, defaults will be used.

To test the camera, simply run the `raspistill` application at the console by typing its name as the command:

```
raspistill -o testcapture.jpg
```

This will show a five-second live preview (see Figure 15-7) during which time a red light on the front of the camera will illuminate. This is an activity light, designed to provide confirmation that the camera is working. If you wave your fingers in front of the camera during this five-second period, you'll see them appear in the preview window on-screen. When the five seconds is up, the light will extinguish and the preview window will disappear.

FIGURE 15-7:
The
`raspistill`
capture
application
showing a live
preview image

Sometimes the position of the Camera Module's cable makes it difficult to place the camera the right way up. If your preview appears upside-down, use the -vf (vertical flip) option to correct the image. Just add the option to the command line along with any other options you are using.

When the preview has finished, the -o (output) option will save a JPEG file with the name test-capture.jpg. When using the -o option, you can change the type of file saved with -e. Currently supported file types include *bitmap (BMP)*, *Portable Network Graphics (PNG)* and *Graphic Interchange Format (GIF)* images. To save a PNG, for example, use the following command:

```
raspistill -o testcapture.png -e png
```

Altering png to read bmp, gif or jpg allows access to the other supported formats. If you forget the -e option, a file will still be saved but regardless of its extension the content will be JPEG data.

Another pair of commonly used options adjusts the width and height of the captured image. This is good for capturing low-resolution stills as part of a computer vision project, or simply to save space.

The width of the captured image is adjusted with the -w option, while the height is adjusted with -h. These options are most commonly used together, to set the overall resolution of the image. To capture an image of 1,920 pixels wide by 1,080 pixels high—the same resolution as a Full HD high-definition TV or Blu-ray film—type the following command:

```
raspistill -w 1920 -h 1080 -o fullhdcapture.jpg
```

The final basic option to know is -t, which controls the preview time-out. By default, raspistill shows a five-second live preview before capturing an image; the -t option overrides this default. The required delay should be specified in milliseconds. To capture an image after a 10-second delay, use the following command:

```
raspistill -t 10000 -o tensecondcapture.jpg
```

To disable the delay and capture immediately—a useful trick if you're running the software from a *shell script*, as demonstrated later in this chapter—use a value of 0 as in the following command:

```
raspistill -t 0 -o instantcapture.jpg
```

The filename after the output (-o) option can be anything you want it to be, with the preceding commands merely using example filenames. When writing the filename, always be sure to add the extension appropriate to your file type: `.jpg` for JPEG images, `.png` for Portable Network Graphics, `.bmp` for bitmap images and `.gif` for the Graphics Interchange Format.

For a full description of all options available to `raspistill`, turn to Appendix B, "Camera Module Quick Reference". Alternatively, type the following command to see a list of options:

```
raspistill --help
```

Recording Video

Just as there is a dedicated application for capturing still images through the Raspberry Pi Camera Module, there is another for capturing video: `raspivid`. Using `raspivid` is very similar to using `raspistill`, but there are several differences you'll need to know before forging ahead.

The most important difference between `raspivid` and `raspistill` is in the -t option: in `raspistill`, the -t option provided the time-out for the preview before the image was captured; in `raspivid`, the -t option provides a limit for the overall length of the recorded video. If a value of 0 is given, the video will record forever—rapidly filling your SD card or external storage device.

As with `raspistill`, the default for the -t option is five seconds. So, to check the camera is working and record a short video, you can simply type the command's name along with the -o (output) option and a filename:

```
raspivid -o defaultvideo.h264
```

This records a five-second video and saves it as in a format known as *h.264*. Unlike `raspistill`, there is no option to save the file in a different format: `raspivid` uses the hardware acceleration available in the Pi's BCM2835 processor to do the recording, and only h.264 is supported as a capture format.

If you play the video back, you'll find that there's no sound. Unfortunately, the Raspberry Pi does not include a microphone input. Although it's possible to record audio by connecting certain USB microphones or sound cards, this will need to be captured using separate software and combined with the video file later using a video editing package.

Other options supported by `raspistill` are also supported by `raspivid`. For example, to set the width and height of the recorded video to 1,920x1,080—Full HD—use the `-w` and `-h` options as in the following command:

```
raspivid -w 1920 -h 1080 -o fullhdvideo.h264
```

To record a longer video, adjust the `-t` option by specifying your required length of video in milliseconds. To record a minute of video, type the following command:

```
raspivid -t 6000 -o minutelongvideo.h264
```

> **TIP** Although h.264 is a reasonably efficient video format, recording at high resolutions can take up considerable disk space. If you're recording longer videos, be sure that you have enough free space on your SD card or consider connecting a USB storage device like an external hard drive.

You can read more options for `raspivid` in Appendix B, "Camera Module Quick Reference" or see a list of available options with the following command:

```
raspivid --help
```

Command-Line Time-Lapse Photography

So far, you've learned the basics of how to use the Raspberry Pi Camera Module—now it's time to find a practical use for the project. The key advantage of the Raspberry Pi over a dumb network-connected camera is the capability to be easily programmed for different tasks. In this example, you can turn your Raspberry Pi and connected Camera Module into a time-lapse photography system.

The `raspistill` program comes with an option for enabling a time-lapse mode, `-tl`, which continuously captures pictures according to a customisable delay in milliseconds. This feature is designed for when `raspistill` is called by an external program, such as a web server or video streamer, and will overwrite the output file each time a new picture is taken.

To use `raspistill` in traditional time-lapse photography, where a new file is created each time, you'll need a way of driving `raspistill` externally. This could be a Python program, a dedicated application or even a web server thread, but the easiest way is to use a process known as *shell scripting*.

A shell script is simply a collection of commands, each exactly as you would type them at the console or terminal. Each command is run in order, from top to bottom, but it's also possible to use loops as in programming languages like Scratch and Python (see Chapter 11, "An Introduction to Scratch" and Chapter 12, "An Introduction to Python" for more details). Coupled with the shell's ability to chain multiple programs together, shell scripting is a powerful tool.

To start a shell script, simply create a new text file in your current directory with the following command:

```
nano timelapse.sh
```

The extension `.sh` is traditionally used for shell scripts, although it's not strictly necessary. Using a file extension like this helps you to remember the difference between a shell script and an executable program, so it's certainly recommended.

At the top of the file (see Figure 15-8) enter a line that tells the operating system to interpret the commands using the default Bash shell:

```
#!/bin/bash
```

FIGURE 15-8:
Editing the
timelapse.
sh script in the
nano editor

Although other shells are available, Bash is the default for most modern Linux distributions and offers a good mix of guaranteed compatibility and advanced features. Everything after this line will be run by the operating system as a command just as though you had typed it at the terminal yourself. The exception is *comment lines*, which are preceded by a # symbol; these lines contain notes that help you remember why the script is written in a particular way, or how to use the script. It's good practice to include comment lines in your shell scripts, although the script will run fine without them.

So that you know what the script is supposed to do when you find the file a few months from now, make the next line a comment explaining the script's purpose:

```
# Captures time-lapse images using the raspistill application
```

Remember to put the # symbol at the start of the line, or the shell will try to run the comment as a command.

Next is to set up a loop that will ensure the script continues to run after the first photograph has been taken. Enter the following two lines to start the loop:

```
while true
    do
```

Note that the second line, do, is indented by typing four spaces at the start; this helps visually illustrate that the code that appears below is part of the loop. Unlike Python, which requires indentation, shell scripts can be written without any code being indented—but it makes the code significantly harder to read and understand. Like comments, indentation is an optional but highly recommended step.

Next, set up the filename that will be saved by entering the following line:

```
filename=`date +%Y%m%dT%H%M%S`.jpg
```

This is a somewhat complex instruction that tells the shell to take the output of the date command and enter it into a variable called filename. The ` symbol, known as a *backtick*, tells the shell to execute the date command; without these symbols, found at either end of the command, the shell would ignore the instruction and treat it as just a string of text.

The date command, as you may have guessed, allows you to find out what the current date and time is on the system. Following the + symbol is a series of instructions on how the date should be printed: %Y gives the year in four-digit form, %m the month in two-digit form, %d the day in two-digit form, and %H, %M and %S give the time in 24-hour format hours, minutes and seconds.

After the final backtick is `.jpg`. This completes the filename, telling the shell script to save the image file in the international date format with the extension of a JPEG file. If you capture an image at exactly two in the afternoon on 17th January 2015, for example, the filename would be `20150117140000.jpg`. Because it takes longer than a second for the camera to take a picture, and there will be a delay later in the shell script, this guarantees that each picture has a unique filename and nothing will be overwritten.

Using the international date format has an added bonus: if you sort the list alphabetically or numerically, your pictures will be sorted from oldest to newest. If you'd prefer a different filename format, however, simply change the order in the command.

WARNING   The `date` command pulls time information from the system clock. When connected to a network, the Raspberry Pi uses the *Network Time Protocol (NTP)* to find the current time, but the Model A cannot do this unless you connect a USB network adapter. In this case, the date in the filename will be wrong unless you manually set a date before running the script.

With the filename set, it's time to tell the script to run `raspistill`. You can use any options you like here, so long as you remember to set the output filename. To capture a Full HD still, enter the following line:

```
raspistill -w 1920 -h 1080 -t 0 -o $filename
```

The $ symbol before `filename` tells the shell that you're addressing the `filename` variable set in the previous line. It's important to include this symbol, as without it the script will write a single file called `filename`, which will be overwritten every time a new image is captured.

It's always a good idea to get feedback from your scripts, so you know when they're running. An easy way to do this is to have the script print status messages to the terminal or console, using the `echo` command. Enter the next line as follows:

```
echo Image captured
```

Next, add a delay to the script by using the `sleep` command. This requires a value in seconds, rather than the milliseconds expected by `raspistill` and `raspivid`. To take a picture every 30 seconds, enter the following line:

```
sleep 30
```

Finally, close the loop by entering the last line of the script (see Figure 15-9):

```
done
```

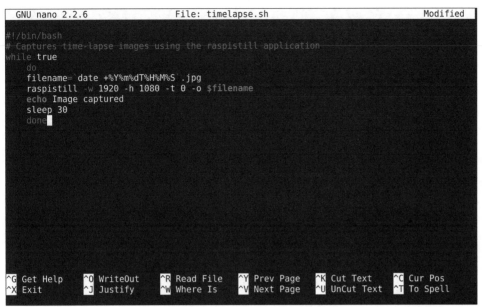

```
GNU nano 2.2.6              File: timelapse.sh                    Modified

#!/bin/bash
# Captures time-lapse images using the raspistill application
while true
   do
   filename=`date +%Y%m%dT%H%M%S`.jpg
   raspistill -w 1920 -h 1080 -t 0 -o $filename
   echo Image captured
   sleep 30
   done






^G Get Help    ^O WriteOut    ^R Read File   ^Y Prev Page   ^K Cut Text    ^C Cur Pos
^X Exit        ^J Justify     ^W Where Is    ^V Next Page   ^U UnCut Text  ^T To Spell
```

FIGURE 15-9:
The complete
timelapse.
sh script, in the
nano text
editor

Although this brings the script to a close, the loop used is known as an *infinite loop*: the instruction while true at the start tells the script to run through the loop until true becomes false, or 1 becomes 0. Because this can never happen, the script runs forever—taking an image every 30 seconds.

Save the file by pressing Ctrl + O, and then change the file's permissions to make it *executable* with the following command:

```
chmod +x timelapse.sh
```

For more information on file permissions, see Chapter 3, "Linux System Administration". Finally, run the script with the following command:

```
./timelapse.sh
```

The script will immediately take a picture and print the status message "Image captured" to the console (see Figure 15-10). After 30 seconds, it will take another picture; after another 30 seconds, a third. This will continue forever, or until your SD card is filled with images. To exit the script, press Ctrl + C.

```
pi@raspberrypi ~ $ nano timelapse.sh
pi@raspberrypi ~ $ chmod +x timelapse.sh
pi@raspberrypi ~ $ ./timelapse.sh
Image captured
Image captured
Image captured
Image captured
Image captured
Image captured
Image captured
Image captured
Image captured
```

Time-lapse photography is often used to compress a long or complex task into an entertaining video. Commercial time-lapse photography rigs, which can be extremely expensive, are often used to film the growth of plants, the construction or buildings or the flow of traffic. A Raspberry Pi running this script can do all of these things, but at a fraction of the cost.

The images you've captured can be transformed into a video, either using video editing software or the ffmpeg tool. While ffmpeg can be run on the Raspberry Pi itself, it's a resource-hungry program that will take a considerable time to run if you have a large number of high-resolution images to convert. If you have the patience do the conversion on the Pi itself, install ffmpeg with the following command:

```
sudo apt-get install ffmpeg
```

Then convert the images by typing:

```
ffmpeg -r 1 -i *.jpg timelapse.mp4
```

This will create a video with images showing at a rate of one per second, or 30 times faster than real-time, from all JPEG images found in the current directory. To speed the video up still further, you can adjust the -r option: -r 10 will show 10 images per second, -r 20 20 images per second and so forth. The finished video can then be shared directly, or uploaded to a video streaming site like YouTube or Vimeo.

Chapter **16**
Add-on Boards

ALTHOUGH YOU CAN use the Raspberry Pi's general-purpose input-output (GPIO) header directly, as you learned in Chapter 13, "Learning to Hack Hardware", a much better idea is to use a specialist prototyping board. Prototyping boards are add-on boards designed to sit between your project and the Raspberry Pi, and range from the relatively simple—such as Ciseco's Slice of Pi—to the complex and powerful Gertboard.

At their most basic, add-on boards simply provide easier access to the Raspberry Pi's GPIO pins. This may mean they can be connected to a breadboard easier, or are spaced further apart and labelled to make connecting other devices simpler. Some boards include circuitry to connect specific add-on devices, such as a small XBee wireless transceiver, and still others provide a small surface onto which you can solder your own components to make a custom board.

The hardware market is constantly and rapidly changing, and the Raspberry Pi Foundation continues to encourage developers to create more add-on devices. It would be impossible to create an exhaustive list of all the add-on boards available or planned for release in the near future, but in this chapter, you'll learn about three of the most common boards and how they can be used.

Ciseco Slice of Pi

The most basic of boards, Ciseco's Slice of Pi (see Figure 16-1) is nevertheless useful. Supplied in kit form, Slice of Pi features a small prototyping area, a space for an XBee wireless module and full access to the Raspberry Pi's GPIO pins.

The compact Slice of Pi is designed to be connected directly to the GPIO headers on the top of the Raspberry Pi, with the rest of the board covering part of the Pi's surface—but not extending beyond the edges of the board nor obscuring any commonly used ports. The Slice of Pi does, however, sit over the DSI video output connector. In most cases where this connector is used, the ribbon cable can be routed underneath the Slice of Pi board without trouble.

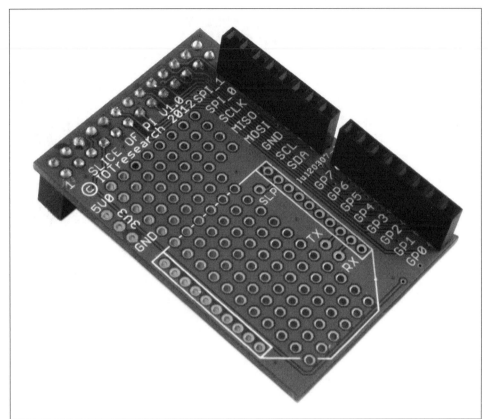

FIGURE 16-1:
The Ciseco Slice
of Pi

The primary advantages of using the low-cost Slice of Pi rather than just connecting directly to the Pi's GPIO header are the labelling on the circuit board, which the GPIO header lacks, and the use of female headers. These allow you to use male-to-male *jumper leads* or even just lengths of trimmed wire to connect the board to a breadboard (as shown in Figure 16-2) or other circuit board—or even to connect components directly into the headers. The Pi's male headers, in contrast, require the use of specialised male-to-female jumper leads.

FIGURE 16-2:
Connecting the
Slice of Pi to a
breadboard

The Slice of Pi also offers a small amount of protection for the Pi. The use of female headers means it's harder to accidentally short-circuit two pins, and the spacing of the headers—with the eight general-purpose pins brought to one header and the other specialised pins brought to another—makes wiring mistakes less likely. More importantly, the Slice of Pi doesn't provide direct access to any of the pins labelled as Do Not Connect (see Chapter 13, "Learning to Hack Hardware"), so there's less risk of damaging the Pi with a wrong connection.

The connections for an XBee wireless interface could also prove useful if you are considering using the Pi in an embedded computing project. When combined with a compatible transceiver—such as an XBee, RF-BEE or RN-XV module—it allows for wireless access to the Pi's UART serial port. Such access could be used to read sensor details from the Pi, take control of the Pi's software or even control a Pi-powered robot from a remote location.

Finally, the prototyping area provides an alternative to breadboards or stripboards for smaller circuit designs. If you are considering developing a small add-on module for the Raspberry Pi, such as a sensor board for reading temperatures or detecting moisture, the required components can be soldered directly to the Slice of Pi. Thanks to the low cost of the board, this provides an easy way to create bespoke add-on modules for the Pi that are entirely self-contained, with no wiring required—just connect the Slice of Pi to the Raspberry Pi's GPIO port and the device is ready to go (see Figure 16-3).

FIGURE 16-3:
The Slice of Pi,
connected to the
Pi's GPIO port

The disadvantage of the Slice of Pi lies in its simplicity. Its compact size means that it is unsuitable for the creation of larger or more complex prototypes, and while the header layout provides some protection against short circuits, there's no protection against the use of 5 V components that can damage the Pi's 3.3 V logic circuits. The labelling is also different to that used to typically describe the Raspberry Pi's GPIO pins, which can lead to confusion when using a GPIO library not written with the Slice of Pi in mind. Table 16-1 provides a mapping from one labelling system to another.

Table 16-1: Slice of Pi GPIO Mappings

Physical Pin Number	Official Designation	Slice of Pi Label
7	GPIO Pin 4 (or General Purpose Clock 0)	GP7
11	GPIO Pin 17	GP0
12	GPIO Pin 18	GP1
13	GPIO Pin 27 (21 on Revision 1 boards)	GP2
15	GPIO Pin 22	GP3
16	GPIO Pin 23	GP4
18	GPIO Pin 24	GP5
22	GPIO Pin 25	GP6

The Slice of Pi is available from Ciseco's web shop at `http://shop.ciseco.co.uk/slice-of-pi/`.

Adafruit Prototyping Pi Plate

The Prototyping Pi Plate by Adafruit is based around the same general principle as Ciseco's Slice of Pi. The add-on is provided in kit form, and offers you a prototyping surface along with easy access to the Pi's GPIO pins (see Figure 16-4). Unlike the Slice of Pi, however, the Prototyping Pi Plate is a full-coverage board built to the same size as the Pi itself. As a result, the plate offers a much larger area to work with than the Slice of Pi, allowing for larger circuits to be constructed. The Prototyping Plate also features 3.5 mm *screw terminals* for connecting the pins, making it easy to use ordinary wire to make strong temporary connections—although 2.54 mm holes for male or female headers are also provided should you want to use those instead.

FIGURE 16-4:
The Adafruit
Prototyping Pi
Plate

The design and layout of the Prototyping Pi Plate will be familiar to anyone who has used an Arduino microcontroller. An add-on board with the same footprint as the target device, designed to connect to on-board headers and sit above the surface of the original board is a common sight in the Arduino world, where such add-on boards are known as *shields*. The idea for the Prototyping Pi Plate, in fact, comes from Adafruit's self-designed Protoshield add-on for the Arduino.

As a full-coverage add-on board, the Pi Plate is designed to connect to the GPIO header and cover the entire surface of the Pi. This positioning above the Pi can make it difficult to access the DSI video output and MIPI CSI-2 camera input connectors, although longer ribbon cables should route beneath the Pi Plate without trouble. If you're planning to use an add-on camera module (see Chapter 15, "The Raspberry Pi Camera Module") or DSI-connected display, be sure to check the length of ribbon cable provided before planning your project around the Pi Plate.

The prototyping surface of the Pi Plate is split into two, with both halves offering through-hole construction in common 2.54 mm spacing. The first half of the prototyping surface is set up in a similar way to a breadboard: copper tracks on the underside link rows together, and a central bus in the middle provides common power and ground connectivity. The second half of the prototyping surface does not have such tracks, allowing more custom circuits to be constructed. Overall, the surface provided for circuit creation is significantly larger than that of the Slice of Pi, making the Pi Plate suitable for more-complex projects. It additionally offers an *SOIC surface*, designed for soldering a surface-mount component for parts that aren't available in through-hole format.

Thanks to its large size, you can also use the Pi Plate with a quarter-size breadboard (sold in the Adafruit shop as a "tiny breadboard"). This small, two-section breadboard comes with a self-adhesive foam backing and can be stuck to the top of the Pi Plate over the prototyping area (see Figure 16-5). Doing so means that it's impossible to use the prototyping area to make a permanent circuit, but the combination offers a self-contained add-on for rapid temporary prototyping of smaller circuits.

As with the Slice of Pi, the Prototyping Pi Plate is at heart a basic device. The kit contains no active components, but simply headers, terminals and the board itself. As a result, it provides little extra protection for the Pi's GPIO ports beyond making it more difficult to accidentally short-circuit two connections. Unlike the Slice of Pi, the Pi Plate provides access to all 26 of the Pi's GPIO header pins—meaning that you could accidentally connect things to the pins marked as Do Not Connect on the GPIO header diagram (see Chapter 13, "Learning to Hack Hardware"). As with connecting things to these pins directly, this is inadvisable and can result in permanent damage to the Pi.

FIGURE 16-5:
A Pi Plate with a
quarter-size
breadboard

Perhaps the biggest reason for choosing a Pi Plate over the Slice of Pi is its clever design. Once connected to the GPIO header on the Pi, there is little reason to remove it unless you need access to the DSI or MIPI CSI-2 camera connectors. Because it only increases the height of the Pi, rather than the width or length, and because it includes the screw terminals for side-on access to GPIO pins, it's also compatible with a surprising number of Raspberry Pi cases (see Figure 16-6). If you're planning to use the Pi and Pi Plate combination with a case, however, be sure to check that the case can be adjusted for height or has access to the GPIO port through its lid.

You can purchase the Prototyping Pi Plate Kit from Adafruit at `http://www.adafruit.com/products/801`.

FIGURE 16-6:
The Pi Plate
connected to a
cased Raspberry
Pi

Fen Logic Gertboard

Properly termed the Raspberry Pi I/O Extension, the Gertboard (shown in Figure 16-7) is named for its inventor, Gert van Loo. An employee of Broadcom and a member of the team that designed the BCM2835 SoC processor at the heart of the Raspberry Pi, van Loo created the Gertboard as a way of unlocking some of the power of the chip hidden by the Pi's overall design and providing a powerful and versatile platform for electronic tinkering.

Unlike the Slice of Pi and Prototyping Pi Plate, the Gertboard is an *active* add-on board with numerous components designed to extend the functionality of the Pi. The Gertboard provides 12 *buffered IO ports* with status LEDs, three push-button switches, six *open collector drivers*, a 48 V 4 A *motor controller*, a two-channel *digital to analogue converter (DAC)* and a two-channel *analogue to digital converter (ADC)*. Additionally, the Gertboard has support for an additional 28-pin microcontroller, such as the Atmel ATmega328 used in the Arduino prototyping system, which can be inserted into a socket on the Gertboard and programmed directly from the Raspberry Pi.

FIGURE 16-7:
The Gertboard,
designed by
Gert van Loo

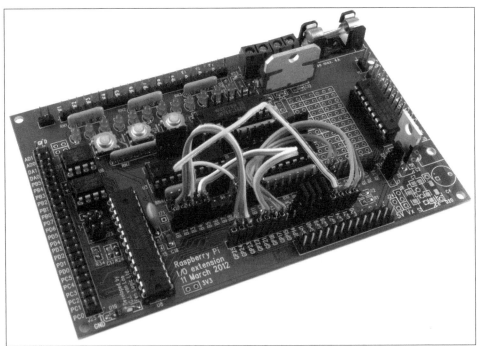

FIGURE 16-7:
The Gertboard,
designed by
Gert van Loo

As the list of features indicates, the Gertboard is a powerful and complex device. Its flexibility makes it a great choice for more complex projects—but that same complexity affects its size. The Gertboard is almost two-and-a-half times larger than the Raspberry Pi itself, making it both the most powerful and the largest add-on board for the Pi available at the time of writing. To counteract its size, the Gertboard connects to the Pi through a ribbon cable terminated in male sockets (see Figure 16-8). This cable allows the Gertboard to sit away from the Pi, or to be mounted in a project permanently yet still be quickly detached from the Pi if necessary.

Perhaps the most important feature of the Gertboard is the protection it offers to the Pi. Using a 3.3 V regulator, the Gertboard is designed to prevent the Pi's GPIO port from receiving voltages it cannot handle. Like the Slice of Pi, it also attempts to restrict access to the six pins labelled Do Not Connect as well as the 3.3 V and 5 V pins to help prevent accidental shorting. Although care must be taken while wiring up circuits, following the instructions included in the Gertboard's user manual guarantees the Pi's safety.

FIGURE 16-8:
The Gertboard
connected to a
Raspberry Pi

The motor controller functionality of the Gertboard makes it easy to integrate the Pi into a robotics project. It's suitable for motors of up to 48 V at 4 A, which is easily powerful enough to drive a small robot vehicle. Sadly, the motor is not included as standard with the Gertboard. Instead, you are asked to supply your own controller—with the L6203 package being recommended—if motor control forms part of your project. With the motor controller soldered into place, the Gertboard can be used to control surprisingly powerful motors either through instructions received from the Pi itself or from the optional Atmel microcontroller module. Figure 16-9 shows an example circuit that's using the Gertboard to drive a 12 V motor from a battery pack power supply.

For project building, the Gertboard offers significantly more functionality than a bare Raspberry Pi. The 12 buffered IO ports, located at the top of the board, can be configured as inputs or outputs and provide more connectivity than the seven or eight general-purpose IO pins provided on the Pi's own GPIO port. The inclusion of LEDs, which indicate when a pin is high or low, helps with both circuit troubleshooting and electronics education, making it easy to see what the various inputs and outputs are doing at any given time.

FIGURE 16-9:
Using the
Gertboard
motor controller

For sensing or feedback projects, the Gertboard's ADC and DAC components are handy additions. Unlike the GPIO pins on the Pi itself, which can only receive and send digital signals, the Gertboard includes two ADC and two DAC connections. The ADC pins, located on the upper-left of the Gertboard, allow analogue components to be converted into digital signals compatible with the Pi. As an example, Figure 16-10 shows how you can use the ADC pins to read the status of a *potentiometer*—a component which varies its resistance according to the position of a slider or knob. This circuit could be used to control the Pi's volume in a media centre application, or to alter the speed of an attached motor. The DAC pins provide the opposite functionality, taking a digital signal from the Pi and converting it to analogue. This could drive a speaker to create audio, or alter the speed of a motor or the brightness of an LED.

For more complex projects, the Gertboard provides an open collector driver, which uses transistors to switch on and off devices that have different power requirements to the 3.3 V used by the Gertboard or that draw a large amount of current and require an external power supply to operate. The open collector driver can control the power supplies of up to six devices simultaneously without requiring any hardware. This gives the Gertboard a large amount of flexibility—although transistors or relays can be used with passive add-on boards like the Prototyping Pi Plate to achieve the same goal.

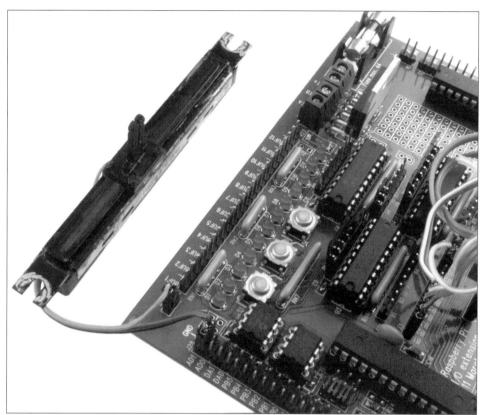

FIGURE 16-10:
Connecting a
potentiometer
to the
Gertboard's
ADC pins

Finally, the Gertboard provides access to a 28-pin microcontroller, which can be fitted to a socket located on the board itself. When fitted, the Gertboard can be wired to address either the Raspberry Pi's GPIO port or the microcontroller, or a combination of the two. The Gertboard is designed to operate with an Atmel ATmega168 or ATmega328 microcontroller—the same type of microcontroller used in the Arduino prototyping project. When fitted, you can write programs for the Gertboards' ATmega microcontroller in the Atmel IDE, giving the Pi a useful level of compatibility with the wide array of existing ATmega-targeted software available to download. It also gives the Pi the ability to address external hardware in a real-time manner, with the microcontroller taking over responsibility for hardware interfacing and simply providing feedback to the Pi.

The Gertboard is a very advanced device, and isn't suitable for every project. For many simple uses, a cheaper passive add-on board like the Slice of Pi will usually be enough. However, for in-depth experimentation of just what is possible with the Raspberry Pi's BC2835 processor and/or to ensure that you'll be able to interface almost any hardware with your Pi, it's a great choice and a powerful extension to the Pi's already impressive abilities.

The Gertboard is available through Farnell at `http://www.farnell.com/`.

Part V

Appendixes

Appendix A
Python Recipes

THE FOLLOWING RECIPES provide the program code for Example 3 and Example 4 in Chapter 12, "An Introduction to Python", and a sample solution for the combined input-output program suggested in Chapter 14, "The GPIO Port". Each recipe is also available for download from the Raspberry Pi User Guide website at www.wiley.com/go/raspberrypiuser guide2e. If you're typing the code in by hand, look out for the ⏎ symbol: this indicates that the line is wrapped due to space constraints in the book. If you see the symbol at the end of a line, don't press Enter until you reach the end of a line that doesn't have a symbol present.

Raspberry Snake (Chapter 12, Example 3)

```
#!/usr/bin/env python
# Raspberry Snake
# Written by Gareth Halfacree for the Raspberry Pi User Guide

import pygame, sys, time, random
from pygame.locals import *

pygame.init()
fpsClock = pygame.time.Clock()

playSurface = pygame.display.set_mode((640, 480))
pygame.display.set_caption('Raspberry Snake')

redColour = pygame.Color(255, 0, 0)
blackColour = pygame.Color(0, 0, 0)
whiteColour = pygame.Color(255, 255, 255)
greyColour = pygame.Color(150, 150, 150)
snakePosition = [100,100]
snakeSegments = [[100,100],[80,100],[60,100]]
raspberryPosition = [300,300]
raspberrySpawned = 1
direction = 'right'
changeDirection = direction

def gameOver():
    gameOverFont = pygame.font.Font('freesansbold.ttf', 72)
    gameOverSurf = gameOverFont.render ⏎
    ('Game Over', True, greyColour)
    gameOverRect = gameOverSurf.get_rect()
    gameOverRect.midtop = (320, 10)
    playSurface.blit(gameOverSurf, gameOverRect)
    pygame.display.flip()
```

```
        time.sleep(5)
        pygame.quit()
        sys.exit()

while True:
    for event in pygame.event.get():
        if event.type == QUIT:
            pygame.quit()
        elif event.type == KEYDOWN:
            if event.key == K_RIGHT or event.key == ord('d'):
                changeDirection = 'right'
            if event.key == K_LEFT or event.key == ord('a'):
                changeDirection = 'left'
            if event.key == K_UP or event.key == ord('w'):
                changeDirection = 'up'
            if event.key == K_DOWN or event.key == ord('s'):
                changeDirection = 'down'
            if event.key == K_ESCAPE:
                pygame.event.post(pygame.event.Event(QUIT))
    if changeDirection == 'right' and not direction == 'left':
        direction = changeDirection
    if changeDirection == 'left' and not direction == 'right':
        direction = changeDirection
    if changeDirection == 'up' and not direction == 'down':
        direction = changeDirection
    if changeDirection == 'down' and not direction == 'up':
        direction = changeDirection
    if direction == 'right':
        snakePosition[0] += 20
    if direction == 'left':
        snakePosition[0] -= 20
    if direction == 'up':
        snakePosition[1] -= 20
    if direction == 'down':
        snakePosition[1] += 20
    snakeSegments.insert(0,list(snakePosition))
    if snakePosition[0] == raspberryPosition[0] and ↵
    snakePosition[1] == raspberryPosition[1]:
        raspberrySpawned = 0
    else:
        snakeSegments.pop()
    if raspberrySpawned == 0:
        x = random.randrange(1,32)
        y = random.randrange(1,24)
```

```
        raspberryPosition = [int(x*20),int(y*20)]
    raspberrySpawned = 1
    playSurface.fill(blackColour)
    for position in snakeSegments:
        pygame.draw.rect(playSurface,whiteColour,Rect ↵
        (position[0], position[1], 20, 20))

    pygame.draw.rect(playSurface,redColour,Rect ↵
    (raspberryPosition[0], raspberryPosition[1], 20, 20))
    pygame.display.flip()
    if snakePosition[0] > 620 or snakePosition[0] < 0:
        gameOver()
    if snakePosition[1] > 460 or snakePosition[1] < 0:
        for snakeBody in snakeSegments[1:]:
            if snakePosition[0] == snakeBody[0] and ↵
            snakePosition[1] == snakeBody[1]:
                gameOver()

    fpsClock.tick(30)
```

IRC User List (Chapter 12, Example 4)

```
#!/usr/bin/env python
# IRC User List
# Written by Tom Hudson for the Raspberry Pi User Guide
# http://tomhudson.co.uk/

import sys, socket, time

RPL_NAMREPLY   = '353'
RPL_ENDOFNAMES = '366'

irc = {
    'host':          'chat.freenode.net',
    'port':          6667,
    'channel':       '#raspiuserguide',
    'namesinterval': 5
}

user = {
    'nick':         'botnick',
    'username':     'botuser',
```

```
    'hostname':    'localhost',
    'servername': 'localhost',
    'realname':    'Raspberry Pi Names Bot'
}

s = socket.socket(socket.AF_INET, socket.SOCK_STREAM)

print 'Connecting to %(host)s:%(port)s...' % irc
try:
    s.connect((irc['host'], irc['port']))
except socket.error:
    print 'Error connecting to IRC server ↵
    %(host)s:%(port)s' % irc
    sys.exit(1)



s.send('NICK %(nick)s\r\n' % user)
s.send('USER %(username)s %(hostname)s %(servername)s : ↵
%(realname)s\r\n' % user)
s.send('JOIN %(channel)s\r\n' % irc)
s.send('NAMES %(channel)s\r\n' % irc)

read_buffer = ''
names = []

while True:
    read_buffer += s.recv(1024)
    lines = read_buffer.split('\r\n')
    read_buffer = lines.pop();
    for line in lines:
        response = line.rstrip().split(' ', 3)
        response_code = response[1]
        if response_code == RPL_NAMREPLY:
            names_list = response[3].split(':')[1]
            names += names_list.split(' ')
        if response_code == RPL_ENDOFNAMES:
            print '\r\nUsers in %(channel)s:' % irc
            for name in names:
                print name
            names = []
            time.sleep(irc['namesinterval'])
            s.send('NAMES %(channel)s\r\n' % irc)
```

GPIO Input and Output (Chapter 14)

```python
#!/usr/bin/env python
# Raspberry Pi GPIO Input/Output example
# Written by Gareth Halfacree for the Raspberry Pi User Guide

import RPi.GPIO as GPIO

GPIO.setmode(GPIO.BOARD)
GPIO.setup(11, GPIO.OUT)
GPIO.setup(12, GPIO.IN)
GPIO.output(11, False)

while True:
    input_value = GPIO.input(12)
    if input_value == False:
        print "The button has been pressed. Lighting LED."
        GPIO.output(11, True)
        while input_value == False:
            input_value = GPIO.input(12)
        print "The button has been released. Extinguishing LED."
    if input_value == True:
        GPIO.output(11, False)
```

Appendix B
Raspberry Pi Camera Module Quick Reference

THE RASPBERRY PI Camera Module comes with software designed to capture still images and videos, each of which has a variety of options that can control the final output. Options for `raspistill`, `raspiyuv` and `raspivid` are included in this appendix. For more information, see Chapter 15, "The Raspberry Pi Camera Module".

Shared Options

The following options, listed in alphabetical order, are shared between `raspistill`, `raspiyuv` and `raspivid`. For application-specific options, see the individual `raspistill`, `raspiyuv` and `raspivid` entries later in this appendix.

○ **-? or --help (Help)**—Displays all options and their uses.

○ **-awb or --awb (Automatic White Balance)**—Sets the colour temperature of the captured image or video according to one of a series of pre-set configurations. If your image or video appears blue or orange, try adjusting this option first. Possible values for this option are: `off`, `auto`, `sun`, `cloud`, `shade`, `tungsten`, `fluorescent`, `incandescent`, `flash`, `horizon`.

○ **-br or --brightness (Brightness)**—Adjusts the brightness of the captured image or video. Possible values for this option are whole numbers ranging from 0 (minimum brightness) to 100 (maximum brightness).

○ **-cfx or --colfx (Colour Effects)**—Allows the user to adjust the YUV colour space for fine-grained control of the final image. Values should be given as U:V, where U controls the chrominance and V the luminance. A value of 128:128 will result in a greyscale image.

○ **-co or --contrast (Contrast)**—Adjusts the contrast of the captured image or video. Possible values for this option are whole numbers ranging from -100 (minimum contrast) to 100 (maximum contrast).

○ **-d or --demo (Demonstration Mode)**—The -d option runs either `raspistill` or `raspivid` in demonstration mode, which displays a preview that cycles through various camera options. In this mode, no image is captured—even if you specify an output file using the `--output` option.

○ **-ev or --ev (Exposure Value)**—Allows the camera to increase or decrease its exposure value, brightening or darkening the captured image or video. Unlike the brightness and contrast settings, this affects the actual capturing of the image or video. Possible values are -10 to 10, with 0 being the default.

○ **-ex or --exposure (Exposure Mode)**—Sets the camera's automatic exposure setting, which controls how long the camera spends capturing an individual image or frame and is largely a factor of available light or the speed of the subject: fast-moving objects need a short exposure time in order to remain in focus, while low-light shooting demands a long exposure time. Possible values for this option are `off`, `auto`, `night`, `nightpreview`, `backlight`, `spotlight`, `sports`, `snow`, `beach`, `verylong`, `fixedfps`, `antishake`, `fireworks`.

○ **-f or --fullscreen (Fullscreen Preview)**—Makes the preview image fill the screen, overriding any other preview option you may have set.

○ **-h or --height (Height)**—Specifies the height, or vertical resolution, of the captured image or video. This should be set to the desired height in pixels; for example, a Full HD capture would require a height value of 1080. The minimum value is 64; the maximum depends on whether video or still images are being captured.

○ **-hf or --hflip (Horizontal Flip)**—Flips the captured image or video along its horizontal axis, as though it has been viewed in a mirror.

○ **-ifx or --imxfx (Image Effects)**—Enables one of a number of preconfigured special effects on the image or video. Possible values for this option are `none`, `negative`, `solarise`, `sketch`, `denoise`, `emboss`, `oilpaint`, `hatch`, `gpen`, `pastel`, `watercolour`, `film`, `blur`, `saturation`, `colourswap`, `washedout`, `posterise`, `colourpoint`, `colourbalance`, `cartoon`, `whiteboard`, `blackboard`. These settings can be seen in action using the Demonstration Mode option.

○ **-ISO or --ISO (ISO Sensitivity)**—Sets the camera's sensitivity to light. A lower ISO value provides a clearer image, but requires longer exposures; a higher ISO value can shoot at very low exposure times to capture fast-moving or badly lit subjects, but creates a 'noisier' image.

○ **-mm or --metering (Metering Mode)**—Sets the light metering mode for image or video capture, which controls the automatic exposure, white balance, and ISO sensitivity options. Possible values for this option are `average`, `spot`, `backlit`, `matrix`.

○ **-n or --nopreview (No Preview)**—Does not display a preview window while capturing; not required when using a timeout value of 0.

○ **-o or --output (Output File)**—Sets the name of the file to be saved. The value for this option can be either a filename, in which case the file will be created in the current directory, or an absolute path. If you are using `raspistill` or `raspivid` along with another application that expects image data through standard input, you can divert the image or video through standard output using a hyphen (–) character as the filename.

○ **-op or --opacity (Preview Opacity)**—Controls how transparent the preview window appears. Possible values are any whole number from 0 to 255, where 0 is completely transparent and thus invisible and 255 is completely visible. Using a value around 128 allows you to see the live preview, but also read the text behind the preview.

○ **-p or --preview (Preview Window Control)**—Sets the size of the preview window, and where it appears. The value should be given as X,Y,W,H where X and Y are the pixel co-ordinates where the window's top-left corner should be drawn, and W and H the width and height of the preview window in pixels.

○ **-rot or --rotation (Rotate Capture)**—Rotates the captured image or video through any arbitrary angle. Values for this option should be given as a whole number of clockwise degrees, where 0 is no rotation and 359 the maximum possible rotation.

○ **-sa or --saturation (Saturation)**—Adjusts the colour saturation of the captured image or video. Possible values for this option are whole numbers ranging from -100 (minimum saturation) to 100 (maximum saturation.)

○ **-sh or --sharpness (Sharpness)**—Adjusts the sharpness of the captured image or video. Possible values for this option are whole numbers ranging from -100 (minimum sharpness) to 100 (maximum sharpness.)

○ **-t or --timeout (Capture Timeout)**—Controls the timeout, in milliseconds, that the preview window will appear. While shared between the tools, the action of the `--timeout` option is different: in `raspistill`, the `--timeout` option will set the time until the picture is captured; in `raspivid`, the option will set the time for which video will be recorded. A value of 0 in `raspistill` captures an image immediately; a value of 0 in `raspivid` continues to record indefinitely.

○ **-v or --verbose (Verbose Messaging)**—Verbose mode tells the capture application to output as much detail of what it is doing as possible to the console or terminal. This is usually only used for debugging errors in the software, as it allows the user to see at what point the capture fails.

○ **-vf or --vflip (Vertical Flip)**—Flips the image through the vertical axis. Most commonly used when the camera cannot be positioned the correct way up, with the connecting ribbon cable exiting from the bottom. If the camera is at an angle other than upside down, try using the `rotation` option to control the final captured image.

○ **-vs or --vstab (Video Stabilisation)**—Attempts to correct for the camera's sensor shaking. Commonly used when the Raspberry Pi or its Camera Module is held in the hand, or attached to a robot, vehicle or other moving platform.

○ **-w or --width (Width)**—Specifies the width, or horizontal resolution, of the captured image or video. This should be set to the desired width in pixels; for example, a Full HD capture would require a width value of 1920. The minimum value is 64; the maximum depends on whether a still image or a video is being captured.

Raspistill Options

Designed to capture still images, `raspistill` has some specific options that do not apply to `raspivid`. These options are listed below.

○ **-e or --encoding (Encoding Format)**—Sets the format of the output image. This does not affect the file extension of the output file, which must be changed manually using the `--output` option. Possible values for this option are `jpg`, `bmp`, `gif`, `png`.

○ **-q or --quality (JPEG Quality)**—Sets the compression level of the saved JPEG, and has no effect when using any other encoding format. The lower the value, the smaller the final image file; a value of 100 will provide the best possible quality, while a value of 0 will provide the smallest file size. A value of 90 is a good trade-off between size and quality.

○ **-r or --raw (Save Bayer Data)**—Saves the output of the camera's Bayer colour filter as metadata in the JPEG image, and has no effect when using any other encoding format. This extra data, the output of the camera's sensor without interpolation, can be used in image editing applications to reconstruct a higher quality or more detailed image, but is not normally required.

○ **-th or --thumb (Thumbnail Settings)**—Sets the size and quality of the thumbnail saved with JPEG images, and has no effect when used with any other encoding format. The value should be given as X:Y:Q, where X is the width, Y the height and Q the JPEG quality from 0 to 100 of the thumbnail.

○ **-tl or --timelapse (Timelapse Mode)**—Puts `raspistill` into timelapse mode, where images will be captured at a set interval. Most useful when using `raspistill` with a script or third-party application by setting the Output file to the standard output with a hyphen (-) character; when used with a filename in the `--output` option, the file will be overwritten every time a new image is captured. The value for this option should be the delay between captures in milliseconds.

○ **-x or --exif (EXIF Tag)**—Allows custom Exchangable Image File Format (EXIF) tags to be written to a JPEG image, and has no effect when used with any other encoding formats. Tags should be formatted as 'key=value' with one possible example being setting the name of the photographer using `-x 'Author=Gareth Halfacree'`.

Raspivid Options

Designed to capture moving images, `raspivid` has some specific options that do not apply to `raspistill`. These options are listed below.

- **-b or --bitrate (Encoding Bitrate)**—Sets the bitrate of the captured video, in bits per second (BPS.) The higher the bitrate, the higher the quality of the finished video—but the larger the file size. Unless you have a specific requirement from your video, this should typically be left at the default setting.

- **-e or --penc (Encoding Preview)**—Uses the preview window to show video frames after they have been passed through the encoder, rather than before. Provides an accurate preview of the final video, and most commonly used when tweaking the Encoding Bitrate.

- **-fps or --framerate (Video Framerate)**—Sets the framerate of the captured video, in frames per second. Higher figures give smoother motion, while lower figures take up less disk space. Recording at a rate above 30 frames per second, which can be turned into slow-motion video with a video editing application, will likely only work at lower resolutions (set with the `--width` and `--height` options).

- **-g or --intra (Intra Refresh Period)**—Sets how often a key frame, also known as an intra-coded picture or I frame, should be captured. A key frame is an entire image, rather than the changes recorded since the last image. More frequent key frames can result in higher quality video when recording rapidly changing scenes, but will result in larger file sizes.

Raspiyuv Options

`Raspiyuv` is an application designed to capture one of two specific formats of colour image—YUV or RGB. Most users will be better off using `raspistill`, which outputs into image formats ready for use; those who plan to edit their images further after capture, however, may find `raspiyuv` a useful tool.

Most `raspiyuv` options are the same as found on `raspistill` with the following exception:

- **-rgb or --rgb (Capture RGB)**—Sets `raspiyuv` to capture red, green, blue (RGB) pixel data rather than the chrominance and luminance normally used.

Appendix C
HDMI Display Modes

YOU CAN USE the values in Table C-1 and Table C-2 with the hdmi_mode option in config.txt to alter the HDMI video output stream. For more information, see Chapter 7, "Advanced Raspberry Pi Configuration".

Table C-1   HDMI Group 1 (CEA)

Value	Description
1	VGA (640x480)
2	480p 60Hz
3	480p 60Hz (16:9 aspect ratio)
4	720p 60Hz
5	1080i 60Hz
6	480i 60Hz
7	480i 60Hz (16:9 aspect ratio)
8	240p 60Hz
9	240p 60Hz (16:9 aspect ratio)
10	480i 60Hz (Pixel quadrupling enabled)
11	480i 60Hz (Pixel quadrupling enabled) (16:9 aspect ratio)
12	240p 60Hz (Pixel quadrupling enabled)
13	240p 60Hz (Pixel quadrupling enabled) (16:9 aspect ratio)
14	480p 60Hz (Pixel doubling enabled)
15	480p 60Hz (Pixel doubling enabled) (16:9 aspect ratio)
16	1080p 60Hz
17	576p 50Hz
18	576p 50Hz (16:9 aspect ratio)
19	720p 50Hz
20	1080i 50Hz
21	576i 50Hz
22	576i 50Hz (16:9 aspect ratio)
23	288p 50Hz
24	288p 50Hz (16:9 aspect ratio)
25	576i 50Hz (Pixel quadrupling enabled)
26	576i 50Hz (Pixel quadrupling enabled) (16:9 aspect ratio)
27	288p 50Hz (Pixel quadrupling enabled)

Value	Description
28	288p 50Hz (Pixel quadrupling enabled) (16:9 aspect ratio)
29	576p 50Hz (Pixel doubling enabled)
30	576p 50Hz (Pixel doubling enabled) (16:9 aspect ratio)
31	1080p 50Hz
32	1080p 24Hz
33	1080p 25Hz
34	1080p 30Hz
35	480p 60Hz (Pixel quadrupling enabled)
36	480p 60Hz (Pixel quadrupling enabled) (16:9 aspect ratio)
37	576p 50Hz (Pixel quadrupling enabled)
38	576p 50Hz (Pixel quadrupling enabled) (16:9 aspect ratio)
39	1080i 50Hz (Reduced blanking)
40	1080i 100Hz
41	720p 100Hz
42	576p 100Hz
43	576p 100Hz (16:9 aspect ratio)
44	576i 100Hz
45	576i 100Hz (16:9 aspect ratio)
46	1080i 120Hz
47	720p 120Hz
48	480p 120Hz
49	480p 120Hz (16:9 aspect ratio)
50	480i 120Hz
51	480i 120Hz (16:9 aspect ratio)
52	576p 200Hz
53	576p 200Hz (16:9 aspect ratio)
54	576i 200Hz
55	576i 200Hz (16:9 aspect ratio)
56	480p 24Hz0
57	480p 24Hz0 (16:9 aspect ratio)
58	480i 240Hz
59	480i 240Hz (16:9 aspect ratio)

Table C-2 HDMI Group 2 (DMT)

Value	Description
1	640×350 85Hz
2	640×400 85Hz
3	720×400 85Hz
4	640×480 60Hz
5	640×480 72Hz
6	640×480 75Hz
7	640×480 85Hz
8	800×600 56Hz
9	800×600 60Hz
10	800×600 72Hz
11	800×600 75Hz
12	800×600 85Hz
13	800×600 120Hz
14	848×480 60Hz
15	1024×768 43Hz, incompatible with the Raspberry Pi
16	1024×768 60Hz
17	1024×768 70Hz
18	1024×768 75Hz
19	1024×768 85Hz
20	1024×768 120Hz
21	1152×864 75Hz
22	1280×768 (Reduced blanking)
23	1280×768 60Hz
24	1280×768 75Hz
25	1280×768 85Hz
26	1280×768 120Hz (Reduced blanking)
27	1280×800 (Reduced blanking)
28	1280×800 60Hz
29	1280×800 75Hz
30	1280×800 85Hz
31	1280×800 120Hz (Reduced blanking)
32	1280×960 60Hz
33	1280×960 85Hz

Value	Description
34	1280×960 120Hz (Reduced blanking)
35	1280×1024 60Hz
36	1280×1024 75Hz
37	1280×1024 85Hz
38	1280×1024 120Hz (Reduced blanking)
39	1360×768 60Hz
40	1360×768 120Hz (Reduced blanking)
41	1400×1050 (Reduced blanking)
42	1400×1050 60Hz
43	1400×1050 75Hz
44	1400×1050 85Hz
45	1400×1050 120Hz (Reduced blanking)
46	1440×900 (Reduced blanking)
47	1440×900 60Hz
48	1440×900 75Hz
49	1440×900 85Hz
50	1440×900 120Hz (Reduced blanking)
51	1600×1200 60Hz
52	1600×1200 65Hz
53	1600×1200 70Hz
54	1600×1200 75Hz
55	1600×1200 85Hz
56	1600×1200 120Hz (Reduced blanking)
57	1680×1050 (Reduced blanking)
58	1680×1050 60Hz
59	1680×1050 75Hz
60	1680×1050 85Hz
61	1680×1050 120Hz (Reduced blanking)
62	1792×1344 60Hz
63	1792×1344 75Hz
64	1792×1344 120Hz (Reduced blanking)
65	1856×1392 60Hz
66	1856×1392 75Hz

continued

Table C-2   continued

Value	Description
67	1856×1392 120Hz (Reduced blanking)
68	1920×1200 (Reduced blanking)
69	1920×1200 60Hz
70	1920×1200 75Hz
71	1920×1200 85Hz
72	1920×1200 120Hz (Reduced blanking)
73	1920×1440 60Hz
74	1920×1440 75Hz
75	1920×1440 120Hz (Reduced blanking)
76	2560×1600 (Reduced blanking)
77	2560×1600 60Hz
78	2560×1600 75Hz
79	2560×1600 85Hz
80	2560×1600 120Hz (Reduced blanking)
81	1366×768 60Hz
82	1920×1080 (1080p) 60Hz
83	1600×900 (Reduced blanking)
84	2048×1152 (Reduced blanking)
85	1280×720 (720p) 60Hz
86	1366×768 (Reduced blanking)

Index